AF438650

Past • an Introduction to the Problem

ŽELIMIR ŽILNIK
*on Film, Communism,
and Former Yugoslavia*

BORIS BUDEN
*in collaboration with
kuda.org, Olivera Jokić and others*

Originally published in BCMS as
Uvod u prošlost, 2013 by kuda.org

This translated edition includes new multimodal content.

TRANSLATION Olivera Jokić

ISBN (kuda.org) 978-86-88567-41-1
ISBN (mi2) 978-953-8469-13-8
ISBN (Iskra Books) 979-8-8691-9071-0

CIP – Cataloging in Publication
Matica Srpska Library, Novi Sad
COBISS.SR-ID 140900361

Novi Sad & Zagreb & Madison · June 2024

Contents

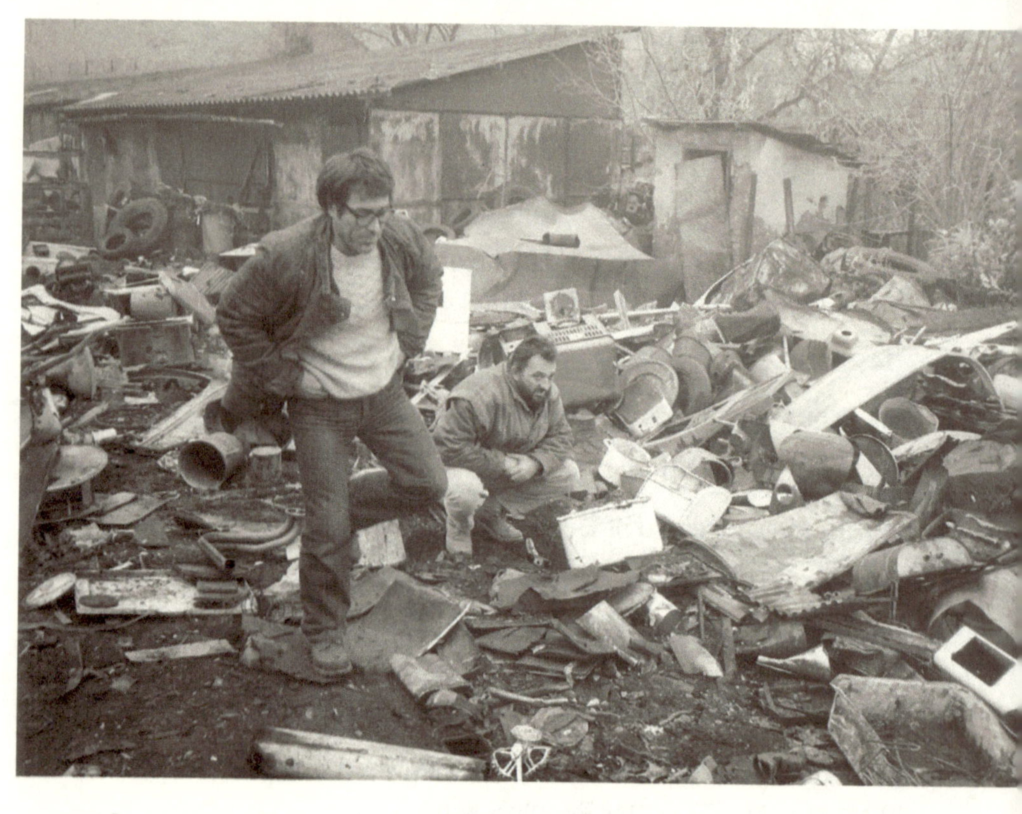

On the set of TV series *Hot Paychecks* (1987) • PHOTO VLADIMIR ČERVENKA

things we still need to do in order to get there."[01] The title of the interview is also telling: "Art Film Does Not Interest Me." These few words take us immediately into a realm radically different from the discourse on the freedom of art and totalitarianism. It is, moreover, a realm that escapes the logic of artistic values and can't be easily subsumed under the concept of art history or film-as-art-history and their canonizations. The brutal truth is simple and is an offense to all who cannot get past the idea of art as an autonomous sphere of human activity: Žilnik is an artist because he is a communist. This still has one further consequence for his own way of art- and film-making.

Film scholar Pavle Levi relates Žilnik's film practice to Karl Marx's famous 11th Thesis on Feuerbach. It reads: "The philosophers have hitherto only interpreted the world in various ways; the point, however, is to change it." Žilnik, he claims, understood this in the sense that "the filmmakers... have only reproduced (represented) the world, in various ways; the point is, however, to produce it."[02] This, in a very concrete manner, reconceptualizes the relation between the filmmaker and the world he films, including the role of his protagonists and of the camera itself. The latter, far from simply depicting the world as it is, intervenes actively in this world, challenges the status quo, mobilizes latent human capacities, generates new social bonds, and so reshapes the social fabric of the reality in which it is deployed. In Žilnik's hands, a camera is not a means of art production that shall, when properly used in a social situation, produce aesthetic effects and, in addition, transform this social situation. For him society is not simply an object before the lens; it is the camera's means of production.

This is also the reason that Žilnik, when shooting documentaries, never hides the camera. On the contrary. All involved in filming should be aware of its presence, so as to actively react to it and co-create the picture the camera makes of

---

01 Quoted in What, How & for Whom/WHW (eds.), *Shadow Citizens—Želimir Žilnik*. (Oldenburg, Berlin, Novi Sad, Zagreb: Edith-Russ-Haus for Media Art and Sternberg Press, 2019), 9.

02 Ibid., 97.

them. The fact that this implies a conscious move away from the position of an individual film author to a socially formative collaboration should be a matter of course. In the 1968 interview mentioned above, Žilnik defines documentary film as a possibility given to people of all sorts directly to express "the pain that sits in one's stomach," a pain genuinely social, which is why it cannot be reduced to "their own private thing." The film director is a sort of technical assistant in the social production of film. In Žilnik's own words, it is all about "the sensitivity of the silver bromide to light, and nearly all the rest I leave up to the characters that my documentaries are concerned with."[03]

One could continue this discussion of Želimir Žilnik's particular film idiom and reflect further upon the influence on him of the materialist aesthetic tradition and Marxism in general, but this is not what this book aims to do. It does not want to extract an aesthetic or ideological essence from his work, nor does it try to historicize an exclusively professional part of his life. It rather evokes the totality of his life and work however contingent, fragmented, contradictory, and even paradoxical it may be.

Take again Žilnik's experience of communism. It can neither be reduced to an external ideological influence, nor to a temporally and geographically limited historical context. Rather it is constitutive of his entire cinematic oeuvre. It is, moreover, constitutive of his most existential experience of life. Žilnik was practically born in a Gestapo-run prison. It was in the year 1942 in the Serbian city of Niš. His mother, a student of philosophy, was a member of the illegal Communist Party. Shortly after giving birth to him, she was executed. His father, a Slovenian communist, was caught and decapitated as a partisan in 1944 by the Serbian anti-communist Chetniks, Nazi collaborators.

It seems impossible to keep these two stories apart, the one about the personal and professional life of a filmmaker and the other about the history of communism as an ideology and political practice. Indeed, in this book the personal is historical as much as the historical is personal. The same is

---

03 Ibid., 9.

true of Žilnik's films. It is impossible to detach them from the historical reality in which they were made and from the lives of those who made them. This is literally so: many protagonists of his films in fact play themselves; that is to say, one cannot differentiate their fictional roles from their real selves. The one who in Žilnik's *Kenedi Trilogy* performs the role of a migrant is in his real life a migrant. Žilnik, who, in his famous *Black Film* (1971) tells the story about a filmmaker who wants to change the world with his films, plays this filmmaker himself and demonstrates in his own existential situation, concretely in his own apartment and within his own family, how the film fails to solve the problem of homeless people. In addition, he publishes a manifesto that makes out of this failure an aesthetic statement and social critique, one inseparable from the other.

As we said earlier, this book is not primarily about the life and work of a filmmaker. It is also about the past, a dimension not so much of historical temporality as of our existence, which has gained in importance over the last several decades to such an extent that it has come to dominate the entire experience of our being in the world. The past has occupied our thoughts, feelings, and fantasies. Not even our utopian imagination has been spared. It has become much easier for us to imagine a better past than a better future.

But what exactly is this past? Is it "a foreign country," as British novelist Leslie Poles Hartley once wrote? This would indeed apply to this book. Not only is it largely about a foreign country; it is about a country that itself belongs to the past, the socialist Yugoslavia that fell apart in the bloody wars of the 1990s. The book tells the story of that country, of its short but fascinating life, as well as of its confused afterlife, haunted by the ghosts of the past. And it tells this story through the life and work of Želimir Žilnik, partly through his own testimonies. Taking all of this into account, this book is neither about a former country, nor about a person. It is not even about the past. Instead, it is a critique of the past, a critique of the idea of the past as an endless accumulation of historical facts and cultural values, a sort of inexhaustible resource from which we can arbitrarily extract the raw material for any purpose of our own, but before all, as the case is today, for constructing our identities.

The story of Želimir Žilnik and his filmmaking, inseparable from the ever-changing historical conditions in which it has been taking place and is now being told, is in itself such a critique of the past—in the name of historical experience. It evokes the meaning of the German phrase "Erfahrung machen," which closely links the notion of experience and the verb "to make." One cannot simply experience something, or just have an experience, one has to make it. It is in this sense that we can say: as far as Žilnik is a filmmaker, he is at the same time an experience maker, a maker of historical experience, his own and, in his films, a shared one.

It is in this sense that the entire story about Želimir Žilnik and his films may in fact not really belong in the history of cinema—as far as this history is, as Godard once put it, that of a missed rendezvous with the history of its century. In Žilnik's case such an appointment seems not to have been missed. This could explain why it is so difficult, if not altogether impossible, to find a proper place for him and his oeuvre in the canons of film history. At the same time, this could make the case for why he should still be important, or most important, to this same history of cinema.

Finally, and once again: this book is a translation. It was originally written not only in another language, but also for a different audience. Now it matters not which language or what audience. Both are preserved and perceptible in the book in what its English reader won't be able to escape—a difficult, arduous, and often awkward encounter with the strange and the foreign. This, however, is unavoidable and at the same time indispensable if the reader wishes not to miss their appointment with history.

Boris Buden · 2023

Foreword

This is not a book about the past. That is not because the past is distant and impossible to recover, so much larger than what a modest writing project such as this could digest. The reason is simpler than that. This book admits openly from the outset that it does not know what the past is and even less about where it is located. To any professional historian this would have been self-evident: the past is what happened in the times past; in a simple linear sequence from the past through the present to the future, it is always to be found behind us. The past is always in the rear view, we have to turn back in order to see it, we are not in it, nor are we going to get a glimpse of it ahead of us. And yet this book is not nor does it aspire to be an authoritative historical account. Indeed, it harbors suspicions about the disciplinary competence of professional historians today, that is, about the relevance of their field of expertise, of history as a discipline of study itself.

The unquestionable assumption underlying historians' confident grasp of the past—the so-called "unity of historical time"—does not obtain in this book. This book presumes, by contrast, the disintegration of such unity and disappearance of such historical time. For this book, the past is a post-historical category. This is something impossible to avoid nowadays no matter which way we turn, moving backwards or forwards, something concerning everyone everywhere, not just historians within the confines of their discipline. That is what is new: the past as ubiquitous, now, here, in everything and for everyone. This past is more contemporary than the present and more uncertain than the future. This is the past that everyone is called on to judge, to remember it in their own way, to understand it and (re)create it. This past is not even a dimension of temporality anymore, but, on the contrary, a cultural artifact.

This is a book that appears to be concerned with a particular segment of the past, something that used to be called cultural history. Yet it does not treat cultural history as a discrete discipline of historiography that takes for its subject something that had acquired the status of a cultural good in the past. For this book, cultural history is the very form in which the past appears to us today. To the degree that we are conscious of the past, we are conscious of it as culture.

Specifically, when this book discusses the cultural production of former Yugoslavia, the films or the so-called "cinematic idiom" of the director Želimir Žilnik; when it discusses conflicts within the culture and among actors in those conflicts; the relationship between politics and art; the economic conditions of film production and its social effects; it does not set these discussions within the disciplinary frameworks of fields such as history of Yugoslav cinema, or the coherent oeuvre of a particular director, so that concepts such as society, politics and the economy could serve to contextualize a narrative that was itself concerned only with culture. Culture does not happen in a preordained economic, political or social context; it is of itself an economic fact, a political factor, and a social product. It does not tell us about how the past really was, but is that past in its presence, currency, uncertainty, openness. It is the past as beyond its difference from the temporal dimension of the present and the future.

This book draws on the conversation with Želimir Žilnik in the final days of 2009 in Novi Sad, Serbia. The conversation, recorded by Hito Steyerl, has been transcribed by the staff of the Center for New Media_kuda.org, also located in Novi Sad. Only a few short snippets of the conversation found their way into the book. It is important to emphasize right away that they do not have the status of documentation, and that, in this form, they are not ready to be archived in any way. They did give generative momentum to this book and remain inseparable from its other texts.

They do not relate to those texts chronologically. While in one place in this book Žilnik's words may comment on a text that was written after the conversation was over, elsewhere in the book they may precede such a text and serve as its prompt and conceptual template. In fact, most of the texts in this book were directly inspired by the conversation, including the greatest part of it which is not even published here. To that conversation these texts are as complements. It is the texts that make the conversation a conversation, and not what it had been in its unprocessed originality—an interview made up of short questions and elaborate answers, and as such just the raw material for a possible document.

All of the above brings into question the status of authorship of this book. As much as the words published here are attributable to this author or that, the book as a whole cannot claim a single author. The idea for the book, the transcript of the conversation, and the editorial work on the book were done by the collective of kuda.org; Želimir Žilnik spoke for nearly twenty hours in front of the camera, and the interview transcript amounts to thousands of words; it also frequently includes extensive quotations from other authors and a number of more or less direct references to a series of other people's ideas; lastly, I personally do not feel that I am the author of this book, although I readily take responsibility for it as a whole.

Why Žilnik of all people?

Let us first clear up a possible misunderstanding: this is not a book about the film director Želimir Žilnik. It is still less a discussion of his body of cinematic work that provides a critical assessment of the aesthetic value of the director's oeuvre or measures its broad cultural or political influence. The book does not claim to create new insights that will advance film theory, or, by way of a public, make society better and smarter.

What is this public anyway? Whose public? The public of this or that small nation state? The public gathered around which national language? Around what communicative or political community, of what society? Even if such a public were to exist, how could this booklet make it smarter? The time of cultivating, civilizing, perfecting, and improving, of the progress happening every-day-in-every-way is gone for good, swept away as long ago as Romanticism, let alone socialism. In the meantime we have learned this: tomorrow could be worse than today, much like today is already often worse than yesterday. Those who inherit the world could be dumber, more backward, and more devious than we are today. In an instant, they could destroy everything their forebears had been building for generations, as the recent history of the spaces of former Yugoslavia has clearly demonstrated.

Thus Žilnik! Because he, in an inimitable way, shares and articulates the experience of trauma: the reality of historical regression, the futility of critique, the mendacity of the public, the vacuity of knowledge, the corruptibility of art, the total disintegration of society, and, finally, the war with all its atrocities. But also because he never shrank before genuine evil or turned his back to it. On the contrary, he faced it straight on from beginning to end. This makes him a creator of experience rather than a mere witness to the past. The difference here is enormous. Even those who used terror to shape the past could bear witness to that past authentically, also when such past had been little more than the past of their crimes; much like we can depend on the witnessing by the miserable little bastard who crawled through that past with shame to be no less authentic, from his crawling perspective, to be sure.

The experience of which we speak should not be mistaken for some accumulated knowledge of the past. Experience is always more than knowledge because it includes the experience of ignorance, not simply as a negation of the former, but as an element of the unmitigated contingency of life that permeates all historical reality. This is the experience of knowledge as dead, the fact of its practical worthlessness and redundancy. So many millions of hours of instruction in history in the schools of former Yugoslavia were dedicated to the evils of fratricidal wars. And what was the use of that vast body of knowledge? It was nil.

This is why this book does not exploit Žilnik as a living archive, a walking collection of documents bearing authentic witness to the past. He does not here play the role of a medium who speaks to us from the past with an immediacy that restores its continuity with our present and future and embodies it as our identity's most valuable element. So that, as it were, we could know ourselves, know where we came from and where we belong. On the contrary, this book, much like what Žilnik discusses in it, shows no interest in identity, whatever or whichever it may be. This is not to say, of course, that identity shows no interest in either, in every word of its famous director and every medium in which this word is published. Canonization does not ask for permission, and neither does national or cultural heritage. It will grab anything it can build into the identity of its nation and culture as if it were self-evident, natural even. That is why it brooks no objection.

And that is precisely one of the primary goals of this book: to give resistance to authoritarian canonization as a god-given right of institutionalized cultural practice; to sabotage the national heritage project; to point to its inherent contradictions, falsifications and manipulations of cultural and social values, to its ideological functions and political abuses. It is not just the cinematic work of Želimir Žilnik but precisely its social, political, and moral dimensions that themselves defy all attempts at canonization, especially that undertaken by a national culture.

To say that Želimir Žilnik is a Serbian director still sounds today like a trite statement of fact. This book wants to make that claim sound like a tasteless joke. The book aspires to make us conscious of the crisis of cultural canonization. Because canons are not dead: they are here and here to stay. But they no longer have the authority they used to enjoy; they are now more fragile, more porous, and more suspect than ever. Above all, their once unquestionable aura of disciplinary authority is dissipating beyond repair. Canons are today, to put it in the terms of one of those nearly forgotten contradictions, a matter of faith, more so than a matter of knowledge. Everyone has the right to bow before them, but equally so to question them, even to deny their existence, be they a professional or an amateur.

Speaking of amateurism, this book openly acknowledges its amateur status. What is worse, it owns up to it proudly. It is not just that the past is handled here by one who has never done it professionally and has no formal qualifications for the job; or that the person writing about film has never made one, nor has he ever shown critical or theoretical interest in it; that culture is being discussed by someone whose academic competence would direct him to do it in a way directly opposed to the way he is doing it here; that the person who speaks about life in what used to be Yugoslavia left the region long ago ... There is more to say here, but the crucial point is elsewhere.

This book was not written in a pre-set, completely apposite and finalized idiom whose words and grammar are applied to the subject, the way it is done, say, in the language of film criticism, the language of cultural theory, the language of political science, the language of this or that faith, worldview, or culture with its specific conceptions, phraseology, fixed meanings, stable and steady references. The language of this book does not arise from either monolingual or homolingual ideology.

On the contrary, it is a language that remains in its heterolingual stage, language that has decided to speak up before it can avail itself of a ready vocabulary, prescriptive grammar, or any claims to a clearly delineated space of transparency and legibility, with clear boundaries from other languages foreign to itself, at a moment when it cannot signal the command of a specific discipline, particular culture, or unique identity. It is a language that, in terms of its discursivity, is clearly amateur. It is therefore not a language of this or that non-professional but a language that, by virtue of its linguistic non-professionalism, is free to go wherever its associations will carry it, to barge in where it was never invited, to meddle in other people's business, and to speak from within the enclosure of another language, in a way that is often inappropriate for the time or the place, but which gives it permission to taste the forbidden, venture into the unknown, experiment with the new.

This is a language that still desires to be the common good, language before it was fenced off and shut into its own fold, the language that dares to speak before it has been subjected to what the English call enclosure, the historical process of fencing off the commons, namely, the meadows and pastures that had once been accessible to all. The process began in the sixteenth century in what is now Great Britain, and announced the epoch of capitalist expropriation of the common property which created a new class of private landowners on the one hand, and on the other their counterparts, the landless, the social forerunners of the modern industrial proletariat.

So the language of this book also wants to remain a common good, free for use outside the control of its expert elites, professional linguists and grammarians, professional archivists of its words and grammatical rules, those language mandarins that Voloshinov called its clergy, the chosen keepers of its obscure secret.

To sum up: this book was not written in the language of amateurism but, on the contrary, in a deliberately chosen amateurism of language, in the disciplinary as well as in the linguistic sense. Not only was it not written in a language used by historians or film theorists; it wasn't even written in the Croatian language.

And for this kind of work it could find no better model than Želimir Žilnik and his work on film. It is true of him more so than of anyone else in these parts, the thing we should all remember. We all started out as amateurs. Only the best of us still are.

The readers will thus search in vain in the pages of this book for expert references, bibliographies and footnotes, the scholarly apparatus typical of academic discussions and highbrow works of nonfiction. Anyone interested in those can use Google to their heart's content. They will find everything they need there.

At the end, to repeat: this is not a book about the past. It is an introduction to the problem called the past.

Boris Buden · 2013

The Past and
How to Acquire One

Life after People

It is said that we are living in post-utopian times which have lost all interest in the future. The reason for this may be as simple as it is unexpected: the future no longer interests us because we have already seen it. This is at least the way it comes across in the television series *Life After People*, a post-apocalyptic science fiction documentary about the world as it may appear after the human race had suddenly vanished from the face of the Earth. The film does not tell us anything about why or how this came about, but it shows us, along the linear scale of time, the human world gradually decaying and perishing. So we see what happens on day one, day two, a month later, three months later, and even ten thousand years later, to human corpses, abandoned supermarkets, empty cities, the buildings in which we now live, the cultural heritage and the works of art. In one episode, for example, we see Michelangelo's frescoes disappear within the ruins of the Sistine Chapel. We also witness the moment when the sea engorges the Manhattan subway system, when the skyscrapers in our cities begin to cave in, and the animal world begins to reclaim the spaces from which humans have disappeared for good.

As a matter of fact, this documentary series does not show simply what we know about the world and about life in the aftermath of the disappearance of us humans. Far more readily it shows the boundless power of our knowledge, which appears here to be greater and stronger than nature itself. The proper subject of this film is the immortality of our knowledge, capable of outliving our own natural mortality. It is a film about the boundlessness of knowledge capable of transcending not only any natural boundary but also any boundary of time. This is the kind of knowledge that knows what the world will look like ten thousand years after the human species has disappeared.

At this point one cannot help but wonder out loud: Are we truly living in postutopian times? Is not *Life After People* an abundantly obvious instance of a utopian vision? But, what kind of utopia is this? The classical kind that concerns itself with the conditions of social life and fires up our imagination in the future dimension? Why, certainly not!

There is a moment in the film when knowledge enters the stage personified in the character of the expert, one of those figures Anthony Giddens calls "the clever people," frequently invited by the media to elucidate competently the "background" of a news item from the strength of their disciplinary knowledge. So, who is this person, this "clever man" called upon to explain to us in the film what will occur in the future and what the future will look like? Is he a futurologist? An expert in social sciences, say, a sociologist? The author of a sci-fi novel? An undead Marxist? On the contrary, in *Life After People*, the expert brought in front of the camera is a forensic pathologist. What in the world could a forensic pathologist have to say about the future? This question is more pertinent than it may seem at first sight.

But, first of all, what is forensics? In his *Rhetoric*, Aristotle defines three main domains of rhetoric, namely, deliberative, epideictic and forensic, relating them to three dimensions of time. While the first, deliberative or political rhetoric concerns itself with the future, i.e., aims to persuade people to take this or that concrete action, the epideictic or ceremonial rhetoric is concerned with the present time in which a rhetorician praises or censures people for what they do. The third, forensic or juridical rhetoric turns to the past. Its goal is to determine the truth or falseness of events that took place in the past.

With this in mind, we could say that the documentary series *Life After People* (which, incidentally, premiered in 2008 on the channel that deals with the past, the History Channel) does not simply show the future of nature after the disappearance of the human species. It rather treats nature as humanity's grave, which, with a kind of forensic anticipation, it digs as if it were an archeological site. In short, it speaks of the future using forensic rhetoric, that is to say, imagines it from the perspective of the past.

The past is another culture

The past is no longer where it used to be. It is no longer behind us as one dimension of time continuous with the present in which we live or the future that is ahead of us. Past is not even what it once had been. Today it is a cultural rather than temporal category. Much like culture, it is everywhere and in everything that surrounds us, just like it is ahead of us and behind us. It is not something we have left behind so that now we could turn back to take a look at it, but also something we have yet to step into, something that is new to the extent that it is alien, unfamiliar, foreign, different, in short, another culture. *The Past is a Foreign Country* was the title

David Lowenthal gave his book more than a quarter century ago. The title is taken from the opening sentence of L. P. Hartley's 1953 novel *The Go-Between*: "The past is a foreign country: they do things differently there." It is nearly impossible to express the main idea more succinctly: the past does not appear to us in the dimension of time, but in the dimension of cultural difference. When we say that something is "old," we ascribe to it a cultural quality that to us could be entirely new. In other words, our very relationship to time has taken on a cultural meaning. This is why today we perceive time in its (three-)dimensionality primarily through a process of cultural differentiation.

It is only in this sense that we can grasp what is meant today by the phrase "culture of the past." It does not refer to a culture from our past, a culture that once was alive but which has, in the kitschy parlance of today, vanished in the vortex of time, so that it remains accessible to us only as memory, more or less materialized as cultural heritage. It does not refer to the idea of culture characterized by clearly distinguished historical periods such as the culture of ancient Egypt, ancient Greece, Rome, the culture of pre-revolutionary, absolutist France, Victorian culture of nineteenth-century Britain, or, in the end, the modernist culture of former socialist Yugoslavia. "Culture of the past" signifies, by contrast, exactly what the word says, namely, that we live in a culture whose primary distinction, its *differentia specifica*, is its insatiable interest in what is past. What is more, to the extent that we perceive such "culture of the past" as our own, we identify (in the sense of belonging) with a very specific historical period, the time in which the obsession with what has passed takes on the dimension of an entire culture. "Culture of the past" names the epoch in which we live and that which distinguishes this epoch from the others, that is, our contemporaneity from the past and the future.

The past today is then not merely a dimension of time, but a cultural dimension of time as such, what we experience through time as time. In Heideggerian terms, in the past as (a) culture we are perceiving the temporality of time itself. To the extent that the past has become culture, it no longer exists "in time" but is temporality itself. This also affects its place, as we said earlier. David Lowenthal starts his aforementioned book about our obsession with the past with the sentence, "The past is everywhere." What is the meaning of this "everywhere?" It means the past is all around us, ubiquitous, *omnipresent* in English, and similarly in French, Italian and Spanish, and *allgegenwärtig* in German. To say that the past is everywhere is to imply its presence in the time in which we live, its presence in the present, its contemporariness. In the grammar of the culture dominant today, therefore, the past is articulated in the present, being nothing more than the (cultural) form of the present.

The unstoppable advent of memory

French historian Pierre Nora, who shares David Lowenthal's sensibilities for this epochal turning of the past, has tried to date the phenomenon more precisely in *Reasons for the Current Upsurge in Memory*. The first symptoms, along with the general social and political, economic and cultural conditions of what Nora describes as "age of ardent, embattled, almost fetishistic 'memorialism'" that has swept the entire world, he discovered in France in the mid-1970s. Nora identifies three general phenomena which brought about this shift from history to memory, specifically, from a historical consciousness France had of itself towards a consciousness founded on memory and through memory.

These are first of all consequences of the oil crisis that seized in 1974 the industrial countries of the West, and which the French society was starting to feel more intensely in those years. The crisis marked the end of a thirty-year period of stability characterized by accelerated economic growth, industrialization, and urbanization. In this postwar period the entire rural world of France, along with its traditions, customs, landscapes, and occupations, the world that had until the beginning of WWII secured the feelings of endurance and stability for the French society, vanished completely. While 50 percent of the French population found employment in agriculture in the immediate aftermath of the war, already by 1975 that number had fallen below 10 percent. This world—this *way of life* of rural France—vanished, leaving its traces only in "rural memory" stored in the emotions of individuals and scholarly publications. This is the period that sees an intensely growing interest in so-called cultural heritage, that is, in its preservation. It was no accident that in 1980, the then-president of the French Republic Valéry Giscard d'Estaing decided to give special attention to national heritage. A representative and symbol of all that was new and urban, European, progressive, and technocratic, d'Estaing discovered in his presidential role an embodiment of the old, traditional, and rural, of everything that survived in memory alone.

The second, political factor that brought about the boom of the new memorialist consciousness and culture Nora locates in the end of the era of de Gaulle. The death of this hero of the French Resistance to the Nazi occupation let into the open the dark memories of the repressed facts of French collaboration and the shameful period of Vichy France which was to become, in Nora's words, "the past that did not pass." Marcel Ophüls's 1969 documentary *The Sorrow and the Pity* (*Le Chagrin et la Pitié*) that spoke openly about French collaborationism and anti-Semitism was banned in the 1970s.

Beyond the Revolution

The period following the death of de Gaulle was marked by another shift in the relationship of the French to their past, a growing interest in the more distant, deeper past. France discovered its pre-revolutionary, royalist past. At this time François Furet wrote in his book *Penser la Révolution française*, "The French Revolution is over." And so the two hundred years of modern post-revolutionary French history were integrated as a brief segment in the history of the nation—that is, of the nation-state—that stretched over millennia. Suddenly the French were a thousand years old, rather than just two hundred.

It was not just the epoch-making meaning of the French Revolution, far exceeding the boundaries of the French nation-state, what once would have been called a world-historic event, that ended up relativized in the context of French national history. The very idea of revolution, which had until then crucially marked the history of the twentieth century, began to fade in the intellectual and in the practical sense. Nora diagnoses "the intellectual collapse of Marxism" as early as the 1970s. The reputation enjoyed by the Soviet Union in those years, at least in the pro-communist political circles worldwide, rapidly declined. The military suppression of the Prague Spring in 1968, re-Stalinization during Brezhnev's rule following the brief "thaw" of the Khrushchev era, and the more flagrant cases of dissidence were some of the reasons for the utter loss of international prestige for the first socialist state and one of the two world superpowers at the time. Finally, a translation of Solzhenitsyn's *The Gulag Archipelago* was published in France in

1975 to enormous success. A new generation of philosophers arrived on the scene in those years, the French *nouveaux philosophes* (the "new philosophers" André Glucksmann, Pascal Bruckner, Bernard-Henry Lévy, Alain Finkielkraut, etc.) who made a radical break with the inheritance of twentieth-century Marxist thought and not only in France. At the same time, the political influence of the French Communist Party, still Stalinist at its core, waned irreparably. In the land of the Revolution, as France had until then identified itself, the very idea of revolution was marginalized in the intellectual and the political life of the country. This shook to the core the concept of historical time. The society that had until then looked to the future with confidence and hope now turned to the past. The vision of radical historical rupture was replaced with the idea of tradition. Nora speaks of "the meteoric rise of the cult of national heritage," revealing its source to be "the disappearance of historical time oriented by the revolutionary idea, (that) restored to the past its freedom, its indetermination, its stature—both material and immaterial."

This transformation affected, of course, the French political scene, not only by weakening the Communist Party. In the early 1970s Jean-Marie Le Pen formed the National Front, a far-right, ultra-conservative party-movement which would establish itself in the coming years as the third political power in the country, taking over the position once held by the Communists.

1970s in Yugoslavia: the conservative turn

It is interesting to mention here that Žilnik diagnosed a similar conservative turn in the 1970s Yugoslavia, also attributed to the tectonic shifts caused by "the earthquake of state socialism following the occupation of Czechoslovakia." He explicitly calls the 1970s the "decade of re-Stalinization" that deliberately renewed the language of party-sponsored, Stalinist repression of the 1950s. It is worth remembering that Yugoslavia was also affected by the oil crisis during this period. The multiple—fourfold, to be precise—increases in the price of oil between 1973 and 1974 alone led the country into a debt crisis and dependence on international financial capital and its institutions, the World Bank and International Monetary Fund. (During this decade Yugoslavia's foreign debt grew from two to twenty billion U.S. dollars.) At the beginning of the 1980s they forced Yugoslavia to introduce what now gets called

Marie-Janine Calic, Dietmar Neutatz, Julia Obertreis, *The Crisis of Socialist Modernity: The Soviet Union and Yugoslavia in the 1970s*, 2011

austerity measures when speaking about a similar debt crisis in the South of Europe. By the mid-1970s, Yugoslavia was also engulfed by the global recession showing the first symptoms of the crisis of classic Fordism. By the late 1970s and early 1980s, the neoliberal economic policies took over the dominant capitalist countries in the West, Great Britain and the United States, supported by the rightwing conservative political forces.

Žilnik thinks the re-Stalinization of the 1970s was responsible for another change whose tragic consequences would not be fully felt until the 1990s. This change concerns the turn to "traditionalist sentiments, from nationalism to some sort of cultural traditionalism," in short, to the embrace of conservative cultural values and their political expression, nationalism. The agents of this conservative break he sees in the intellectual and academic elites of the former country, that is to say, not in its overt enemies, the defeated pro-fascist forces of WWII. In other words, the turn was a consequence of an immanent political development. An analogue to France in the same period, we can say that Yugoslavia also experienced an epoch-making exhaustion of the revolutionary idea, and therefore the withdrawal of historical time along with its general orientation towards a future. Here, like in France, the past gradually replaces history, and interest in traditionalist values, for what in France gets called national or cultural heritage, eclipses what had been the dominant interest in radical social transformation fed by the visions of social justice and carried by the energy of modernist progress. In those 1970s, then, Yugoslavia, within the framework of its own socialist system, followed the global epoch-making trend whose fallout, roughly ten years later, it would not survive.

The age of commemoration

Pierre Nora called this the "memorialist" trend (*mouvement de la mémoire*) and declared the entire period "the age of commemoration." He saw the cause of this tidal wave of memorialism in two important historical phenomena coinciding. The first can be encapsulated in the concept of the "acceleration of history," which refers fundamentally to the fact that the central feature of today's world is no longer its permanence or its continuity but its changing. Accelerating change turns everything around us immediately into the past, which results in the transformation of the way our remembering is organized. Remembering can no longer hold together historical time, guarantee its unity, and connect the present and the past to the future in a linear fashion. We do not know today what we should remember from the past in order to secure a future. We know even less about what those who come after us should know about us in order to understand their own lives. That impossibility of anticipation of the future forces us to hoard, randomly for the most part, any possible trace of our existence that could testify to what we are today or to what we may one day represent to those in our future. At the same time, this acceleration of history has cut us off from the past. It is no longer a part of our lives. The only communication with it is possible through its traces and imprints. We can restore it only through detailed reconstruction using documents and archives. The notion of memory has become in that sense so broad and all-encompassing that we could take it to mean the same as the past. Thus Nora, "In other words, what we today call 'memory'—a form of memory that is itself a reconstruction—is simply what was called 'history' in the past."

Democratization of history

There is still another reason for this surge of memory that Nora defines as social and calls the "democratization of history." It is the rising interest in memory across broad segments of society, especially among ethnic minorities and individuals. Nora sees in this interest emancipatory motivation and potential. In most cases there is desire in people to rehabilitate their past and in this way reaffirm their identities.

This trend, in the broadest sense, is made possible by a threefold process of decolonization: international, in which entire societies re-discover their past that the colonial power had suppressed; internal, in which a range of newly mobilized minorities, sexual, social, religious and other, within the framework of traditional western societies now use their memory to demand from a larger community a recognition of their difference; finally, there is the ideological decolonization in which individuals and groups rediscover their past that had been confiscated by totalitarian regimes, in a way that has been most evident in Eastern Europe and South America.

The phenomenon discussed here is often encapsulated in the notion of "collective memory." Nora writes,

"History was the sphere of the collective; memory
that of the individual. History was one; memory, by

definition, plural (since by nature individual). The
idea that memory could be collective, emancipatory,
and sacred turns the meaning of the term inside out."

The ascendance of collective memory coincides with the intensifying politicization and commercialization of the past, as in its use for tourism. Yet there is an even more important consequence of the collectivization of memory: historians lose their monopoly on the exclusive interpretation of the past. The moment the relationship between collective history and individual memory is inverted, once memory has become collective, the control over the past has slipped from the historians' hands. They are no longer in charge of establishing the facts, producing evidence, and delivering the ultimate truth about what really happened in the past. In other words, the aura of scientific truth has vanished from their works and discussions. As Nora writes, today the historian, when it comes to "manufacturing" the past, shares his role "with the judge, the witness, the media and the legislator." The aura which always distinguished the "truth" of the past did not only just shift towards the side of memory. It has dissolved over the limitless sphere of amateurism. What now goes for knowledge about the past is like what goes for an artistic skill, say, acting. Of the amateur actors he hired for his films, Žilnik will say,

"So, if you were to ask me now, is the talent that
graduated from acting academies and other schools,
could you compare them with nonprofessionals, I'd
say yes, I could compare them, like I could compare
the perfect pitch in a musician who went to the music academy and a man who's just a wedding singer
but you can tell he has the perfect pitch."

The past remembered by amateurs is no less authentic than the past "apprehended" by historians.

Life after society

But, let's return to the beginning, to *Life After People*. There is also a scientific, or, more precisely, a sociological conception of sociality "after people." For this notion we could use the term "transhuman sociality." It fundamentally questions the persistent understanding of sociality as an exclusively human phenomenon. This conviction seems obsolete today.

Sociologist Karin Knorr Cetina proposes that we separate the notion of sociality from its fixation on purely human groups. The kind of sociality she has in mind also includes objects. This is, as she writes, an "object-centered sociality." In other words, what we used to call sociality and believed it only had to do with humans, today belongs in the past. It has been exposed to something this sociologist calls "objectualization," which implies that today objects have replaced human beings as our social partners and as our social environment, that is, that objects to an ever-greater degree mediate human relations. The ascendance of sociality focusing on objects is just a moment in what Karin Knorr Cetina calls the "postsocial" development.

To live "after society" does not mean we are finally rid of society, but rather that our sociality has been supplemented by objects. In other words, we are still social beings, but now we share our sociality with objects.

Objectualization of the post-social conditions of contemporary life is the other side of the simultaneous experience of individuation. This is the experience that Giddens calls "being disembedded" from the classical, or, as Paolo Virno put it, "substantial community." Individuation in this sense is a symptom of the postsocial turn. It does not happen within society but is itself just a moment in society's dissolution.

This obviously has very concrete historical significance: the end of industrial societies—the nation states which developed in response to the social consequences of capitalist industrialization. The phenomenon of the social appears historically in conjunction with the development of social policy, or, as some authors call it, the nationalization of social responsibility. They include here labor regulation, pensions, and various forms of social care, including care for the unemployed, public education, etc. These developments brought to the historical scene new forces that decided human fate, the so-called impersonal social forces. Phenomena such as individual risk, poverty, inequality, are now understood to have social causes.

In short: industrialization has facilitated the development of various forms of social welfare, social embedding, and social interpretations, all of them mediated by the nation state, that is, by the political forces typical of industrial modernity such as trade unions, labor movements, etc. The pinnacle of this historical development is the institution of the (Western) social welfare state with its social policies and collective insurance for protection against individual catastrophes. Today, however, this development has stalled. The welfare state has been subjected, as Knorr Cetina argues, to a kind of general overhaul. She does not say in whose political interest. We can therefore add that today the welfare state is subjected to the process of general dismantling in which the leading roles are played by very concrete—neoliberal—political forces.

This is the historical context of what Karin Knorr Cetina calls the "postsocial objectualization," the context that articulates a society focused on objects.

Still, not all objects take equal parts in this new kind of postsocial socialization. Those related to commodities and instruments, which have been of primary interest to traditional sociology, seem to be excluded from the idea of new sociality focusing on objects. In fact, at play are only the so-called objects of knowledge which enable and participate in the expansion of sociality into the sphere of non-human objects, i.e., into the sphere of things.

Knorr Cetina claims that the postsocial transformation is closely related to the dispersion of the processes and structures of knowledge into social life. In this scenario, the postsocial relations are not simply a-social or non-social. They are, writes Knorr Cetina, "creolized" with other cultural principles not encompassed by the social in the past, foremost among them knowledge, culture, and expertise. This is, of course, about the so-called knowledge society. But the emphasis here is on "society," not on "knowledge." Society is now more likely to be inside the knowledge processes than outside them. Knowledge has become constitutive of social relations. But as knowledge cultures revolve fundamentally around the worlds of objects that are of interest to experts and scientists, we could say that in the knowledge society object relations replace social relations, that is, they have become constitutive of social relations. In short, the paradigmatic relationship of all social relations today is precisely the relationship of scientists and experts to the objects of their expertise and research.

This is after all the historical and social context in which the documentary series *Life After People* was made and viewed. But this is also the context in which we could ask about the meaning and the relevance of the old, familiar question about the social character of artistic creation. Or, to put it even more concretely, what is in this context the meaning of that practically self-evident thesis, for example, that Želimir Žilnik in his movies deals mostly with characters from the social margins, the social outsiders, and that it is precisely this, that is to say his social inclusivism, that gives his films their emancipatory meaning? What is the meaning of this thesis now that any clear boundary has been erased between what is outside and what is inside society; now that it no longer seems possible clearly to distinguish between human and non-human societies; now that what used to be understood as "social causes" have disappeared from the horizon of social interpretation and political action; now that social experience also includes objects, primarily objects of knowledge; now, finally, that what was once called social solidarity has expanded into the sphere of things and objects?

But, while we're talking about the arts, let us take a look at the most significant event in the arts today, documenta 13, which is winding down in Kassel as we write these lines.

Comrade Strawberry

Roman David-Freihsl begins his commentary on documenta 13 in the Viennese *Standard* with these unusual words:

> "What is really on the mind of a strawberry? She hangs out all day and seems to care about a good complexion more than anything. But, who knows? Great discontent may be raging among strawberries (*Erdbeeren*) because they are generally known just as berries (*Beeren*), and hardly anyone knows that they actually belong to the much more genteel family of roses (rosaceae). Are they happy, the strawberries? If organic fruits are also happier—like, as we know, organic chickens—then they are an absolute minority in any case. Only one to two percent of Austrian strawberries live in organic happiness."[01]

Strawberries could actually decide one day what they want. That, at any rate, is the intention of Carolyn Christov-Bakargiev, the curator of documenta, who wants to give to animals and plants in equal measure the political right to participate in decision-making:

---

01 "Sie hängen nur rum—aber sind sehr beliebt: Die Erdbeere gehört emanzipiert, sagt die documenta-Chefin," *Der Standard*, June 8, 2012. http://tinyurl.com/58wt6vsa

"The question is not whether we should give the permission to participate in elections to dogs or strawberries, but how a strawberry could articulate its political intent," she explained in an interview with the *Süddeutsche Zeitung*. "I don't want to protect animals and plants, I want to emancipate them."

This is no wonder in a postsocial society centered on objects. Karin Knorr Cetina claims that there is a kind of solidarity that centers objects.[02] Scientists and experts, for example, develop relationships with objects they study, relationships which encompass love, passion, ecstasy even, and, of course, solidarity. So this sociologist quotes the biologist, cytogeneticist Barbara McClintock, the Nobel Laureate for physiology and medicine in 1983, who has said of herself that she has been in the state of subjective fusion with the objects of her knowledge, "in a love relationship with the world of objects:" "Every time I walk on grass I feel sorry because I know the grass is screaming at me."

And yet, we could ask if this grass, or that strawberry from documenta, if they would get sad if the scientist, or the curator, lost their job due to the government-imposed budget cuts and austerity measures in education, scientific research, and culture? What, in fact, if the social sensibility which has expanded into the sphere of objects has simultaneously abandoned the society focused on people? A cut is supposed to be painful. And it is hurtful in any case, but only to individuals. A cut no longer hurts socially. And it doesn't hurt objects, the grass or the strawberry.

Whereas classical society developed the means and mechanisms to control and reduce social pain mostly in the form of the welfare state, which is itself a sort of social analgesic—the social painkiller of industrial modernity—today's postsocial condition no longer needs this remedy because it is already completely socially anesthetized. Social sensitivity seems to have forever disappeared from "life after society."

That much the better

What confusion! The past which calls to us from the future, society without people, strawberries as political activists, amateurs who

---

02 See Karin Knorr Cetina, "Sociality with Objects: Social Relations in Postsocial Knowledge Societies," *Theory, Culture & Society* 14, no.4 (1997): 1–30.

know more than the professionals... But what is actually wrong with this confusion? Would we prefer false certainties, tired self-evidence, faded auras? We no longer know if the past is in front or behind us, don't know who's in charge of the truth about it, don't know any more if it's part of the society of people or the society of things. That much the better. In his essay about the collector and historian Eduard Fuchs, Walter Benjamin warns that the so-called cultural history, we could say as a historical form of our knowledge about the past, amasses its wealth on the backs of humanity, but does not eventually give it power to throw that weight off its back and take it into its own hands. Is today, then, when the cultural form, the only form in which we can still access the past, has slipped the control of the "officials" and rolls freely down the street, is today not the time to take it into our own hands? And to do it with the self-consciousness of amateurs come aware of the pile of shit all those mighty professionals had got them under?

From Uprising
in Jazak (1973)

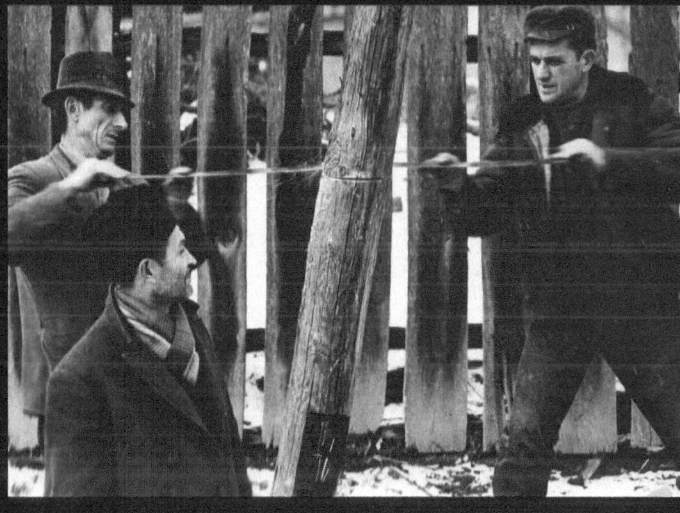

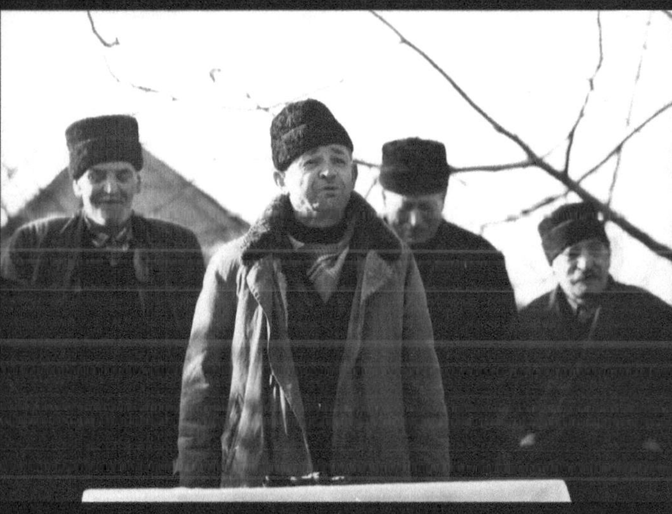

Out of Your Mind

Reading a book about the Yugoslav Black Wave cinema and the films of Želimir Žilnik, right there in the opening pages I came across this phrase: "Žilnik is one of those Serbian directors…" Nothing out of the ordinary, one would think, just as I did at the time. This is an entirely banal categorization that can be found in any text concerned in the broadest sense with cultural production anywhere, in any one of its elements. Instead of Serbian, it could have equally been about a Croatian, French or American director, or a Russian realist writer, German idealist philosopher, Renaissance painter, etc. Normally we skim over these phrases barely noticing them and rarely wondering about their actual meaning. It is as if they were punctuation marks that structure the text and facilitate its comprehension but in themselves have no substantive signification.

This is how I also quickly gobbled up that phrase, albeit not without some sense of discomfort, and went on to consider, much like the book, the questions of Žilnik's cinematic language, the influence of other cinematic poetics on his work, analyses of individual films he had made, the problems of activism and documentation, etc. Still, the discomfort about that phrase from early in the book never really left me. With each new subject the author raised it kept growing, casting a dark shadow over the entire discursive content of the book and eventually putting in question the very value of its insight. "Želimir Žilnik, the Serbian director"—maybe this time we should not let it all go just like that.

A dirty little compromise

At first it seems perfectly clear where this discomfort might have originated. Was not the bulk of Žilnik's work created in former Yugoslavia? Was not the society of former Yugoslavia, its ideological and historical assumptions, its political reality and cultural life, the formative influence on the director's work, not only when it came to the work's context, but first of all as the motivation or the subject of his cinematic creation? How did it all suddenly become "Serbian?" This question becomes even more pressing if we bear in mind that Žilnik's ideological-political habitus, which makes itself clear in his films' political engagements, has formed in direct opposition to, if not unambiguous criticism of, any "nationalization," thus also "Serbification" of social life and artistic creation. After all, "Serbian" always implies "not Yugoslav," and therefore also "not Slovenian, Macedonian, Croatian, Bosnian…." On what grounds are Žilnik's films now forcefully being seized from all of those not included in the notion of "Serbian," be they "non-Serbian cultures" or "non-Serbian" individuals, creative collaborators who once either directly participated in the creation of his films or made up the immediate intellectual and artistic environment for cultural production in which these films were made and which made up the films' subject matter? The same goes for the audiences today, that is, for the critical recipients of those films. Would you show, say, Žilnik's *Early Works*, a film made in 1960s Yugoslavia, in Sarajevo today as a foreign, Serbian film? Is a film critic, a student, or a PhD candidate writing in Zagreb today about the films of Želimir Žilnik critically evaluating the work of a foreign, Serbian film director, while their colleague in Belgrade treats of the work of one of "their own" filmmakers on whom they can lay a claim more authentically? And in what sense of authenticity? Referring to the cinematic idiom? To culture, politics, or history? To identity?

The uneasiness prompted by the phrase "Želimir Žilnik, the Serbian director" does therefore have its perfectly good reasons. This is a normal reaction to the falsification of the work itself, to the cultural and social reductionism, that is, to the forcible appropriation of cultural heritage implicit in that phrase. The fact that it is being tacitly normalized speaks first of all to the abnormality of the dominant cultural paradigm. More than that, it points to the violence that has been a constitutive element of that paradigm, the violence to which we have become completely inured. The thick skin that cannot feel the pain of injury is itself a result of countless blows and injuries to which it has been exposed for a long time and which have transformed it into an anesthetized lump of dead cells. These are the anesthetic presuppositions of (cinematic) aesthetics, the calloused feet of a beautiful cinematic soul that can walk barefoot over the hot coals of reality and not feel any pain.

"Želimir Žilnik, the Serbian director" is a dirty little compromise that remains unremarkable amidst the general corruption of the time that turns to look for a different kind of past. This is the past in which it was precisely not compromising that was the fundamental condition of creative expression. One could call this the avant-garde, but such categorization solidifies the meaning of the past without reviving its attitude. There is no compromise, no matter how wise, that could grasp the non-compromising nature of the past over which it desires contemplative dominion. After all, why would a time which has in many respects fallen behind the standards of its past get to pass sovereign judgment on that past? This is not a moral problem. It is that the knowledge it commands is insufficient. A knowledge that has confused its *a posteriori* vision for superiority, that believes it knows more because it comes after, cannot be the final arbiter of the past.

Would it not be more legitimate in this case, at least for the sake of an experiment, to reverse the relationship and call on the past to make a judgment on the present, to pry open its dead mouth so it can, at least in fantasy, lash out at this present and its arrogant bluster? Without compromises, of course.

Hommage à Tom

There is a character from the past, a creative player in the time whereof we speak, a man who could not distinguish reality from film. "The second I open my eyes," he used to say, "I see a film." No thick skin, no dead epithelium stood between the film Tomislav Gotovac was living and the reality that surrounded him. Just the iris of an open eye, full contact. After all, was it not Gotovac himself who used his body not only as an aesthetic medium, but precisely as an aesthetic sensation, the one for whom film as a medium was not a McLuhanesque extension of bodily sensations, but the exact opposite, the one for whom bodily sensations were an extension of the medium of film?

So, let us imagine this Tom Gotovac, sometime in the 1970s, in one of the booths of the theater café in Zagreb, the famed Kavkaz, gesturing with great animation in conversations with friends, most likely about film. Let us assume then that one of those friends uses the phrase "Želimir Žilnik, the Serbian director." Tom would, we assume, immediately cut them off, brusquely and without compromise, but never arrogantly: "Oh come on! You think I'm out of my fucking mind!"

Profanity aside, the question remains. How has the radical attitude that clearly made up a crucial part of past cultural production—was even its very precondition—how could it subsequently be re-valorized by non-radical means: by cultural or film theory (in our case), by art history, by archiving and preservation, by curating cultural heritage, national canonization, etc.? Does this past attitude not oblige us to a comparable one today? Can it be otherwise understood, that is, remembered? Or is its product, fetishized in

41

the form of the so-called original work of authorship, all that remains? Does the relationship with the past not also entail a moment of repetition, re-actualization, re-cognition, in short, an act
of reenactment that transcends the cult of authenticity? This is
not just about the new dressed up as the old in order to experience
the past as it ostensibly really was, reduced of course to a cultural
way-of-life; on the contrary, this is about the work of translation
that enables what has passed to speak the language of the present,
and, quoting the work, to revive the attitude that had made that
work possible and gave it form.

Because, what is the alternative?

Only in accordance with the ego

On the final pages of the book mentioned above—it matters not
which one; it is one actually excellent book about the cinematic
work of Želimir Žilnik—so, in the last paragraph of that book that
at the beginning speaks unremarkably about this filmmaker as a
Serbian director, we shall read this:

> "The work of Želimir Žilnik ... functions exclusively
> in accordance with his ego which is the foreground
> for each of his individual works on film or television.
> In the process of accepting all the characteristics
> of his cinematic language it is necessary to be *a
> posteriori*, or else encounter a strong barrier at the
> level of communication."

Only now can we understand the meaning and function of the
phrase "Serbian director." Whereas "Serbianness" vouches for
continuity between the past and the present at the level of cultural
generality—as well as a criterion of selection between that which
passes irretrievably and that which remains—the artist's "ego"
does that job at the level of an individual work of art. They are two
complementary registers. The "Serbianness" is an organ of cultural
memory beyond temporality. It persists through all historical ca-
taclysms, through feudalisms and capitalisms, though socialisms
and communisms, nationalisms and neoliberalisms; it outlives its
every captain, king, and politician, every victim and every villain;
it is renewed in each historian and linguist, poet and painter, actor
and director that it has. Žilnik is safe there, stored for safekeeping
in time immemorial. Immortal. In the company of other immortals
inseparable from that cultural genealogy, from Saint Sava to Žika

Pavlović and beyond.

"Serbianness" is an obscure medium of cultural canonization. It is obviously not made up of individuals but of their bodies of work which are themselves nothing less than mini-canons of their works compiled in a no-less obscure medium that is the artist's "ego." This trivial psychological category figures as the sole attestation of the unity, continuity, and completeness of the work. It holds the work together through all social and political changes, through economic crises and cultural transformations. And it clearly discriminates between this work and any other cultural and artistic production, as well as the work's own technical conditions of possibility, that is, its collective character. The "ego" brings harmony to the historical chaos in which the work had been created and homogenizes the heterogeneity of artistic, especially cinematic creation, and retroactively inscribes necessity into the contingencies of reality. Let us say that again in the words of the author of the said book: "The work of Želimir Žilnik... functions exclusively in accordance with his ego which is the foreground for each of his individual works on film or television." No doubt remains here: without Žilnik's "ego" his work will not function. Not in any place, not in any way, not for anyone.

The psychological category of "ego" revives the cult of the author, declared dead by Roland Barthes way back when Žilnik was making his first works on film and when the most important works of the Yugoslav Black Wave cinema were created. Although trivialized to the point of psychological abstraction, where it functions as a self-contained and non-contradictory entity, this "ego-author" still manages to accomplish its crucial goal—to maintain the aura of the work of art over the works of an author and to secure to them as a whole the old romantic qualities of originality, authenticity, and inimitability. It is ironic, of course, that Walter Benjamin recognized as early as the 1930s that it was precisely film, that is the mechanical nature of film production, that announced the historic end of the artistic aura. This is the paradox that haunts the idea of auteur film like a specter, since it tries to assign exclusive artistic quality to such films, to differentiate them from so-called genre films by their superior aesthetic values lacking in the regular film production. This is how the difference, the critical tension and even contradiction between auteur film and "Hollywood" appears to us as the difference between art and not-art, pushing aside all its presuppositions and implications, be they social, ideological, political, etc. Art or not art? That is the wrong question.

This makes itself clear in the fact that it is not just the work that needs the aura; Serbianness needs it even more. It makes not just the work of a "Serbian director" but Serbianness itself original, authentic, and inimitable. It is a symbiosis, or, better yet, a pragmatic deal: I give you aesthetic sublimity, you give me immortality.

Fruitless, hollow, impractical, ineffective, ineffectual

While we are on the topic of death and immortality, it is interesting to note that the author of said book insists that the correct understanding of Želimir Žilnik's cinematic work, of his original style, that is, his cinematic language, only becomes possible after the fact, to wit: "In the process of accepting all characteristics of his cinematic language it is necessary to be *a posteriori…*" What is the meaning of this "a posteriori?" *A posteriori* in relation to what?

The key word in the answer to this question is "language." Once we symbolically sum up the practice of film production in the concept of language, we have no choice but to look at it *a posteriori*. The reason is simple. One should recall that the understanding of the structure and content of modern languages follows the model set up for the understanding of a dead, foreign language. This is what Voloshinov called abstract objectivism in linguistics. In other words, the grammars and dictionaries of Serbian and Croatian, German and French or English treat their languages as if they were dead and foreign, that is, as if they were, say, Latin. In fact, it was only after Latin stopped being a vernacular language that it became possible to enumerate all of its characteristics and write down all the words mentioned in Latin manuscripts. Ancient Roman linguists did the same for Homer's Greek, and Buddhist monks for the holy Sanskrit scriptures. We are doing the same with the cinematic language of Želimir Žilnik when we want to "accept all its characteristics." (Really ALL? What happens if we miss any?) We have to approach it *a posteriori*, i.e., we have to treat it as if it were dead. It's an ugly job. Virtually impossible. What makes it worse is that it is "fruitless, hollow, impractical, ineffective, ineffectual." (These adjectives are listed online as possible Croatian translations for the English word "futile." Serbian online dictionaries add: worthless, unpromising, etc.) I borrowed this word "futile" from the brilliant book by David Bellos, *Is That a Fish in Your Ear? Translation and the Meaning of Everything*. A sentence on page 97 reads, "To try to capture 'all the words of a language' is as futile as trying to capture all the drops of water in a flowing river. If you managed to do it, it wouldn't be a flowing river any more. It would be a fish-tank."

When we apply this to the case of the "Serbian director" Želimir Žilnik: if you manage to "accept all characteristics of his film language," it is not a language of the moving image. It would be the language of a box of dead pictures, maybe of a photo album. It would not be the language of a filmmaker and culture worker who makes films, not just in different social and political conditions and different historical periods, but mostly against those various social and political conditions and often at odds with the dominant currents that marked those different historical periods. It would be the language of a Serbian ego-author, a Serbian language.

And in fact, any philosophy of language that starts from this, let's call it necrophiliac position, which in order to understand a language has to treat it as dead on arrival, on the model of the study of dead classical languages, culminates in the Romantic identification of language with the spirit of the nation. What goes for Humboldt's and Herder's Germanness must go for Serbianness. It is built, renewed, and perfected in language and through language, and so in the cinematic language of a film director, say, Želimir Žilnik.

Caretaker, undertaker, safekeeper

For the phrase "Serbian director," as we said, "Serbianness" is not just the organ of cultural memory out of time, but the medium of cultural canonization.

Here it is worth remembering a few facts of its history. Modern literary canons emerged as national languages were being established in the eighteenth and nineteenth centuries, also on the model of Latin as the universal, superior language, and at a remove from it. At the same time and in a similar way—through the profanation and transformation of Latin and Christian dogmas—emerged the modern artistic canons grounded in the homogenizing concept of so-called fine arts (*les beaux arts*). The central feature of this process of canonization was its thoroughgoing segregation from social relations. That process had started earlier, during the Renaissance, with the elevation of painting into a so-called true liberal art (*artes liberales*), which resulted in the emancipation of artists from the bonds of their guilds and their differentiation from artisans. In the eighteenth and nineteenth centuries, the distinction between arts and crafts sharpened and reached its pinnacle in the concept of art for art's sake and the cult of artistic genius. Genius and near-godlike creativity separated artists not only from their social relations and mundane labor, but also from time and space as such. The aim of canonization is to save the artist and his work from social death and oblivion, that is, to make him and his work immortal. As much as canonization may rest on the idea of art as a sublime sphere of life, elevated beyond the reach of social and historical realities, modern artistic canons are, by contrast, deeply rooted exactly in social and political life, in the concrete reality directly contingent on being institutionalized. Even the most sublime aesthetic value still has one very concrete, real function—it serves to cultivate the nation, it is used for what the aforementioned Humboldt and Herder called *Bildung*, that is, for education, refinement, general cultural uplift, etc. To keep it brief: the immortality of great men who took their places in the sublime spheres of the canon has depended directly on the social-political substrates of these canons, on their institutional infrastructure, on schools, universities, and museums, on academies, theaters, and libraries...in short, on the nation state as their material safekeeper.

This is why there is nothing personal in the critique of that strident phrase "Želimir Žilnik, the Serbian director." The phrase is perfectly suited to the social reality, to the material, that is institutional preconditions of artistic canonization and cultural memory. "Serbian" means one thing only: a concrete, existing form of immortality. Whenever whoever digs your grave, the state will be there to preserve you forever!

This is why the canon is not to be imagined as the said sublime sphere of the pure aesthetic, that is, as cultural values elevated far above the paltry realities of social life. On the contrary, the canon is a very concrete, material thing, a room, a building, a shelf, some archival materials; the canon are the actual canonizers, archivists, curators, teachers, actors, directors...the circle is complete.

From Pale to eternity

In the year 2005 I had the dubious good fortune to see the canon, and the cinematic canon at that, in the instance of its creation, at the moment it appeared in its sheer institutional form without any content. As a participant in a film project I was present at the meeting—the first one and perhaps the last, I don't know—of the directors of two national film archives: Devleta Filipović, director of the National Film Archive of Bosnia and Herzegovina located in Sarajevo, and the director (I forget the person's name) of the National Film Archive of Republika Srpska located in Pale.[01] The latter institution was actually just undergoing the process of creation, so it did not yet exist as such, or, to put it another way, its director existed as did the group of his administrative collaborators, and also the rooms existed in which they worked, but the films did not, nor did any other supporting infrastructure, the archive, the cinema, etc. A national film archive *in statu nascendi*, a mere institutional shellwith no content.[02] Its counterpart in Sarajevo,

---

01 A town situated southeast of Sarajevo, the capital city of Bosnia and Herzegovina. During the Bosnian war (1992-1995) it was the administrative and command center of the Serbian forces.

02 This is what you can read today, in 2012, about the creation of the Film Archive of Republika Srpska (FARS) on the state's culture portal online: "FARS was established by the government as an institution of special interest for RS in early 2009, when Srna Film officially ceased operations and FARS became its legal successor. Previously, the archiving was done within Srna Film, the public film production company of RS, founded in 1992 with the aim of collecting and permanently preserving the archival film materials related to the immediate wartime developments in the region of RS, Bosnia and Herzegovina, and Serbian regions more broadly. From these materials was sourced the documentary production of Srna Film, the first and long the only production house in RS. One of the youngest institutions of culture in RS, FARS was created and developed authentically, not like other institutions, from the inherited material, human, or infrastructural resources. The greatest contributions to its creation and development came from a group of enthusiasts once gathered at Srna Film, who, as early as 1993, in addition to creating documentary footage and producing documentary films began the work of collecting cinematic works and creating the conditions for the founding of FARS. The film archive now holds a significant collection of fiction film (more than 1,000 titles) on 35mm and 16mm, including Yugoslav and foreign productions, largely of a recent date (latter half of the 20th century). The film collection also includes several hundred documentary films on 16mm and 35mm, made in former Yugoslavia between 1945 and 1991, as well as 300 negatives, various archival film material, newsreels, and a large collection of BETA, SVHS, and VHS recordings, digital recordings, audio and audio tape recordings, etc."

by contrast, had a wealth of material, but the infrastructure of the National Film Archive of Bosnia and Herzegovina was in decay, underfunded, kept afloat more by the fantastic enthusiasm of its workers than by the systemic care and support of the state. The encounter itself was completely absurd. The two people who undoubtedly shared one general interest most succinctly called "film," who were capable of having a rational and tolerant conversation, were at the same time infinitely divided by the institutional and political presuppositions underlying their shared interest and their work. Their conversation was pleasant, smart, moving, and meaningless, not to say completely futile ("fruitless, hollow, impractical, ineffective, ineffectual"). The only thing they had in common, aside from their genuine general interest in film, its preservation and proliferation, was the prospect not of their collaboration but of their bilateral leaning onto the "Big brother," the Yugoslav Film Archive in Belgrade. One side was to use it to renew what was decayed or destroyed; the other, so to say, to "imagine," if we can borrow the term from Benedict Anderson's *Imagined Communities*, which reminds us of the constructed, "imagined" character inherent to the process of creation of any national identity, or, in this case, of cinematic cultural heritage.

Besides all this, in the emptiness of this not-yet-film-archive one could feel the sublime distance from the dirty reality that had just given it life. In some uncannily self-evident way, it had already arrogated to itself the right to the utopia of a new, guileless beginning and began to draw energy from its high cultural goal, the preservation of the cultural heritage from whose destruction it had just emerged. Despite all that, these two modest ground-floor rooms, better suited for a dentist's office, the two or three women in the administrative jobs, pleasant, warm, and hospitable, and the director, a reasonable, tolerant film buff, could not do enough to hide the truth—the emptiness of the promise of eternity that could legitimize their existence.

What was said was then done. The National Film Archive of Republika Srpska is no longer empty. To a growing number of filmmakers and their works it not only promises but actually guarantees immortality, much like it provides cultural content and secures for the nation state that founded it the refinement of pure aesthetic values, original, authentic, and irreproducible. Would it be odd to find on the shelves of this film archive, among those more than one thousand features and hundreds of documentaries (see the footnote) a film or two by the Serbian director Želimir Žilnik? (A private message: Želimir, wouldn't it be better if they forgot all about you, if they used your films, as they are said to have done after WWII, to make some pairs of sandals out of them, so at least some people over there no longer had to walk barefoot?)

What was I actually going to say? Ah, yes, "Želimir Žilnik, the Serbian director?" Out of my fucking mind!

In the Graveyard of Dead Words *(fragments)*

The cinematic language of Želimir Žilnik? If it really is
a language, then we can go on to ask questions about its
lexicon. There seems to be no doubt, however, about who
is supposed to be in charge of its contents—film theory
is. Film theory commands the difference between what
is "purely cinematic" and what is non-cinematic: what is
social, broadly cultural, political, historical, and so on. It
supposes to know how much of the non-cinematic it can
permit within the ambit of its discourse without jeopar-
dizing its own authority, that is, bringing its own competence into question. Each time it makes a specific decision
about how many and which biographical facts, for example,
it will take into consideration in its critical assessment of
an author's filmography, to what degree it will interrogate
social and historical contexts, the cultural assumptions
of the films it valorizes and the political circumstances in
which they were created, it maps anew its disciplinary bai-
liwick and cuts up a new narrative patch to sew onto its
grand narrative called film. Outside this narrative, beyond
its language and its lexicon, remain the words and meanings undeserving of its attention.

Time has not been merciful to some of them either. It
ran over them and threw them onto the garbage heap, not
just one of film theories but the one of history itself. It's
as if they never meant anything to it. As if they had had
nothing to do with film or with life. As if they were not
worth mentioning, at least not after the fact, at least not
on some list of rejected, forgotten, dead words.

In his book, *Is That a Fish in Your Ear? Translation
and the Meaning of Everything*, David Bellos quotes a passage from the "novel" *La Vie, mode d'emploi* by Georges
Perec, which he translated into English as *Life, A User's
Manual*. Perec, incidentally also a documentary film director, lost both of his parents in WWII; his father was
killed in 1940 and his mother perished in Auschwitz in
1942; he was taken in and raised by his uncle and aunt,
and worked for seventeen years as an archivist in a library,
which affected his writing to a significant degree. In the
passage quoted he describes the career of one of his fictional characters who works for Larousse dictionaries as a

"word-killer." While others collect new words, his job is to make room for them by removing all the words and meanings that have fallen into disuse. This is not to say that he was not creating a dictionary of his own. A list of words removed is also a dictionary, a kind of graveyard for words, which, like any graveyard, is a place of memory, an opening into the past.

Should not we today, as we look back to films and their creators in our past, also work on a dictionary like that, on a list of words departed from life, but which once played decisive roles in the narrative called "Yugoslav film?" Should we not give them a dignified burial, like we do with people, even the worst of them? Let us start with **UDBA** (Uprava državne bezbednosti), the State Security Administration, that is, the Yugoslav secret police, often mentioned today in a packaged deal of a phrase, with the qualifier "notorious."

Zdenko Radelić, "The Communist Party of Yugoslavia and the Abolition of the Multi-party System: The Case of Croatia," 2016, essay in the book *Revolutionary Totalitarianism, Pragmatic Socialism, Transition*

UDBA, State Security Administration
(off screen)

Immortal Youth

BORIS BUDEN

<u>You say that one of the first cultural activities organized after the liberation of Belgrade was precisely filmmaking. When does that actually begin?</u>

ŽELIMIR ŽILNIK

In the summer of 1944, a film office was established as part of the Central Command of the National Liberation Front, to be run by Radoš Novaković. After Belgrade was liberated, the Central Committee for Cinematography was formed as part of the Government of the Federal People's Republic of Yugoslavia, and after that the national film company Zvezda film, and then the production houses Avala film and Filmske novosti (Newsreel) at the level of federal republics. Beginning in January 1945, *Kinohronike-informativni žurnali* (*Cine-chronicles–info journals*) were being filmed and screened in theaters ahead of the main features. Radoš Novaković made the feature documentary *The New Land* (*Nova zemlja*), about the resettlement in Vojvodina of people who had come from the burned-down villages of Bosnia and Dalmatia. In 1947, the first feature film *Slavica* was made, directed by Vjekoslav Afrić, and in 1948 Vojo Nanović directed *Immortal Youth* (*Besmrtna mladost*). Afrić had led the partisan theater which moved with the Central Command during WWII, and Nanović had been in charge of youth actions against the occupiers in Belgrade. The shooting of those first films would take five or six months. The crews could comprise a few hundred members. They were almost like war operations.

Film a continuation of war and socialist reconstruction with celluloid weapons!

BB

<u>Filmmaking as a medium of propaganda?</u>

ŽŽ

Above all, definitely that.

As early as 1946 Voja Nanović was shooting *the documentaries Victory Parade (Parada pobede) and The Pan-Slavic Congress (Sveslovenski kongres). He became the most prolific director. In 1950, he made the film fairy-tale The Magic Sword (Čudotvorni mač),* Hollywood-style in its use of imagination and technology.

The plot is set in the Middle Ages, with amazing costumes, makeup, scenery. They even built stages in the Postojna Cave and the ancient Roman arena in Pula. The evil giant Baš Čelik abducts the girl Vida, and the young hero saves her using the magic sword. The hero is played by Rade Marković, and he is willing to sacrifice his life for truth, love, and freedom. It's a film that totally works in the spirit of Peter Jackson's *Lord of the Rings.*

I remember, this was the first film I saw at Cinema Sloboda (Freedom) in Zemun. Among the cast are the actors who would dominate the scene for the next half century: Pavle Vujisić, Stevo Žigon, Milan Ajvaz, Milivoje Živanović. Another film Nanović made in 1953, titled *The Gipsy Girl (Ciganka),* based on the novel *Koštana* by Bora Stanković, was a wonder. For the first time on the screen, you see bare female breasts. Selma Karlovac was the name of that beauty, and the cast was made up of the most distinguished actors: Raša Plaović, Janez Vrhovec, Vladimir Medar, Pavle Vujisić... By 1960 Nanović had made eight feature films, which is, if we know the technical conditions and the size of these projects, the kind of productivity to match that of Fassbinder or of Michael Curtiz in America. And then, out of the blue—the news that Nanović had fled to the US.

BB

Do you know anything about the fate of this partisan and film director in the US?

ŽŽ

I met him in New York in November 1969. This happened at the moment when The Museum of Modern Art, Department of Film, invited twelve Yugoslav films to be screened between November 13 and 25. Us authors also came. The program was called *The New Yugoslav Cinema.*

They showed *The Event (Događaj)* and *Kaja, I'll kill you (Kaja, ubit ću te)* by Vatroslav Mimica; *When I Am Dead and White (Kad budem mrtav i beo)* and *Ambush (Zaseda)* by Živojin Pavlović;

The Museum of Modern Art

11 West 53 Street, New York, N.Y. 10019 Tel. 956-6100 Cable: Modernart

CONTEMPORARY YUGOSLAV CINEMA
FIRST TIME IN USA

The contemporary Yugoslavian scene, as reflected on the screen in New Yugoslav Cinema by ten major filmmakers in twelve feature motion pictures, will be presented in mid-November by The Museum of Modern Art. The twelve-day series, starting November 13th and continuing through November 25th, is the result of several trips made to Yugoslavia by Willard Van Dyke, Director of the Department of Film, who has viewed the most recent Yugoslav production from which the present selection was made. All the films were produced in the past three years and have been sub-titled for this occasion.

Five Yugoslav directors will come to this country to participate in the Museum showings. Represented by their own works in the series, they are among the youngest and most conspicuous filmmakers in that country today: Boro Drašković, who filmed "Horoscope;" Želimir Žilnik, director of "Early Works;" Dušan Makavejev, who directed "Innocence Unprotected;" Živojin Pavlović of "Ambush" and "When I Am Dead and White;" and Branko Ivanda, whose film "Gravitation" will open the series. Prior to the opening a private reception will be given (November 12) in the Founders Room of the Museum to honor the Yugoslav guests.

"The new Yugoslav cinema is inquiring, doubting, enigmatic and sometimes deeply critical of the society from which it springs. Its heroes are the defeated, the bewildered, and the unsatisfied savage young," states Mr. Van Dyke in announcing the series. On his frequent trips to Yugoslavia in the past year Mr. Van Dyke saw as many as twenty films a day, viewing miles of film footage before arriving at his final choice. The films chosen have not been seen here* and offer the American public and critics the opportunity to evaluate the most recent cinematic developments in this Eastern European country.

The themes, according to Mr. Van Dyke, are beginning to embrace youthful protest and revolt. "Gravitation," for example, tells of a young man who returns from the army completely listless, undirected and passive, his life ebbing in a sense of futility except for a brief fantasy of revolt. "Early Works," which won the Silver Bear at the Berlin Film

* with the exception of "Kaya, I'll Kill You" shown once at the Lincoln Center Film
Festival.

(more)

Press release for "New Yugoslav Cinema" series at the
Museum of Modern Art, New York (1969)

Innocence Unprotected (*Nevinost bez zaštite*) by Dušan Makavejev; *Gravitation* (*Gravitacija*) by Branko Ivanda; *The Journey* (*Pohod*) by Đorđe Kadijević; *Playing at Soldiers* (*Mali vojnici*) by Bato Čengić; *I Have Two Mummies and Two Daddies* (*Imam dvije mame i dva tate*) by Krešo Golik; *Horoscope* (*Horoskop*) by Boro Drašković; *Crows* (*Vrane*) by Mihić and Kozomara; and my *Early Works* (*Rani radovi*).

Major American newspapers wrote about the films and the theater was always full. Elia Kazan and Miloš Forman, who was then still adjusting to emigré life, came to the screenings, and so did Vojislav Nanović. He was skeptical at first, but when he saw the movies, he said,

> "I thought you were all revisionists, but now I see
> there are also some artists among you."

He invited me and Svetozar Udovički, who came along as our "chief of delegation" to visit him at home. Udovički knew him from before. He had an editing station in his apartment and told us he was making documentaries for ABC television and also making commercials for the auto industry. He explained to us the strict, almost dictatorial rules set by the filmmakers' union about how to put the crew together, technical standards, and movie content.

He stressed the advantages of a huge market, so one could live off the short pieces alone if they became successful. He asked about our situation and was puzzled by the prolific and free-ranging production. Visibly surprised, he explained to us that some of the biggest names of the "New Left" scene in New York were writing about our films, people like Dotson Rader, whose position and impact in America, among the youth, was comparable to the influence of Rudi Dutschke in Europe.

The man who killed two thousand men and
shagged two thousand women

From the conversation we realized that Voja probably withdrew when Avala Film, where he reigned supreme, brought in Ratko Dražević to take his place as director. Production policies changed. Instead of state-sponsored projects that shot for a long time, which occupied the entire studio for several months, which is what Nanović made, they decided to encourage co-production, to find co-financiers, and hire foreign actors.

Ratko Dražević, a high-ranking officer of the UDBA, with

'Early Works,' Yugoslav Romanticism

EARLY WORKS, directed by Zelimir Zilnik; screenplay (Croatian with English subtitles) by Mr. Zilnik and Branko Vucicevic, additional dialogue by Karl Marx and Friedrich Engels; photography by Karpo Godina Acimovic; produced by Avala Film (Belgrade) and Neoplanta Film (Novi Sad); released by Grove Press International. At the Bleecker Street Evergreen Cinema, 144 Bleecker Street. Running time: 87 minutes. (Not submitted at this time to the Motion Picture Association of America's Production Code and Rating Administration for rating as to audience suitability.)

Yugoslavia	Milja Vujanovic
Dragisa	Bogdan Tirnanic
Kruno	Cedomir Radovic
Marko	Marko Nikolic
Father	Slobodan Aligrudic

By ROGER GREENSPUN

"SO MY FILM is about the impossibility of changing the world by romantic means . . . ," but it is a romantic film nonetheless, an evocation of lucid idealism and of a dim reality that turns everything to confusion and defeat, but that does not lose its hold upon the imagination. "Early Works" is the first feature of Zelimir Zilnik, Yugoslav, not yet 30, revolutionary, and with the sense to know from what, as well as for what, he speaks.

At one point he even has somebody cry "Down with Romantics!," but the scene belies the sentiment: a broad calm river, a drifting raft, the early mist—a little like the great farewell to the River Po in Bernardo Bertolucci's "Before the Revolution," another young man's movie about the futility—and beauty—of romantic means. And once he holds his camera, for maybe 10 whole seconds on his sleeping heroine's profile, an enraptured, reticent and wholly romantic homage to her breathtaking and challenging beauty.

Her name is Yugoslavia, and together with three males shouting slogans and even conversing in aphorisms ("additional dialogue by Marx and Engels"), she sets out to persuade the peasants that the world must change. The four comrades fail, and as their revolutionary play grows more serious, it also becomes a self-destructive testing of intent, ending in a real killing and immolation for which all the practice, the "political theater" of Molotov cocktails and torture games, has been a preparation.

In style, "Early Works" resembles middle-period Jean-Luc Godard, looking a bit like "Band of Outsiders," and sounding a bit like "La Chinoise." In its borrowings, and in its many (sometimes academic) technical excesses, it is clearly a young man's movie. But Zilnik has managed to fuse his insights and his imitations into a form of personal expression that is often deeply moving and is always under conscious and complex control. The film builds upon a series of rhetorical positions — but for each, there is a point of view that transforms didacticism into drama.

●

None of the performers seems especially distinguished, except for Milja-Vujanovic (Yugoslavia), but when she is on the screen it is really difficut to look at anybody else. In a sense the film is a tribute to her beauty, her toughness, her naiveté, her pathos,. She is, of course, a heroine of a picaresque romance that is disguised as diatribe, and emerges finally as tragedy.

I liked "Early Works" when it played last fall in the Museum of Modern Art's Yugoslav series. Seeing it again, at its commercial opening at the Bleecker Street Evergreen Cinema, I like it even more.

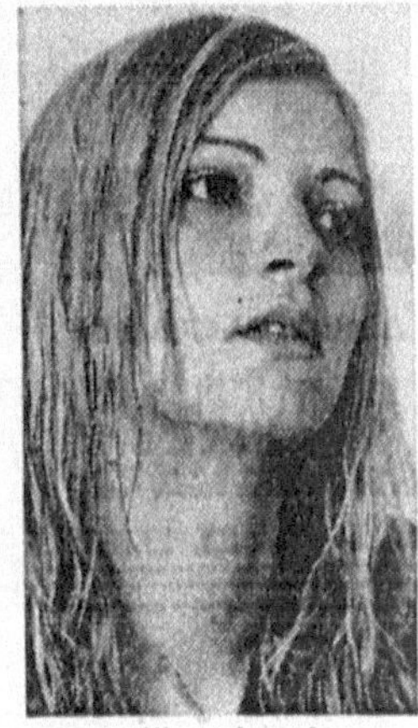

Milja Vujanovic

Review of *Early Works* screening in New York City, *New York Times* (April 24, 1970)

experience in postwar diplomacy and international trade, was
the man for the new assignments. He was a close friend of Krcun
Penezić, the Prime Minister of Serbia, formerly chief of UDBA's
Serbian branch, and he focused on implementing the new policy,
not on his own body of work.

Obviously, Avala Film became too small for two commanding
officers, Ratko and Vojo. The new director had a free hand in hir-
ing new, younger authors, and this also made Vojo a thorn in his
side. He had liked our movies at MoMA in New York. He told us
he wanted to go back. A few years later he showed up in Belgrade,
unfortunately already ill. He collaborated with Žika Pavlović on a
script, but I don't know what became of it...

> **BB**
> So you're saying that Ratko Dražević was the
> third-ranking man of UDBA, and what he was
> really doing was making international co-pro-
> ductions?

ŽŽ

Yes! In Croatia you had Sulejman Kapić, probably from a similar
background, who made movies at Jadran Film based on the novels
by Karl May about American Indians, the saga about Winnetou and
Old Shatterhand. Avala was filming co-productions with Americans,
Germans, Italians, and the French.

Ratko was an accomplished businessman and superb com-
municator. At the Košutnjak Park studios you could meet Clint
Eastwood, Burt Lancaster, Telly Savalas, Orson Welles...

ŽŽ

Dražević told affecting stories. Before he joined a party, walking
very slowly like Steve McQueen, one of his people, his driver or
the art director, would whisper to us, youngsters,
> "Better watch out, Ratko has killed two thousand
> men and shagged two thousand women."

He sits down, they pour him whiskey on the rocks.
He lights a cigarette and mutters,
> "We eliminated the chetniks quickly, but now it's
> complicated, after the war."

Everybody stirs up:

"Can it really be harder now, Comrade Ratko?"

"Well, with these foreigners, you have to rub them the right way, gotta be politicking. They are suspicious, they want to check everything."

Someone acts surprised:

"Why are they suspicious, aren't we allies?"

Ratko then opens the floodgates:

"When we went to Geneva in 1945, to abolish the League of Nations and found the UN, our delegation were Đilas, Kardelj, Velebit, lawyer Bartoš, and I was their security detail. I ordered the guards to bring three suitcases of prosciutto, cheese, sauerkraut, and brandy.

Switzerland was covered with snow and ice, all around us the ruined cities. Who knew if we'd have anything to eat. We got to the hotel, in the middle of a huge park. I go out with the guards, we take those suitcases, dig out holes in the snow and store our food and drink there. Then in the evening, after the discussions are over, the Yugoslav delegation heads to the park. We sit around the trench and dig into the ham and the brandy. That Bartoš, he was a big guy, ate like a tornado. On the third day, we were scarfing down the ham when a platoon of armed American marines popped up. Huge, muscled, and half of them were Black. They cock their machine guns and shout:

'Hands in the air! Hand over the radio transmitter!'

Kardelj's glasses fell off his face. Bartoš almost choked to death on the food in his mouth.

'What radio transmitter?'

They say:

'We have been watching you for three days. You were hiding in the park, you dug the radio transmitter into the snow and you are reporting directly to Stalin what we were talking about at the conference.'

I jump to my feet:

'Fuck Stalin!' I scream and offer them brandy. I was wrong to do that. They didn't leave until they had gobbled up all of our food and drink.

He also had a story about how international trade got initiated after the war. Krcun gave him a list of supplies he should get so that offices could function: carbon copy paper, typewriter ribbons, pens, mimeo machines, cameras and films, and most of all spare parts for automobiles. Ratko reported that none of that was available in the country.

He proposed to cross the border and acquire the goods abroad. Our army was in Trieste and Klagenfurt, and in Italy and Austria he could pick up everything we needed. He was told that seizure by force was not allowed anymore. Germany had capitulated. Things had to be bought, in the civilian capacity, for money. Ratko explained that there was no foreign currency available. There was only trading for gold abroad, as the war had washed away everything else.

He proposed to load a train full of goods he could exchange: potatoes, onions, beans, charcuterie, logs of firewood. He set up the whole train, ready to head to Austria. But how was he going to go through the military checkpoints and across borders? As a military unit or as humanitarian aid, or how? Plus, his task was to come back loaded with goods needed by the new government. From Border Control they said they had to register as a trading company. Draževič told it like this, but who knows if that's how it really happened:

> "I ordered the rubber stamps which said General Ex-
> port, International Trading Company. I was hoping,
> if everything went well, they would promote me from
> the rank of colonel at UDBA to the rank of general."

That is how the famed Genex got its start. There may be some truth in all of this because it has been well established that Genex routinely hired UDBA cadres. As quickly as he suddenly came to Avala Film in the early sixties, he suddenly left six or seven years later, having put the company on the international map. After the mysterious death of Krcun Penezić, the Prime Minister of Serbia, his friend and patron, he went to Italy and there he started his own private film production company called Prodi. Of him Olivera Katarina, the biggest movie star of that time, his lover and wife, had said:

> "Ratko had a forceful personality, volcanic, funny and
> strong. He was a rough man, imposing, with bushy
> eyebrows, large, tall. But with me he was soft as silk."

BB

Early Works was made as a co-production, between Avala film and Neoplanta film?

ŽŽ

After Ratko, Dragiša Đurić became the director of Avala film, a postwar cadre. Previously he had been an official in the League of Socialist Youth and then president of a municipality in Belgrade. He was also a skillful manager and very cooperative with film workers.

In the summer 1968, at the Pula Film Festival, someone from Avala Film comes up to me and says:

"Gile"—that's what they called the director—"is
inviting you to come to the terrace of Hotel Riviera."

At the time, I could no more expect this kind of invitation than I can expect Barack Obama today to invite me to be the best man at his daughter's wedding.

First of all, by then I had made only the first three documentaries and had just finished shooting the material at the student demonstrations in Belgrade, but we had not finished editing *June Turmoil.*

Second, during the film festival there was never any place to sit on the terrace of Hotel Riviera. All the tables were reserved for the biggest production companies, and the long tables were for the actors to sit at before and after the screenings in the Arena.

Us younger people went to that old, elegant hotel, built while Pula was the main naval base for Austria-Hungary, only after the festival was over. We would order a cup of ice-cream and listen to the waiters' stories about champagne flowing, about who got wasted and threw around large bills, and which actress had danced on the tables. I was taken to the table reserved for Avala Film. Đurić sized me up:

"So you are that Žilnik. I hear you got some awards
in Belgrade, and also the Grand Prix in Oberhausen two months ago. They wrote a lot about your
ugly documentaries. Do you have the script for a
feature film?"

Without hesitation I said, no, I don't. And he shoots back, like he
enjoys toying with me:

> "Go on, think of something by August 15, write it
> up and bring it to Avala Film. Each year we give an
> opportunity to at least two first-timers."

I mumbled something back about how I had heard "many stories
from students who were demonstrating."

> "Bring it all in, so I can take a look at it," said Gile
> Đurić by way of ending the conversation. The middle
> of that summer was a mess, when the tanks rolled
> into Prague, and then I went to Avala with my script
> for *Early Works* in early September.

BB

<u>And then it went through the regular procedure:
artistic council, workers' council, to the Fund
at the Ministry of Culture?</u>

ŽŽ

It sounds incredible, but you could look into it, Gile Đurić is still
alive. He called me on the phone three or four days later. He said
he had read the script, that it was interesting, and I have to come
in for a meeting immediately. The next day, he is looking at me,
making faces, throwing the script on the table:

> "How am I supposed to give this to screenwriters
> when there is no drama in it? And the bureaucrats
> in the Ministry will latch onto the sausage links
> of quotations from Marx right next to nudity and
> scenes of lovemaking."

I explained the atmosphere at the occupied University of Belgrade
and how the nights there were anxiety-provoking. He waved me off:

> "Forget about that! This film, by the time you pay for
> technical services, the lab, editing, the crew, trans-
> portation, you'll end up spending at least 200,000
> dollars."

I realized my chances were slim. I suggested that I should come
back in a month or two with a different project. Gile was sniggering:

> "Are you scared? Come on, let's the two of us go to
> the bank, and we'll take out a line of credit. Do you
> own an apartment?"

I said that I do.

"Okay, you'll sign that apartment over to Avala film
in front of the bank director, so you can pay us back
if this movie does not recover the costs."

Two days later he called me back:

"Money is in the account, get your crew together!"

**And then you found at Avala the profession-
als and technicians who ended up being your
crew?**

ŽŽ

First, I tried to do that. But many who read the script for *Early
Works* were not much interested in collaborating. Either the
characters were not properly "fleshed out," or the relationships
between characters were "too cool." The story was fragmented.
At the same time the film is simple, but complicated to work on
because it is set in multiple locations. In the end no reputable location manager at Avala would agree to do it for 150,000 dollars,
which is the amount we received from the bank.

Another problem was casting. We spoke to the movie stars
of the day: Milena Dravić, Snežana Nikšić, Radmila Andrić. They
all refused, primarily over the nude scenes, which until then had
never appeared in domestic films.

BB

**And then you got support from Neoplanta in Novi
Sad, because you had the film finished as early as
November 1968.**

ŽŽ

I saw it was difficult to work through the obstacles at Avala film. I
was turned down also by Aleksandar Petković, the great director
of photography who had worked with Makavejev and Žika Pavlović.
I had known him from our days of amateur filmmaking because he
was one of the founding members of the Belgrade Cinema Club. It
occurred to me that I could suggest to Gile to transfer the money
to Neoplanta film and have the post-production done there.

I figured, there I have my crews from my documentaries, and there is no crowding there like there is at Avala where they were also working on four or five other films. Dragiša Đurić, I think the next day, accepted this idea. He signed a contract with Svetozar Udovički and that connection became a solid foundation for the work.

So, Neoplanta had collaborators in all filmmaking professions, as well as technical services?

ŽŽ

No, but now we could invite the skilled people from Belgrade, offer them honoraria and per diem, hotel accommodation. Plus, I was free to choose people with whom I had great communication but who did not enjoy professional status.

So I invited Branko Vučićević to Novi Sad, to work with me on the final version of the script. He proposed that we draft it as we visit the filming locations. We got good suggestions for locations from a seasoned producer and actor from Novi Sad, Ilija Bašić. We said: Take us around Vojvodina to the places that bear traces of the beginning of modernization, from the mid-nineteenth century. From the time when Marx wrote his letters to Arnold Ruge.

He chose the cement factory in Beočin, remains of a silk factory, old brickyards, abandoned villas of former landowners. I thought of Karpo Aćimović-Godina, my friend from the time of cinema clubs, because his films were visually the most expressive. I called him on the phone in Ljubljana and told him to come at once, that we had to start shooting within a week. He said to me:

> "I'm coming, but I'm finishing my degree at the academy in film directing and not in cinematography."

And he said he had never done anything on the 35mm negative before. I replied, that much the better. We shot the film in three weeks in the atmosphere of freedom, enthusiasm, and friendship...

What happened with the line of credit from the Belgrade bank? Did they take your apartment?

That also ended well. According to the co-production contract, Neoplanta held the rights to the revenues from domestic distribution, and Avala to international sales. In the local markets, *Early Works* did relatively well—stayed for two to three weeks in bigger cities.

But after it got the award at the Berlin Festival, there were polemics and political disqualifications, so that by autumn 1969 it was no longer showing in theaters. This was not a problem for Neoplanta because Avala had supplied full financing. The sales abroad continued. The film was released in 45 countries. Avala made four times the amount they had put in the film.

Censorship (**Purging of the Cadres**)

Censorship is the word believed to have lost all meaning with
the fall of communism. This may or may not be true. But something else is more important. It is implied that in socialism censorship had a completely distinct, clearly recognizable, ideologically and institutionally precisely defined purpose and function;
that it was an important lever in the machinery of communist
totalitarianism, in other words, an institution of the totalitarian
state. The problem with this understanding of censorship in the
cultural and artistic production of socialist Yugoslavia is that
it relegates the experience of censorship entirely to the past,
cutting all of its ties to the present, that is, to the world in which
we live today. This understanding also ascribes censorship—and
in its exclusive sense—to an experience strictly delimited
in space and time, to the experience of so-called historical
communism located in the space we now very generally call the
East, referring to Eastern Europe, that is the space of formerly
actually-existing socialism, including Yugoslavia. It goes without
saying that this precise locating of censorship in the past of the
East implicitly assumes that the democratic, capitalist West
has had nothing to do with this experience, not today and not
yesterday. The forgetting of censorship, or rather its denial, thus
becomes one of the ideological presuppositions of the memory
of that censorship.

This is why, and precisely in order to sabotage said ideological presuppositions of memory, we return to the time in which
Žilnik and his comrades in socialist Yugoslavia began to create
their "black films" which were quickly to run head-on into what
was the Yugoslav form of censorship. The year is 1964, only not
in Tito's Yugoslavia but in far-away America, in Hollywood. The
book is titled: *The Face on the Cutting Room Floor: The Story
of Movie and Television Censorship*, and its author is Murray
Schumach.[01]

It is interesting that the book opens with an "eastern" quotation and that at the pinnacle of the Cold War, a couple of years

---

01 Murray Schumach, *The Face on the Cutting Room Floor: The Story of
    Movie and Television Censorship* (New York: William Morrow and
    Company, 1964).

after it nearly became, by way of the Cuban crisis, a hot, nuclear
war—from the pre-Bolshevik time, that is the time of Tsarist
Russia. The author takes as the motto of his book the words of
Tolstoy:

> "You would not believe how, from the very com-
> mencement of my activity, that horrible Censor
> question has tormented me! I wanted to write
> what I felt; but at the same time I felt that what I
> wrote would not be permitted; and involuntarily I
> had to abandon the work. I abandoned, and went
> on abandoning, and meanwhile the years passed
> away."

Even more interestingly, already in the first sentence of the fore-
word the author explicitly relates the experience of censorship
to democracy:

> "The first law of censorship—and probably the
> only important one not inscribed on the statute
> books—is this: in a democracy, the more popular
> the art form, the greater the demands for censor-
> ship of it."

Specifically, he claims that in the first third of the twentieth century, the problem of censorship in America expanded along with
the movie business, from the peep shows in moldy closets to an
industry worth billions of dollars, when frequent sickening scandals brought about the first compromises and when "the industry worked out a method of self-censorship that is unique in the
world."

What he had in mind was the Motion Picture Production
Code, issued by the Motion Picture Association of America,
Inc. in December 1956. This motion picture production "code"
provides, in addition to the general principles that emphasize
requisite conformity with moral standards, with the standards
of living that comply with the format of cinematic drama and
entertainment, as well as with the law (whether "god's, natural
or human"), an exhaustive list of subjects of concern, detailing for each what is allowed and what is not, and how. Some of
these subjects are crime (murder, drug addiction, kidnapping,
etc.), brutality, sex (detailing how "scenes of passion, seduction,
rape," etc. are to be shown), vulgarity, obscenity, blasphemy and
profanity, costumes, religion, national feelings, etc. The logic of

censorship is simple: "American movie is the original mass medium of the arts. To survive, it needs a vast audience. The price of mass appeal is conformity to mass morality." Very clear and unambiguous.

The book also offers lots of details related to specific cases of censorship, that is of the directors' struggle with censorship. Nearly all the movies considered today to be Hollywood classics have gone in one way or another through the hands of censors. Here is, as an illustration, one of the more bizarre cases. It concerns the Oscar winner *From Here to Eternity* directed by Fred Zinnemann, an important movie because it acquired the permission of censors to show adultery without sanctioning it narratively with horrific punishment. Still, the censors, not lacking in creativity of their own, demanded from the director that, for the famous kissing scene on the beach with Burt Lancaster and Deborah Kerr in swimsuits, there had to be clothes strewn around in the sand around the pair of lovers.

But the details of the story of Yugoslav censorship are surely no less bizarre.

So, he said: Cut out the women. And I said:
Comrade Lule, but how

BB

Is there anything relevant regarding censorship that you think is worth recording?

ŽŽ

It's not unimportant to expose the mystifications and memory loss of today's "whitewashers of the past." Mystifications have legitimated confusion. One side will say that the censorship was total, the other that there was none. Let's start from the beginning.

First, about censorship through the ministries of culture of the federal republics. No matter how deep we dig, we won't find a domestic film of any significance that did not see the light of day, that is the darkness of the cinema, because it was stopped by censorship. That just didn't happen. All movies, the best and the worst, went through the Federal Commission for the Supervision of Film—the so-called censorship. And all with their labels were certified by the state office and had a card that was attached to each copy of the movie in distribution.

WR: Mysteries of the Organism (*Misterije organizma*) by Dušan Makavejev; *It Rains in My Village* (*Biće skoro propast sveta*) by Aleksandar Petrović; *The Sacred Sand* (*Sveti pesak*) by Miroslav Mika Antić, *Do not Mention the Cause of Death* (*Uzrok smrti ne pominjati*) by Jovan Živanović; *The Man from the Oak Forest* (*Čovek iz hrastove šume*) by Mića Popović; *Handcuffs* (*Lisice*) by Krsto Papić; *Life of a Shock Force Worker* (*Slike iz života udarnika*) by Bato Čengić; *Crows* (*Vrane*) by Mihić and Kozomara; *Young and Healthy As a Rose* (*Mlad i zdrav kao ruža*) by Joca Jovanović; or *Early Works*, like all the others, had a stamped and signed "Certificate granting permission for public screening" ("Rešenje o izdavanju odobrenja za javno prikazivanje"), which was the official document issued by the censor, whose name was the Federal Commission for the Supervision of Film.

Not only were they approved and screened, but nearly all of the movies listed also got a bunch of awards at the Pula Film Festival, and then at international festivals too. The Commission, which would issue the mandatory document, was not a group of people wearing hoods and Stalin's mustaches. They were appointed, I think, by the Ministry of Culture, and comprised roughly ten people, mostly film critics and makers, and also managers of distribution companies, theaters and museums. I don't think any professional politicians were involved. They weren't needed anyway because every person on the Commission, I suppose, was a member of the League of Communists of Yugoslavia (LCY).

The author and the producer could attend the censorship commission screening. They were welcome in a way. I "accompanied through censorship" the first six of my short films: *Newsreel on Village Youth, in Winter*; *Little Pioneers*; *The Unemployed*; *June Turmoil*; *Black Film*; and *Uprising in Jazak*, as well as the feature film *Early Works*. This took place between 1967 and 1973. The screenings were held inside a cozy little screening room at Jugoslavija Film, which was the one and only official film importer and exporter, for all producers and distributors.

I know personally at least three or four members: Dušan Makavejev, film critics Slobodan Novaković and Milutin Čolić, and the Commission president Antonije-Lule Isaković, then the director of the publishing house Prosveta. A good writer. He wrote the first remarkable short stories about the war, outside the socialist-realist script, and several novels. On the basis of his scripts they made three or four movies including *Three*, the anthologized work by Saša Petrović. "Comrade Lule" was also known as the youngest fighter in the First Proletarian Brigade.[02] And he was a high-ranking official of the LCY in Serbia.

When the commission came together to watch and decide, on their program they had several short films or one feature film. Within the purview of the commission were questions about whether the film was calling for a violent overthrow of the government, offending morality, spreading ethnic or religious hatred, or having a corrupting influence on the youth. Institutions of control in

---

02 The First Proletarian Brigade (FPP) was the first formalized unit of the People's Liberation Army, formed in December 1941 of volunteers and under the command of Communist Party cadres, to become the core of the army that emerged victorious with the Allies at the end of World War II. December 22 was celebrated in post-war Yugoslavia as Army Day, and membership in the FPP suggested that the volunteer or the officer was a true believer in the cause, someone who joined the scrappy anti-fascist army from the first.

other countries have similar authority. In Germany, a few years later, I could see this for myself when their censorship, under the prim name of *Freiwillige Selbstkontrolle* (voluntary self-control), banned my documentary *Öffentliche Hinrichtung* (*Public Execution*). The subject of this film: the police murders, foregoing trial or legal procedure, of the members of the Baader-Meinhof group. So, the Commission did their viewing in an atmosphere that was not tense, there was running commentary on the films, some were even praised. There were two occasions when comments on my work required "an intervention in the material."

First, in late 1967, for the film *The Unemployed* (*Nezaposleni ljudi i žene*). This documentary is a reaction pamphlet, registering the fury of the men and women laborers who were left jobless by the economic reforms. They were sent to the Unemployment Bureau to sign up for collective departures for Germany, through the German Arbeitsamt. German doctors and educators would come at some point also, to certify their ability to work and their health. The film runs at about twenty minutes, in the form of episodes— *Men* is the first part, *Women* the second.

BB
This was the time of the introduction of the market economy.[03]

ŽŽ
Government wanted to make the production more efficient and therefore <u>a few hundred thousand people went unemployed—what was a big shock for all of us and especially for us from the young generation.</u> *The Unemployed Women* we shot partly in the bar of Hotel Putnik in Novi Sad.

When I went down the stairs, where the bar was, I felt 'I am in hell.' Small light, some people were dancing, others drinking whisky. So, who could be those people? Either some from the police, others may be managers of the trade firms, who were traveling here and there. We approached a lady who did striptease:

"We heard you have been a functionary in the trade
union, in a textile factory."

Susan L. Woodward,
Socialist Unemployment: The Political
Economy of Yugoslavia, 1945-1990,
1995

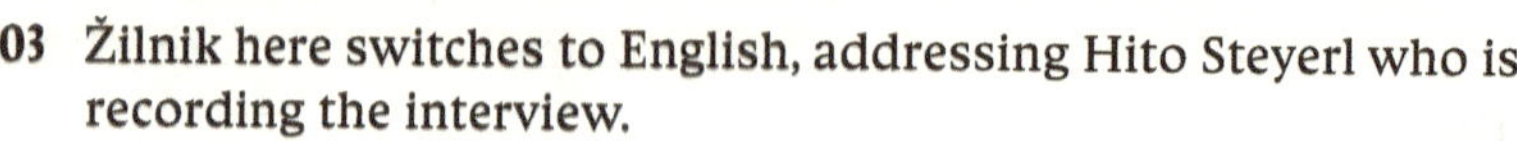

03   Žilnik here switches to English, addressing Hito Steyerl who is
recording the interview.

"Yes," she said.
"But the workers' council fired me. Some friends told me that
I still have a good body, so I work now here, why not. It is
not my own wish, I got unemployed, this bar is also socialist
enterprise, and many customers are members of the party."
When Comrade Lule saw the film, he reacted:
"Žilnik, those workers are unemployed now, but
they are going to Germany. That country is under
social-democratic rule, they will become there again
class conscious.
They will enter the Party, maybe there, so the depression they are suffering will disappear. But those
women, they went into prostitution, they went deeply into sins, and I am afraid they will not be able to
come out of it. They are no longer of use in the class
struggle. So, cut out the women."
I was upset:
"Comrade Lule, but how."
Other members of the Commission supported the president. They
started arguing, how two parts of the film do not follow the same
style. And that I insult women. Lule concluded:
"I'm not going to sign the paper if you leave the part
with the women."
I just went into the projection room and cut out the poor women. So,
this famous film which even got the Grand prix in Oberhausen and
Silver Medal in Belgrade is actually one half of the original version.[04]

BB
So, you were a victim of censorship after all.
One half of the film, as you said, was cut out.

ŽŽ

But it wasn't lost. A few years ago, when the archive of Neoplanta
Film was transferred from Novi Sad to the Film Archive in Belgrade,
they found the reel with *Women* that was cut. I saw it and then
decided to leave the shortened version as it was. I don't know if
others had similar experiences with censorship. I suppose I was
not the only one.

---

04 Buden and Žilnik are no longer speaking in English here.

The next time I had to deal with the Commission was when they saw *Early Works*, in February 1969. They started to complain about too much nudity. They listed sequences. The film critic Milutin Čolić, who was the oldest person there, insisted on cutting out at least roughly twenty seconds from the bathroom scene in which a young couple after taking a shower lie on the floor and start to make love. At which point president Isaković interjected:

> "Listen, Žilnik, you start your provocations right from the opening credits. How can you say A COMEDY OF IDEOLOGY right after the title? There is never any comedy in ideology, and it's rare to see ideology in comedy."

And word by word, I realized they were going to object to a whole lot of things, so I agreed to cut out 30 seconds. If you watch *Early Works* today, you will notice in the opening credits that there are four seconds of black blank screen. This is where the word IDEOLOGY used to be, and now it just says that *Early Works* is a COMEDY. And of that love making, the intention remains in that scene, but no execution.

Constant, secret fighters for the multi-party system and democracy

BB

So that was the Commission for the Supervision of Film. And the effect of manhunts and public campaigns was more powerful?

ŽŽ

Those were the populist tools in the struggle for political influence. They are rarely mentioned or analyzed for the simple reason that many manhunters of the past quarter century emerged onto the public stage in countless new roles and colors, switching from one party to another, swearing by various ideologies and role models. That is how the Great Evil was finally pinned on Yugoslavia, so that the movers and operatives in all kinds of shenanigans could surface as "the constant, secret fighters for the multi-party system and democracy."

In the campaigns and manhunts the normative principles were set aside, on account of "political necessities"—in the interest of maintaining authoritarian rule or for competitions over budget allocations among the local cadres or the governing structures at the federal level.

From the early 1960s I remember three major public campaigns, which then escalated into actual manhunts. Two of them barely scratched the sphere of culture, but the third one was comprehensive.

The first, in 1962, was initiated by Tito's speech in Split. On the Riva, the Split waterfront, he demanded that the role of the party be reinforced. Against the negative phenomena, primarily in the economy, which was "out of control." After the speech, a manhunt was launched against artisans, enterprising managers, and local officials. As a result, the self-management potential of independent subjects, which was nominally in place, was restricted.

The second campaign took the form of a shocking political earthquake in the summer of 1966 against the omnipotence of the State Security Administration (UDBA). At that time the second most powerful man in the country, Aleksandar Ranković, was removed from every position he held. This campaign went in a direction totally different from the one four years earlier. Probably because that one had gone too far, back to administrative, directive socialism. The one to blame for that failure was not Tito who initiated it, but UDBA, that is, the organizing secretary of the LCY Ranković who took his orders too seriously.

This campaign, however, did have a certain effect on the media, on culture, on the university. The dogmatic cadres withdrew. The atmosphere was more relaxed afterwards—there were more translations published, a mass import of newspapers, books, and films, and public discussions opened up about all kinds of questions.

ОДЛУКЕ ЦЕНТРАЛНОГ КОМИТЕТ[А]

Централни комитет Савеза комуниста Југославије на Четвртој седници, одржаној на Брионима, 1. јула 1966. године, после уводне речи друга Тита, извештаја комисије Извршног комитета ЦК СКЈ и свестране дискусије једногласно

УСВАЈА

Извештај комисије Извршног комитета Савеза комуниста Југославије о стању, методу руковођења и појавама злоупотребе у органима државне безбедности.

Централни комитет такође усваја политичку оцену комисије о узроцима и могућим последицама да се служба државне безбедности претвори у силу изнад друштва.

На основу предлога комисије и дискусије Централни комитет Савеза комуниста Југославије доноси следеће

ОДЛУКЕ:

1. Препоручује да се одмах приђе реорганизацији органа државне безбедности како би се прилагодили насталим променама у нашем друштву и развијеном систему самоуправљања. Потребно је да представничка тела и њихови извршни органи обезбеде фактичку друштвену контролу над радом државне безбедности на бази уставних норми и законских прописа. Такође се препоручује одговарајућим органима да се у циљу кадровског појачања и олакшања спровођења реорганизације на дужности руководилаца органа унутрашњих послова бирају и политички функционери и пре коначне реорганизације државне безбедности.

2. Препоручује се Савезном извршном већу да посебно формирана комисија настави истрагу, како би разоткрила све материјалне чињенице, праве намере и смисао појединих подухвата и злоупотреба положаја и власти, као и да се кривци позову на одговорност.

3. Да је друг Светислав Стефановић као непосредно одговоран за рад органа државне безбедности у читавом овом периоду када су се појавиле истакнуте деформације и озбиљне злоупотребе као и због његовог неискреног држања пред комисијом и на седници Централног комитета, а то значи према Савезу комуниста Југославије, онемогућавања рада комисије и акција које је у том правцу водио код других у самом току рада, искључи из Централног комитета Савеза комуниста Југославије и из Савеза комуниста Југославије. Централни комитет СКЈ такође препоручује Савезној скупштини да га разреши дужности члана Савезног извршног већа.

4. Прихвата се оставка коју је друг Александар Ранковић поднео на функцију члана ЦК СКЈ и Извршног комитета Централног комитета и прихвата се да поднесе оставку Савезној скупштини на функцију потпредседника Републике, јер је његова политичка одговорност за рад органа државне безбедности таква да на овим функцијама више може остати.

5. Доносећи ове одлуке [...] трални комитет Савеза комуниста Југославије обраћа се свим комунистима и радним људима Југославије да уложе максималне напоре у даљем развоју самоуправљања и непосредне демократије и остварења уставних права, учвршћујући на тај начин поверење у демократске институције нашег друштва. Само у тим институцијама могу се доносити политичке одлуке и у њима сваки човек треба да остварује право на пуну контролу свих друштвених организама. Кадровску политику у друштву треба ослободити сваког субјективизма и монополизма и остваривати најпуни утицај јавности у за то створеним институцијама.

Безбедност демократског система треба пре свега да лежи у јавним институцијама, а служба државне безбедности да буде орган против деловања класног непријатеља и спољне опасности. Сваки противзаконити поступак нужно мора да повлачи правне санкције.

Централни комитет СКЈ поводом позива комунисте у служби државне безбедности да најактивније заложе за остварење ових одлука, рашчишћавање негативних појава и да допринесу да рад ове службе усклади са нашим целокупним друштвеним развојем и да служи интересима социјализма и циљевима за које се бори Савез комуниста Југославије.

"Resolutions of the Central Committee of the League of Communists of Yugoslavia," front page of *Borba* (July 3, 1966)

BB

How did this general relaxation of society reflect on film, its production, distribution, public reception?

ŽŽ

Those were the years when pluralism in cinematography was being promoted as the new norm. The first filmmaker work groups were starting to form on the principles of self-management, which was a form of private-public entrepreneurship in the realm of culture. It is in this context that Neoplanta film was founded in Novi Sad in the autumn of 1966.

The amateurs from the Cinema Club in Novi Sad got a chance to make professional movies on 35mm. The administrative service, two or three clerks, was going to supply the technical equipment, and all the filmmakers were freelancers. This idea of sustainability was market-oriented, towards local and international markets. So, the manhunts continued while the old adage applied, "one man's meat is another man's poison."

Towards the end of 1966, I filmed my *Newsreel on Village Youth, in Winter* at Neoplanta film. The following March the documentary was screened at the festival. At the largest theater in the country, Trade Union Hall, all the producers showed up surrounded by their "teams." Around Vicko Raspor: Škanat, Štrbac, Gilić, Nikola Majdak, Dragoslav Lazić. In the group around Petar Ljubojev, the "forwards" from Sutjeska Film, Vefik Hadžismailović, Bakir Tanović, Žika Ristić. Zagreb Film "brought into the game" Nedjeljko Dragić, Dovniković, Krešo Golik, and also the young players, Krsto Papić, Zafranović, Zoran Tadić. At the time, the jury was also the selection committee.

My film was not included in the official selection. It was screened in the afternoon, and still met with substantial interest. It won two awards, but not from the official jury: the Žaromet Award from the film journal *Ekran* (Screen), and the youth award called 25th of May [Youth Day in socialist Yugoslavia, marking Tito's birthday]. Both were being awarded by great film critics. The usual "difference of opinions" happened, which seemed like a routine thing: Ranko Munitić quit the official jury and used the press conference to criticize the jury's rigidity and concerns with "regional representation" in making their selections and decisions about prizes. The journalists in attendance asked for another screening of *Newsreel*. The film was shown in the large theater, for everyone present at the press conference. In the period we are discussing—mid-sixties, early seventies—regardless of the opposing opinions and critical polemics that filled the press of the day, there were no bans and no manhunts.

At the next festival, when they showed the documentary *Little pioneers*, I remember there was a newspaper article that said how the film was causing outrage and worry in Novi Sad. The underage prostitutes in the film calmly discuss their most intimate relations with elderly gentlemen, and they chew gum and smoke cigarettes besides. "That is not a true picture of the lives of young people in the city," it said. A few days later, that same journalist reported that the film was awarded "the Silver Medal." Then he gets into a comparison of the mockumentary method used in the film with Buñuel's in *Las Hurdes*.

Even the later administrative interventions could hardly be called "unprecedented threats," like when *Early Works* was temporarily banned by the District Attorney's Office in Belgrade on June 19, 1969. This intervention occurred three months after the film had passed censorship and had been shown in theaters all over the country with considerable success and to mixed reactions in the media. The court held a public hearing on June 24 and 25, heard the prosecutor and my defense, saw the film, questioned witnesses, and issued the Decision to reject the District Attorney's motion to ban the film. Copies of the film *Early Works*, confiscated by the order of the public prosecutor, were to be returned to their owners.

BB

Early Works **subsequently triumphed in Berlin, right?**

žž

Yes, it was shown on July 3, 1969 in the official competition of the Berlin Film Festival, for which it had been selected as early as April. The jury awarded it the Golden Bear on July 7, and the students of Berlin gave it the Young Generation Award. In the short film competition, *Transplantation of Feelings* (*Presađivanje osećanja*) by Dejan Đurković was awarded the Silver Bear.

That same year at Berlin there was a retrospective of the Yugoslav "youth film." At the same time, the domestic press vehemently attacked the jury in Berlin since the largest daily papers—*Politika*, *Vjesnik*, and *Borba*—which all had foreign correspondents, never gave much support to *Early Works* or any "new films" at home to begin with.

The Golden Bear is a gross disservice, wrote Božidar Diklić in *Politika*. "Award for a delusion" was the headline for Mira Boglić's article published in *Vjesnik*.

One detail that shows you what an enormous arena this opened up in which to exchange blows you can find in the debate at the Federal Assembly, its Education and Culture Committee, which also met on July 3, 1969, the day the film was screened at the Berlinale. The debate centered on the selection process for domestic films going to international festivals. The discussion that lasted hours made apparent the contradictions of the hybrid system.

There was a national commission selecting films to go to international festivals. It was ostensibly deciding on how to put together a representative sample. But their choices were obviously not binding at all for the selectors at international festivals. So there were instances when an international festival refused the movie proffered by the commission. The producers who had invitations from international selectors, and their movie didn't "pass" our commission, could file a complaint claiming infringement of rights available to them through the system of self-management and claim damages sustained if their participation in the festival competition were blocked.

The Assembly debate specifically considered the case from a few months prior, when the festival at Oberhausen, where they show national selections, selected two films produced by Neoplanta that were rejected outright by the Federal Commission for International Cultural Cooperation. These were the documentaries *Merry Working Class* (*Vesela Klasa*) by Bojana Marijan and my *June Turmoil*.

This is why the Yugoslav selections were screened one evening, and these two films as independent selections produced by Neoplanta. The loud and long Assembly debate ended much like the court trial: it was decided that the responsibility for films produced would rest on the self-management bodies and the authors.

BB
But the manhunt didn't end there?

ŽŽ

No, campaigns as tools were not abandoned, which we can see in two Party-press publication initiatives in the summer of 1969. The first occurred after the unsuccessful judicial and parliamentary efforts to "suppress the negative phenomena in film art," and the Municipal Committee of the League of Communists of Novi Sad organized a discussion among the communists about the development of filmmaking in the Vojvodina region.

The Committee secretary, Dušan Popović, a prewar cadre, hardened in the party's factional struggles, who happened to be from a distinguished bourgeois family in Vojvodina, and consequently extra woke and "class-conscious," added his tone to that discussion:

> "Žilnik was impressed by anarchism. Especially Cohn-Bendit's ideology. It is true Žilnik also invokes the letter Marx wrote to Ruge in 1843, in which—as is well known—he calls for a ruthless criticism of everything existing. It's not just the anarchism of the four protagonists of his film, but primarily the author's anarchism, that negates and ridicules in this film the Revolution and People's Struggle for Liberation.
>
> The film's main idea is that there is no way out. Its message is nihilistic. That worldview has been defeated here in the struggle for social affirmation of the working class and for socialism. And it is being overcome daily in the struggle for socialist self-management.
>
> To the degree that *Early Works* is an anarchist film, we could also speak of it as an anticommunist film."

I listened to all that and couldn't figure out why the film was being read as a factional political program or as a five-year action plan. I tried to change the subject and mentioned movies we were seeing in theaters in Novi Sad: *Black Peter* by Miloš Forman, Věra Chytilová's *Daisies*, and movies by Miklós Jancsó. I spoke about

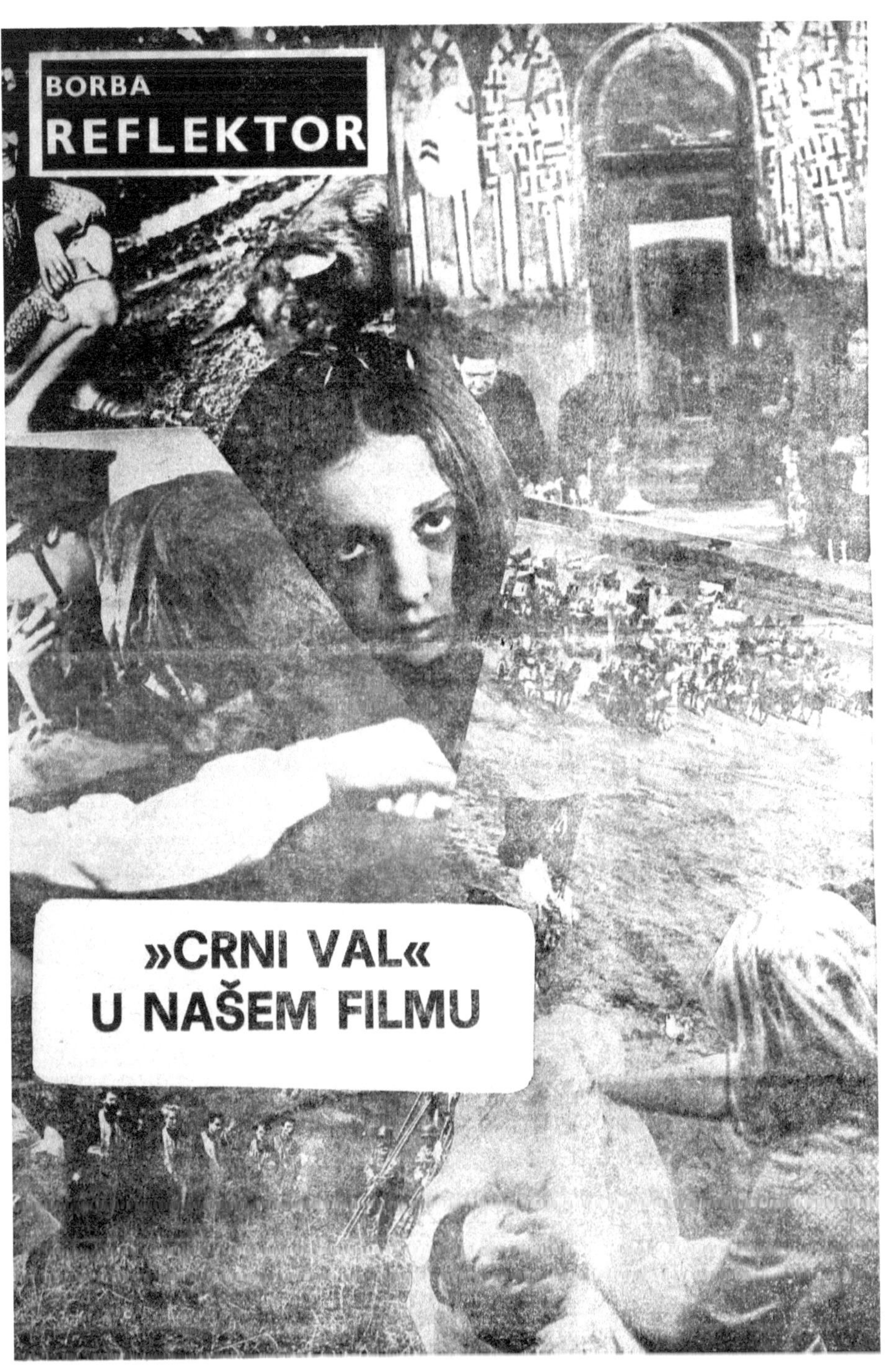

Vladimir Jovičić, "The 'Black Wave' in Our Cinema,"
Borba supplement (August 3, 1969)

young people's desire to make space for themselves in the world, to separate themselves from the past. I avoided mentioning Jonas and Adolphas Mekas, because who knows, maybe they were members of some anarchist group. My approach was rejected but the judgment passed on me was mild:

> "As an artist, you are an anarchist, but subjectively, as
> a man, we don't believe you are an anticommunist."

After that, I no longer received invitations to attend Party meetings. This counseling session did not pass up the documentaries either. Comrade Popović added,

> "Authors of short films only want to see one side of
> reality. They insist at all cost on the darkest sides
> of life, using partiality in their selection, and from
> complex social conditions they direct a warped
> picture about man and the times, such that a docu-
> mentary film stops being a document and becomes
> a forgery," etc.

This rhetoric probably brought up memories of the diktats of socialist realism, so there were no immediate consequences for the programming and repertory at Neoplanta Film, regardless of the publicity given to the slaps we received. In the next few months production started on *WR: Mysteries of the Organism* by Dušan Makavejev, and on the short films by Karpo Godina and Boto Šajtinac, and on my *Black Film...* In the summer of 1969, at the Pula Film Festival, they showed *The Ambush* by Živojin Pavlović, *It Rains in My Village* by Saša Petrović, *Crows* by Mihić and Kozomara, *Happening* by Mimica, *Horoscope* by Bora Drašković, *When You Hear the Bells* by Vrdoljak, and many other films by first-time filmmakers.

Unexpectedly, a long article appeared in *Borba*, signed by Vladimir Jovičić, an official of the Central Committee of the party in Serbia, under the headline "The 'Black Wave' in our cinema." It was published as a supplement to the newspaper, which gave it the "appearance of a directive." But we thought of this intervention as a kind of trial balloon. There were no aggressive political disqualifications in the text, but rather sentimental lamentations about how the films would not leave for the younger generations a pretty enough and accurate enough picture of the enthusiasm and the happiness of the working people building socialism.

The author must have had in his mind's eye the Soviet posters with laborers on them from the 1930s, to become as appalled as he was by Petrović's movie *It Rains in My Village*, based on the work of Dostoevsky. The essay was written in the style encouraged by provincial high school literature teachers.

And if he doesn't take his words back, I'll resign
from the League of Communists

BB
But here we can't get around the question of your membership in the Party. You were a member at the time...

ŽŽ
As I said, I dropped out at the "anarcho-liberal curve," in the summer of 1969.

BB
When did you become a member?

ŽŽ
In the final year of high school. They admitted the students who excelled academically and those who were active in "the fields of culture or sports." When you are outside, you feel on the one hand that you've been left out to dry, that nobody is "counting on you."

At the same time, if you don't find that depressing—and I didn't, because I figured the accusations were all clichés and careerism, that the apparatchiks were trampling over the "libertarian promises" of their organization—you could get more confidence from it, develop a response, because it was clear that one should not hope for much sympathy or solidarity.

BB
But how precisely did you fall out?

ŽŽ
At that meeting I described, of the Board of the League of Communists of Yugoslavia, of the Municipal Committee of Novi Sad, which discussed the film. I didn't "accept" the report and the criticism from the secretary Dušan Popović, but openly opposed his views. And I left the meeting.

The element of suspense was in the fact that I had known Comrade Popović since we were children, because my grandfather's family were friends with his family. And I knew not only that he was a man of solid education, but that he had occupied high-ranking positions in diplomacy, media, and culture since the end of the war. He had been the ambassador to London, the first director of Belgrade Television, president of the Education and Culture Council at the Federal Assembly, and the managing director of a theater.

I was surprised that the person who was certainly aware of the significance of free and critical artistic practice in the specific context of Yugoslavia, that he could mount such a facile attack on a production house that had just been formed in Novi Sad, which launched several new authors in three years who were recognized on the local and international levels.

It was clear that the political elites were constantly looking for opportunities to score points, no matter the price, because the secretary of the local Municipal Committee knew us very well, all the nuances of schisms and clashes on the cultural left, going all the way back to the 1930s. He knew how fragile and rare it was to have an artistic breakthrough, and still he got on the high horse of Stalinist storeroom rhetoric.

I saw that his harsh and long text was reminiscent of ABC's (Bogumir Hermann) attack on Krleža on behalf of the Party. And I was shocked that Popović and others like him were unable to get out of their prewar trenches. Although they were leading the party and the state, they had no idea where they were. Or, they knew exactly where they were, but they were afraid that if things were to get normal or relaxed, they would lose their monopoly on power.

The local Municipal Committee in Novi Sad organized a formal campaign against Neoplanta, its director Udovički and myself, and in fact against the "insufficient vigilance of the Municipal Court in Belgrade," because it had lifted the ban on the film in regular procedure. In essence, the so-called consultations were careerist sycophancy, showing solidarity with Tito who left the screening of *Early Works*, which must have all been discussed among the "inner circles."

Dušan Popović sent his reply to Comrade Tito, to his question, "What's it these lunatics want?" He replied,

> "They are just acting, Comrade Tito, pretending to
> be lunatics. Really they are anarchists. They negate
> our Revolution, the leading role of the League of
> Communists and the dictatorship of the proletariat.
> What they really want is to topple us over."

And then this Dušan Popović, just before these consultations, he talked to me and he said:

> "Come over so we can discuss a plan. You all are
> making these films that are very provocative. Are
> there any foreign contacts involved there, any foreign
> money?"

I said:

> "Wait a minute, do you know who is in charge there?
> This guy Svetozar Udovički is in charge."

BB
You were on a first-name basis with him, right?

ŽŽ

Yes, yes. I said,

> "You know all that, and you could check. That's all
> nonsense. We are making films the way we think
> they should be made in this country."

And that was the end of that conversation. He said:

> "There's no reason to check anything if that's how
> it is. I guess you would tell me."

And he's holding in his hand a report that was published in the papers where he is analyzing our films and saying they are Trotskyist and then also anarcho-liberal.

BB
**The term anarcho-liberal was already in use?
I thought it was created after 1968.**

ŽŽ

It appeared, you see, in these matters. He was clearly testing the stringency rules, so to say, and declared of this film, as he said,

> "Insofar as the film is Trotskyist and anarchist, we
> could also argue that it is anticommunist."

**And so, this was a person who knew you, with
whom you were on a first-name basis?**

žž

A person who knew me. And I stood up (even while still a Party
member) and said,

> "The tragedy of the League of Communists is that
> in important places we have people who are clearly
> bogged down by some familial complexes and who
> are trying to be greater Catholics than the Pope."

BB

You said that?

žž

I did! I said,

> "Comrade Popović spoke to me the day before yes-
> terday, and he has just told you sheer untruths, and
> if he doesn't take his words back, I will resign from
> the League of Communists."

Now they were all looking at me like I was crazy, and I practically
left in the middle of the meeting. And that's how I resigned from
the League of Communists. Then, obviously, by the autumn of
that year they decided to withdraw the film from distribution, but
at this point it was not the court or the production company that
was pulling it, but the party group affiliated with the distributors,
so that was happening, but the atmosphere in the entire country
was not such that a totalizing formal dogmatic wave came over us.

That something had been said about us wanting to remove
them from power was confirmed for me in the mid-1990s. I was
walking down Vase Stajića Street, where lots of party "executives"
had their apartments. Someone came up to me from the back and
put a hand on my shoulder.

> "Želimir," said an elderly man. "We steered our strug-
> gle in the wrong direction. Did you see how those
> we least expected threw us out in the end?"

I turned around and recognized Mr. Popović.

I replied briefly,

> "You missed it, you weren't vigilant enough..."

BB

But much of what was happening in Yugoslavia in those years, those manhunts in the culture, was also happening in a very turbulent international context. We are talking about the late 1960s, right?

ŽŽ

Yes, it's obvious that some party ideologues found appealing the news about the wave of re-stalinization taking over the Eastern bloc after the occupation of Dubček's Czechoslovakia in the summer of 1968.

I learned first-hand about the strength of pressure from that side when I visited the Film Archive in Moscow a few years ago. They showed me the resolutions of the Ministry of Culture of the USSR and their Central Committee's Ideology Commission, which say that "there should be a drop in the distribution of Yugoslav films and co-productions because Yugoslavs have permitted anti-socialist phenomena in their cinematography."

Still, the top-ranking officials in Yugoslavia condemned the tank invasion of Prague. There was open talk about the plans for the "troops of brotherly countries" to keep moving south. In the summer of 1968, all of us who were army reservists were called up to dig trenches on the slopes of Fruška Gora, in anticipation of attacks from the north. Everyone knew about the Soviet tank divisions on the southern Hungarian border. I used the personal experience of digging trenches to plan several sequences in *Early Works* which were shot in November 1968.

The state policy was that the possible occupation would be countered using partisan tactics, and that's where we got the foundations of the "comprehensive people's defense." It was decided that regions and larger enterprises should be able to arm themselves and prepare for self-defense.

Twenty years later, as we know, those weapons would be used in the bloody internecine war, but now we are in the year 1969. Near the end of that year, there was a political meeting at the highest level of authority concerning film production: the Commission for Culture of the Presidency of Yugoslavia organized consultations on the problem of cinematography.

ВАНРЕДНО ИЗДАЊЕ

БЕОГРАД, СРЕДА, 21. АВГУСТ 1968.   ГОДИНА XXXIII БРОЈ 231   ЦЕНА 50 ПАРА / СУБОТОМ 60 ПАРА

ПРОЛЕТЕРИ СВИХ ЗЕМАЉА УЈЕДИНИТЕ СЕ

БОРБА

ОРГАН СОЦИЈАЛИСТИЧКОГ САВЕЗА РАДНОГ НАРОДА ЈУГОСЛАВИЈЕ

Уређује редакцијски колегијум ★ Директор и главни и одговорни уредник Мома Марковић

Председништво ЦК КП Чехословачке сматра да је упад оружаних снага супротан не само основним принципима односа међу социјалистичким земљама, већ да представља гажење основних норми међународног права.

ЧЕХОСЛОВАЧКА ОКУПИРАНА!

Синоћ у 23 часа трупе Варшавског пакта умарширале у ЧССР и за шест часова окупирале целу територију

Синоћ око 23 часа, трупе СССР, Пољске, НДР, Мађарске и Бугарске прешле границу Чехословачке. — ТАСС јавља да је интервенција уследила због тога што су „чехословачки државни и партијски руководиоци позвали Совјетски Савез да им пружи хитну помоћ укључујући и помоћ оружаних снага". — Стране трупе, обележене белим крстовима, опколиле зграду ЦК КП Чехословачке. — Совјетски авиони бацају летке који садрже саопштење да је „Антоњин Новотни председник Републике." — Западне агенције јављају да грађани Прага граде уличне барикаде и да је дошло до првих сукоба у којима младићи и девојке покушавају својим телима да зауставе надирање тенкова. — Према последњим извештајима западних агенција, у прашким улицама почеле уличне борбе.

— Председништво Народне скупштине Чехословачке упутило саопштење Подгорном, Улбрихту, Гомулки, Кадару и Живкову у коме се тражи хитно повлачење свих јединица са територије Чехословачке. — Захтев о хитном повлачењу трупа поставило и Председништво ЦК КП ЧССР

Јединице Совјетског Савеза, Пољске, Немачке Демократске Републике, Мађарске и Бугарске окупирале су прошле ноћи Чехословачку.

Прелазећи са свих страна чехословачку територију, ове трупе су прошле ноћи почеле да продиру око 23 часа и већ у 4,15 изјутра, Радио-Праг је јавио да су снаге Варшавског пакта запоселе читаву Чехословачку.

У званичном саопштењу ТАСС каже се да је интервенција уследила на захтев „чехословачких државних и партијских руководилаца који су позвали СССР да им пружи хитну помоћ укључујући и помоћ оружаних снага због опасности по социјалистички систем".

Према саопштењу Радио-Прага, интервенција се догодила без знања председника Републике, председника Народне скупштине, председника владе и генералног секретара ЦК КП Чехословачке. Председништво ЦК КП Чехословачке затражило је хитно повлачење трупа Варшавског пакта са чехословачке територије. Председништво Народне скупштине Чехословачке упутило је исти захтев Подгорном, Улбрихту, Гомулки, Кадару и Живкову.

Приближавање трупа чехословачкој престоници пратило је масовно надлетање совјетских авиона над Прагом. Авиони су бацали летке у којима пише да је председник Чехословачке Републике Антоњин Новотни.

Пошто су продрли у Праг, совјетски тенкови и возила опколили су зграду ЦК КП Чехословачке. Неколико хиљада омладинаца којима су се прикључили грађани, викали су „слобода", тражили Дубчева и захтевали повлачење совјетских војника. После тога уследило је пуцање из машинских пушака.

Према последњим информацијама грађани Прага граде уличне барикаде. Како јављају западне новинске агенције, на улицама Прага почеле су борбе. Грађани на централном престоничком тргу Вацлавским Намјести, покушавају телима да задрже совјетске тенкове који надируду.

ПРВИ ИЗВЕШТАЈ НАШЕГ СПЕЦИЈАЛНОГ ДОПИСНИКА

СОВЈЕТСКИ ТЕНКОВИ У ЦЕНТРУ ПРАГА

Специјални извештач нашег листа Риста Бајалски који се налази у Прагу јавио се телексом редакцији јутрос у 9,25 часова и послао извештај о догађајима у Чехословачкој:

(Праг 21. августа, у 9.25) (телексом) — Војна интервенција против Чехословачке извршена је синоћ око 23. часа. Оружане снаге Совјетског Савеза, Пољске, ДР Немачке, Мађарске и Бугарске почеле су надирањем преко државних граница Чехословачке Социјалистичке Републике. У року од највише 6 сати совјетски тенкови су већ запоселу главне зграде у центру града. Чехословачка је окупирана у току једне ноћи.

Грађани Чехословачке могли су сазнати о војној интервенцији између 2—3 сата ујутру. Тада је Радио Праг у 3 наврата емитовао проглас Председништва ЦК КПЧ. У 2 сата радио је први пут покушао да емитује тај проглас, али је — после неколико изговорених речи — прекинут глас спикера. Како смо касније сазнали, то је учињено на интервенцију бившег директора радија који је пре пола године уклоњен са те функције. Он је дошао у радио станицу и рекао да се не чита проглас — јер је то провокација. Редакција је брзо успоставила везу са партијским руководством и добила потврду да је то њен проглас.

Нешто касније, прочитан је проглас Председништва ЦК КПЧ који гласи: „Свим грађанима Чехословачке Социјалистичке Републи—

(Наставак на 3. страни)

ПРЕГОВОРИ У ПРЕДСЕДНИШТВУ ЦК КПЧ

(Праг, 21. августа) — У 9.40 спикер прашке телевизије, чије речи преноси АФП, јавио је да се у згради Централног комитета Комунистичке партије Чехословачке управо одржава важно заседање.

У просторијама Председништва ЦК, додао је спикер, воде се важни преговори. Ништа подробније о карактеру ових догађаја није, међутим, досада познато.

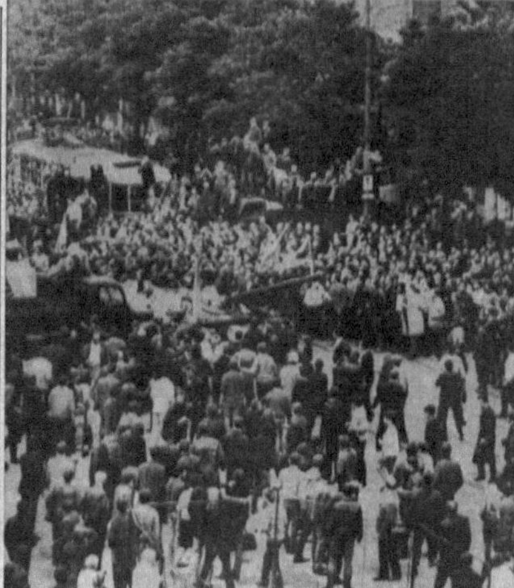

(Праг, 21. августа, Рејтер) — Прашке трговине с храном, чим су јутрос отворене, завеле ограничење продаје. Купци, који образују дуге редове, могу да купе само четврт килограма бутера и по пола килограма брашна и шећера.

У међувремену, такође према извештају Рејтера, људи окупљени на Вацлавским намјестима, домахују посадама совјетских тенкова и возила — „Руси, идите кући"!

Пред зградом прашке радио-станице један совјетски тенк сударио се с трамвајем пуним путника, и топовском цеви разбио његове прозоре. Чује се, додаје агенција, и узвици — „фашисти"!

Како јављају стране новинске агенције, грађани Прага покушавали су да својим телима спрече продор совјетских тенкова у главни град. НА СЛИЦИ: Совјетски тенкови окољени грађанима који носе чехословачке државне и партијске заставе.

ВЕЧЕРАС СЕДНИЦА ПРЕДСЕДНИШТВА ЦК СКЈ

Председник Савеза комуниста Југославије Јосип Броз Тито сазива седницу Председништва Централног комитета Савеза комуниста Југославије која ће почети рад вечерас у 20 часова на Брионима.

The working group, led by our only Oscar winner Dušan Vukotić, collected a wealth of material on the conditions and problems in domestic film. Newspapers reported that the discussion lasted six hours, among Avdo Humo, Rudolf Sremec, Oskar Davičo, Milutin Čolić and Vukašin Mićunović, all top-notch intellectuals-officials.

They discussed all possible contradictions and "dangers" that lurk in free creativity and production initiatives but concluded that abolishing freedom would be worse. There was no campaign. For the next two years, the energy of film production and the polemics about films were still there, and the end of 1971 saw the completion of *The Role of My Family in World Revolution*, *WR: Mysteries of the Organism*, *Plastic Jesus*, *Knockout*, *Young and Healthy Like a Rose*, *Freedom or Cartoons*, and others.

WR was finalized at Neoplanta and got invited to the Cannes film festival. But, again, the Municipal Committee of the League of Communists of Novi Sad proposed an initiative that would give the film "a public critical evaluation." There was a screening in the large theater of Cinema Arena, followed by discussion. The theater was full, although it was noon. There were activists, veterans, filmmakers, and around twenty intellectuals from Belgrade. In contrast to the event held two years earlier, where the debate was purely bureaucratic, this one was organized to be a "rally of discontent" full of sound and fury. War veterans and presidents of local councils would take the microphone and shout:

"Makavejev must be exposed! He is a western spy
in the service of hostile enemy forces."

Nikola Božić, president of the Commission for the preservation of traditions with the Federation of Veterans' Associations of the People's Liberation War of Yugoslavia (SUBNOR):

"We were finished with Comrade Stalin, but the way
Makavejev attacks him really crosses the line. Is it
okay to masturbate to Comrade Stalin? Makavejev
is dead to us!"

There were also heated defenses of the film, saying it was successful and spectacularly interesting, funny and essentially "pro-Yugoslav." There were protests that some discussants were returning to Stalinist mythomania. But WR found itself in a tight place: the censorship commission had approved it and signed its card. It went to Cannes, because it was made as a co-production with the German partner Telepool so there were copies abroad.

In Cannes, the film was received euphorically and got enormous publicity. But, at the Pula Festival there were inconceivable administrative and technical difficulties, completely unrelated to the festival rules, and the screening was made impossible. Apparently, WR was at the top of the Soviet list of "ideological failures and falsifications of history."

Cut the cock out

BB
But that year, 1971. It was one of the most dramatic years in Yugoslavia after the war.

ŽŽ
That's right. The domestic political conflicts that spring escalated into the "Croatian Spring," led by the younger generation of Tito's favorites—Savka Dabčević Kučar and Mika Tripalo. A space was created for nationalist rhetoric, most of all among the intellectuals, both Croatian and Serbian, and it took over the media. The ethnic narcissism and the coming together were the means that would ostensibly break up the party monolith and authoritarian rule.

Ante Batović, The Croatian Spring: Nationalism, Repression and Foreign Policy Under Tito, 2017

The "reinvigoration" of discourse by returning to the past and to traditional values was ostensibly going to help to revitalize the socialist concept. This nonsense, or that dead-end, was designed at the top, by the structures working in individual Yugoslav republics. They put together crowds of people to be the backdrop for the rallies. Their actions, however, called to mind the old wounds from the war.

There were call-outs, there was counting of employees by ethnic categories, and organizing of romantic-nationalist events. It was pretty chaotic. This was the period when my generation asked itself for the first time if Yugoslavia could keep it together. Tito hesitated, first gave support to the "Spring people" then took it back. Then he decided to replace the Croatian leadership.

In January 1971, we were shooting a documentary, it was actually a happening-intervention called *Black Film*. The occasion for the film was the question about whether "activist film" could change anything in society. The flier for the film came with my explanation:
    "...Since I have failed to warn the public about so-
    cial disparities, or to exert any influence anywhere,
    I make do with what is within reach for me—to

acquaint my wife and my child with where we live.
The film shows to my family in a direct way how it
is for those starving, dirty, those without property..."
This documentary enraged the film critics, and even more my colleagues the filmmakers. That spring 1971, the team from *Early Works* came back together—Karpo Godina, Branko Vučičević and the others, and we were running around the jittering Yugoslavia. In Zagreb, we filmed the coup at the student assembly launched by Čičak, Budiša and Paradžik.

In Ljubljana, we filmed demonstrations, held under the banner of ecological protest, with Leninist and Maoist ideas and slogans, led by Jaša Zlobec and the editorial board of the student magazine *Tribuna*.

In Belgrade, we filmed student demonstrations against constitutional reforms that would make the federation less centralized. That documentary material for the film *Freedom or Cartoons* was one part of the collage about the dissolution of a Yugoslav family.

BB
In that turbulent political context, the film
***Freedom or Cartoons* was ultimately blocked.**

ŽŽ
In the summer, we were editing the film at Neoplanta. The heat was unbearable. Makevejev was on the island of Lastovo, on vacation after being blocked in his country and celebrated at Cannes. The phone rang, I picked up. The voice from the receiver said:
"Hello, this is Colonel Marković from the office of the
Secretary General to the President of the Republic.
Was that film about mysteries made with you? I'd
like to come over with my driver, in a couple of hours,
to fetch a copy. I need it for tonight's screening."
I immediately called the company director Svetozar Udovički and he was so relieved.
"Finally, Tito is going to see *WR*. Stalinists could
attack the film until now because he didn't get
around to seeing it."
I told Udovički we should call Makavejev. Although he didn't think we should, I called Mak, and barely managed to get through. Makavejev was gritting his teeth:

"Why did you tell him there was a copy there?"
I tried to explain how excited Udovički was that it was going to be
screened for Tito that day. Makavejev screamed:
> "Cut the cock out of every sequence where you see
> it in the film!"

I said, okay, we have an editing table right here.
Makavejev was yelling,
> "There's cock in four places, cut them all out!"

And the phone operator, when I called the second time, said:
> "I can't put you through to mister artist, he was just
> begging some friend of his a minute ago, if you'll
> excuse my language, to cut his cock off. I'm afraid
> our guest is not completely with it."

I called Udovički again and told him what Makavejev ordered me
to do. And now Udovički was crying:
> "You two want us to lie to Tito. There's no way! He
> should see it all. When Tito sees it he will under-
> stand that Mak is on his side."

The copy was taken there that same day. We had no news of the
reaction. But early that fall, regional officials removed director
Udovički. They left him jobless. He went to Belgrade. There he met
up with Dragiša Đurić, the other director who was removed, this
one from Avala Film, with whom he had co-produced *Holy Sand*
by Mika Antić and *Early Works*.

Following his removal, Đurić was appointed director of the
Belgrade parking service. From there he hired Udovički to work in
a booth at a parking lot taking payments. A few months later, the
newly installed director of Neoplanta, Draško Ređep, was putting
pressure on us in the editing room to take out sequences from
Freedom or Cartoons. In his written orders, Ređep was practicing
vigilance,
> "I draw the author's attention, in consideration of
> the request from the investigative judge in Zagreb,
> to the request to exclude all materials pertaining
> to the student events in Zagreb. The producer also
> requests that the film exclude all documentary and
> other materials pertaining to student events in Lju-
> bljana, especially those which mention Jaša Zlobec,
> considering that, on several occasions, the magazine
> *Tribuna* was sued in response to his writings.

It is also necessary to cut out frames 564, 565, and
566 because they contain unacceptable political
allusions and negative implications..."

Realizing that Ređep's political toadyism had no bounds, the crew refused to cooperate. An order followed for us to leave the premises of Neoplanta and forfeit our permission to enter the production house, and we would continue in this status until the moment Ređep led Neoplanta into bankruptcy over the financial and artistic collapse of the mega-project *The Big Transport* in 1985. And that was thirteen years later...

BB

After that you went to Germany.

ŽŽ

Before that, all I had left to do was to follow through with the censorship on two of my shorts, *The Women are Coming*, which was left behind at Neoplanta, and *Uprising in Jazak*, which I made for Pan Film. There was a "purge" underway in Novi Sad. This is how the Film Review Commission of Vojvodina came into existence. Because the one in Belgrade was clearly too liberal.

In early 1972, the censors in Vojvodina banned three shorts: *Cross With a Star* by Karolj Viček, *I miss Sonia Henie* by Karpo Godina, and *The Women are Coming*. Karpo had invited as collaborators on his film the guests at the Belgrade Film Festival, a few well-known film directors—Miloš Forman, Paul Morrissey, Frederick Wiseman, Puriša Đorđević, and Dušan Makavejev, to make the film experiment with him.

This the censors declared to be objectionable, and that ban lasted for about ten years. The fate of *Uprising in Jazak* was a bit more cheerful. I had intended to react to the latest trend of shooting partisan-themed spectacles at enormous expense, with grand costumes, weapons and aviation, and big international stars, so I went to the village of Jazak on the Fruška Gora mountain and proposed to the locals to reconstruct in front of cameras their life as it was during the war.

What we ended up with was an authentic piece with phenomenal characters, but the censors in Vojvodina understood that I had hired vagabonds and drunks to make fun of the People's Liberation War. So the film was banned. The next day, we let the participants

ПРВИ ИЗВЕШТАЈ ПРИВРЕМЕНОГ ПОСЛОВОДНОГ ОРГАНА „НЕОПЛАНТА-ФИЛМА"

Грешка до грешке – финансијски крах

О несолидном пословању, утврђеним али још неупотпуњеним махинацијама главних антера краха „Великог транспорта" и „Неопланта-филма" ускоро ће расправљати Извршно веће и Скупштина Војводине. — Дуг „Шервуду" 3,1 милион долара!

У форми извештаја привременог пословодног органа, одмерена анализа крцата подацима о пословању продуцентске куће „Неопланита филм и бројним њеним неоствареним и непословним уговорима са копродуцентима филма „Велики транспорт" — била је предмет јучерашње краће расправе на седници Покрајинског комитета за образовање и културу. Извештај привременог органа је прихваћен и, испуњавајући своју обавезу према Скупштини Војводине, Комитет га је упутио Извршном већу и Скупштини Војводине.

Како се очекује, Скупштина Војводине ускоро ће дати свој коначни суд о првом извештају привременог пословодног органа, догађајима у „Неопланта-филму", закон ским и финансијским прекршајима и одговорности појединаца за финансијски крах „Великог транспорта".

Утврђује се одговорност појединаца

Извештај није потпун, али је Комитет прихватио образложење да је рок од два месеца недовољан да привремени пословодни орган сагледа све чињенице и финансијско пословање „Неопланта-филма" и све противзаконите радње које су се у овој области десиле за по следњих неколико година, а посебно у време снимања „Великог транспорта". Очекује се, како је и у извештају речено, да ће и други државни органи који истражују пословање у „Неопланти" начинити ускоро сопствене извештаје — налазе и да ће они послужити привременом органу да ваљано одмери одговорност појединаца.

Опширно, на основу постојеће документације у „Неопланти", привремени пословодни орган је образложио да су сви уговори склопљени са америчким копродуцентом „Шервуд" и италијанском фирмом „Латерна едитриче" — начињени мимо знања самоуправних органа „Неопланта-филма" и Савета филма „Велики транспорт". Савет филма је два пута врло упозорено, према записницима сачуваним у „Неопланти" на које се позива пословодни орган — прихватио интернационализације пројекта. У закључцима своје друге седнице од 25. септембра 1981. Савет каже: „Остварише се контакти и у смислу интернационализације пројекта". Закључак следеће седнице гласио је: „Прихвата се и информација о настављању копро-

мом" из Москве". У то време „Неопланта" је већ склопила четири уговора са италијанским копродуцентом и два са америчким и ни је остварила сарадњу са земљама Источне Европе и Француском.

Привремени пословодни орган, према томе, нуди закључак: „Најбитније одлуке о интернационализацији донете су без верификације од стране Савета филма, као и без одлуке самоуправних органа радне организације".

Неовлашћени па и шверперски послови

Образлажући ову тезу пословодни орган доказује да су редитељ филма Вељко Булајић и директор „Неопланте" др Драшко Ређеп све уговоре потписивали на своју руку, тргујући неовлашћено, на велику штету „Неопланте", само делимично одмерену пресудом лосанђелеског суда свотом од 3,1 милиона долара. У својим трговинама прешли су и преко одлуке збора радника „Неопланта-филма" који већ први уговор са италијанским копродуцентом није прихватио тражећи да се цео посао са евентуалним страним копродуцентима води преко „Југославија-филма", што је „Неопланта" била и законски дужна да чини, јер није била судски регистрована за спољнотрговинску делатност.

Међутим, ствари нису текле тим током. Да би задовољили свог првог копродуцента „Латерну" др Драшко Ређеп, Вељко Булајић и адвокат „Неопланте" Раде Микијел су 1982. и у наредне две године склапали са Ђанијем Масаром, представником ове фирме, десетак уговора, протокола, различитих аранжмана, на рачун „Неопланте" док потпуно ова продуцентска кућа није остала кратких рукава и од италијанског копродуцента за право снимања италијанске ТВ серије о „Транспорту" и право на дистрибуцију филма у неколико земаља Европе — није добила само аранжман са Хелмутом Бергером. А за уговор са глумцем „обештећена" је и фирма „Веркли" из Лихтенштајна правом на дистрибуцију три југословенска филма по целом свету, без накнаде. Од уговорена три филма „Неопланта" је била власник само филма Александра Ђорђевића „Стићи пре свитања", али је понудила и „Човека кога треба убити" „Јадран-филма" и „Поглед из поткровља" три друга продуцента, као и шест анимираних филмова које је она произвела.

Два играна филма које није поседовала, „Неопланта" је откупила од југословенских продуцената и у пакету оцарињеном као „материјал од Великог транспорта" прошверцовала преко границе. На несрећу излезени су филмски оригинали и на тај начин, како се констатује у извештају „ови филмови су практично за сва времена отуђени из наше културне баштине".

Заплет са „Шервудом"

Много злосрећнији уговор др Драшко Ређеп и Вељко Булајић су склопили са америчким фирмама „Инковентом" и „Шервудом". Овим уговором партнери се нису

садржи све ставке трошкова. Филм је за америчко и остало светско тржиште, сем социјалистичких земаља, требао бити снимљен по себном сценарију кога је на основу сценарија „Великог транспорта" Арсена Диклића и Вељка Булајића написао амерички сценарист Доналд Бојл.

Такође овим уговором „Неопланта-филм" је била обавезна да обезбеди филмску траку, али како није имала девиза, филм се у почетку снимао са позајмљеном траком од „Јадран-филма" из Загреба, а онда је „Шервуд" анексом на уговор прихватио да „Неопланти" купи филмски материјал у вредности од 200 хиљада долара. Амерички копродуцент је платио и три глумца из Америке, али је на крају све своје трошкове, због лабавости уговора, на суду заокружио на 3,1 милион долара.

Због дугова — на добош

„Неопланта-филму" још није приспела пуноважна судска одлука југословенског суда којом би морала да исплати ове доларе, али два изгубљена судска спора са Основном банком Нови Сад (девет милиона динара) и Државом СФРЈ — ЈНА (двадесет милиона), довели су је у ситуацију да је по мишљењу привременог пословодног органа евентуално потребно да се распрода њена једина имовина која има вредности: зграда „Неопланте" и аутомобил „застава 101"!

Опширан извештај, поред већ реченог, представља и финансијску конструкцију филма „Велики транспорт" која је у зачетку износила 70 милиона динара да би се код завршетка филма попела на око 250 милиона. Оцењујући све што се дешавало са филмом и у „Неопланти" председник привременог пословодног органа Дору Трифу је покушао да образложи на јучерашњој седници Комитета кратким запажањем:

— Генерална оцена која ми се намеће је да је екипа „Великог транспорта" имала изузетну сталност у односу на продуцента, фактички она је била неформална филмска радна заједница, којој је продуцент давао фирму и средства.

Дору Трифу је још додао да за „Велики транспорт" Вељко Булајић никада није спремио књигу снимања и да је филм снимљен без ње, а исто тако да је проду-

know that the film wouldn't be allowed to show. A few of them, who had fought in the war from the beginning in 1941, and had those esteemed papers that said they held the Partisan Commemorative Medal of 1941, entered the Secretariat of Culture and screamed at the regional minister Đole Popović,

> "Say, are you a chetnik or an ustasha, to be banning us
> and showing *Early Works* and other trash like that."

Poor Đole was scared to death, found the censorship card and tore it up in front of them.

> "Forgive me, comrades, there has been a misunder-
> standing," he muttered.

I remember this little anecdote, from before I took off for Germany. The entire year 1972 was marked by smear campaigns and man-hunts. The Yugoslav model was deadlocked, and a solution was being sought in purges, which only made things worse.

After disposing of the Croatian Spring, the equilibrium was to be restored by purging liberalism from Serbia. There was new confusion and new striving by the careerists, so it became difficult to recognize the cultural milieu in which we had worked just a year or two earlier. A functional collapse of Tito's state, twenty years before its actual disintegration, was underway.

A document was put together called "A letter from Comrade Tito and the Executive Bureau of the Central Committee," an instructive epistle to the apparatus which calls on the dogmatists to take charge. A new position was introduced, the coordinator of all intelligence agencies, and the apparatchik Stane Dolanc was now it, with a strange stain on his biography—as a young man he had been a member of the Hitlerjugend, and he got to the new position to prove his worth.

He became the right-hand man to Tito in his old age. Those who climbed the ladder then would become the state's undertakers in the early 1990s. The death of the new Yugoslav cinema was pronounced. Newspapers were full of articles with headlines like, COLLAPSE OF AUTEUR FILM, BLACK WAVE IS OVER, THE BIG CLEANUP AHEAD.

The authors and producers were self-critiquing, and those who refused were expelled from the LCY, like Makavejev was in November 1972. Božidar Rančić, Mak's colleague, explained that

> "The enemy successfully got us to use our resources
> to make the films they couldn't make in their own

countries—*Parade, Little Pioneers, Early Works, The Ambush, Red Wheat, WR, Master and Margarita.*"
Dean of the Film Academy Kosanović:
  "Živojin Pavlović has the feeling and talent, but he was directed by foreign agents to make hostile films."
Gojko Miletić, Minister of Culture in Serbia:
  "A false free thinking blossomed in cinematography. The roots of it were at Avala Film where managerialism won the day amidst flirtations with foreign producers."
The newly formed LCY working group at Neoplanta declared, "Black Wave is history." The communists of Neoplanta decided to withdraw more than 20 films from distribution although the relevant commission did not ban them.

The potential created when self-management was introduced, through international contacts and alternatives to the Soviet model of socialism, was exhausted by its own contradictions. And there was simply no room anymore for the kinds of films that were being made just a few years earlier.

> *Here it's not possible to make such explicitly activist films the way you do it down there*

BB
For you, was going to Germany not also a moment of liberation after your experience with censorship in Yugoslavia?

ŽŽ
It wasn't a matter of censorship, but the fact that all the producers' doors were shut for a few authors who had been "marked by infamy." However, in Germany at that time, to say you were being persecuted by Yugoslav censorship was like if we had a filmmaker come to us from Monaco today, tell us the weather is beautiful there, and then keep on talking about being persecuted by censors.

What would we say back to him? We would nod and think, What a moron!

BB
And why did they so blindly believe in Yugoslavia...?

СЕДНИЦА ИЗВРШНОГ БИРОА ПРЕДСЕДНИШТВА СКЈ

ПОЛИТИЧКА ДИВЕРЗИЈА У ПОЈЕДИНИМ ФИЛМОВИМА

Извршни биро Председништва СКЈ закључио је на јучерашњој седници да се редна седница Председништва СКЈ закаже за 5. март.

тој седници би се расправљало о припремама и нела одлука о заказивању четврте конференције СКЈ. Расправљајући о неким питањима међународних односа, Извршни биро размотрио је и изјаву Нородома Сиханука, шефа државе и председника Уједињеног националног фронта Камбоџе, и руководства Националног фронта у вези са ситуацијом у Камбоџи после потписивања споразума о окончању рата и успостављању мира у Вијетнаму. Наглашено је да ће СКЈ и социјалистичка Југославија и даље пружати подршку и помоћ народима Камбоџе, Лаоса и Вијетнама и у садашњој фази њихове борбе за независност, мир и прогрес.

Разматрајући појаве политичких диверзија, које су дошле до изражаја у неким филмовима антисоцијалистичке и дехуманизаторске садржине, Извршни биро је закључио да организације, односно активи Савеза комуниста у филмским кућама — уз активно учешће градских организација СК, централних и покрајинских комитета — неодложно изврше идеолошко-политичко рашчишћавање и утврде политичку одговорност оних који су филмску уметност користили у реакционарне сврхе. Извршни биро подржава акцију коју је започео један број истакнутих филмских стваралаца у листу „Комунист“ на сагледавању и рашчишћавању идејних и друштвених проблема на подручју филмске уметности.

Look, Yugoslavia was, first of all, the country to which Germans rushed in long lines every summer to cool their feet in the Adriatic.

Second, it was the country from which came the films that often got a bunch of awards in those years at the German festivals. Pavlović, Makavejev and Petrović were more familiar to the German critics than Herzog, Kluge, and Fassbinder.

I had already received the Grand Prix from Oberhausen and the Grand Prix in Berlin, plus four or five other awards. Yugoslav films were shown on TV as a package, and five or six of them were in regular distribution. Yugoslavia was held in high esteem for the things we now forget or despise, and that is workers' participation, self-management, and non-aligned politics. With our passport you could cross more borders freely than you could with a German passport.

I met Alexander Kluge, who was also the president of their filmmakers' association, in Munich, in their film workers' collective *Filmverlag der Autoren*. He asked me if I could urgently acquire a copy of our law regulating film production and the codebook regarding budget support for domestic production based on the revenue from ticket sales. I asked him why he was interested. He said,

> "That is the best funding system in Europe at the
> moment. We want to copy it!"

I phoned Vuk Babić, who was planning to visit me, to tell him to bring those papers with him. We spent a week with Kluge and his secretary, translating our codebook and praising the so-called "fusion of labor and material resources," as we used to call it when freelancers contributed to the production from their own wages...

BB

In Germany, you were not really received as a dissident from communism?

ŽŽ

It was the exact opposite. I was hanging out with them and they asked me what I was planning to do. I told them about a couple of outlines for documentaries and for a longer project called *Das Paradies*. They agreed to provide technical support. The well-known cameraman Thomas Mauch got in touch, wanting to shoot. He did end up doing a couple of projects with us. Herzog took me to visit him at home, to see his editing table and some camera he owned. Herzog said that he could understand a little of our language.

"How come?" I asked. And he said:

"My father is Stipetić, a Croat. But he is not living with my mother. When she sees us, let's speak English, she is angry at you Yugoslavs."

They advised me to be careful, because "here it's not possible to make explicitly activist films the way you do it down there."

They told me that the script for *Das Paradies* would never see the light of day because it talks about how the state manipulates the dangers of anarcho-terrorism to make more space for reinforcing police power and the beginnings of the country's militarization. They were right about that. We finished the film in 1976, and after the premiere, they declined to distribute. Then a couple of friends, film critics, openly told me that they could not write anything about the topic at that time. Lastly, a few days later we had a police search and a financial audit of the production and we were advised to leave the country.

Still, those two or three years I spent in Germany were crucially important for me. I learned the meaning of private production and personal financial risk. I gained the experience of filmmaking on small budgets and realized it was also possible. In those years the big German filmmakers worked along the same lines.

All in all, I made seven short films and one feature film. At Oberhausen in 1975, of the eight films produced in Germany, four were mine...

Stalinism

"Stalinism" nowadays is a term that has been historically used up. It had once played a crucial role in the development of what we call historical communism, that is, the ideology and political practice of the communist movement from its historical beginnings in the nineteenth century until its breakdown in the so-called democratic revolutions of 1989–90. "Stalinism" is a concept inherent to its dynamism, to its historical, ideological, and factional differentiation.

In the figure of Stalinism, the communist movement discovered its immanent negation around which it tried not only to draw historical boundaries and distance itself from it as the period of its own deviance and decadence, but indeed to look in that negation of the negation, in its delimitation from Stalinism, for its immanent renewal.

Without the notion of Stalinism it is impossible to understand the case of Yugoslavia, the peculiar Yugoslav path to socialism, Titoism, the politics of non-alignment, self-management, including the unique achievements of cultural production and the particular forms of dissidence in Yugoslavia, the now-forgotten leftist, democratic critique of totalitarian practices within the Yugoslav socialist system. It was not only the Yugoslav communist movement that re-discovered the authentic democratic and emancipatory legitimacy it had carried from the period of antifascist struggle and social revolution, its entitlement to distinctiveness, to political, ideological, and historical experimentation in the negation of Stalinism; its critics, within and without the Party, the overt deniers of its bureaucratic, totalitarian perversion, of the cult of personality it used as a crutch, those who struggled for freedom of artistic creation, of cultural and intellectual work, they also found their legitimation in the overt negation of Stalinism.

Without the notion of Stalinism, the Yugoslav past makes no sense. With the so-called collapse of communism, this internal differentiation of the communist movement became irrelevant. The idea of Stalinism lost any use value, any particular referentiality. It became empty and redundant. The past appeared in its trivial uniformity, literalness, and transparency, or, which is the same thing, it appeared ahistorical and apolitical. Even that

most banal of differences between socialism and communism,
the difference once apparent to any elementary school student
in formerly socialist states—the difference between the idea
itself, communism, and its concrete historical realization, socialism as a particular social order, political system, a form of
property ownership, etc.—completely lost its meaning after
the years 1989–90. Everything got rounded up to the notion of
communism which could then be thrown onto the garbage heap
of history. This is how, already at the level of naming, a huge
erasure came over a vast experience of social conflict, factional
struggles, open international conflicts including real wars, as
well as the experience of difficult ideological and cultural dis-
putes, in brief, the entirety of the political dynamism of historical communism.

The concept of communism today connotes oblivion to the
concept of Stalinism. But the notion of communism itself could
not defy forgetting for long. It was soon swallowed up by the notion of totalitarianism. At this point the difference between communism and fascism has become irrelevant, much like the experience of conflict between those "two forms of totalitarianism"
has become historically insignificant and worthless. All those
many millions of people who died in the struggle over life and
death between those two ideologies and political movements in
their mutual war to the extinction, they may appear to us today
as accidental victims of a blunder, a tragic misunderstanding
between friends, between brothers, as unfortunate casualties of
one fundamentally fratricidal war.

In this conceptual transformation many see the progress
made in our consciousness about the actual truth of the past.
The one thing, however, which has made progress on the way
from Stalinism via communism to totalitarianism has been the
forgetting.

žž

These days the picture has completely faded of the global marathon race between Democracy and Capitalism of the West against Communism of the East, which began with the Cold war, in the late 1940s.

The case of Yugoslavia, that is whatever gets mentioned today with a great deal of incredulity as the so-called clash between Stalin and Tito in 1948, was actually an event of world proportions. After the war ended, the victors celebrated. On one side, Churchill, Truman, and de Gaulle; on the other, with the same merits and same contributions—Stalin. It was his troops that marched into Berlin, and the number of Red Army soldiers sacrificed exceeded the number of soldiers killed in all the other Allied armies combined. Each side took some of the spoils. General McArthur ruled in Tokyo; he received the Japanese emperor Hirohito as a visitor who had to report to him. Stalin's generals ruled in Bucharest, Sophia, and Budapest. Each one defined the rules in their own backyard.

Suddenly, in this just-established balance, the Balkan bag full of cats whose nationalist nails had barely been clipped, the Federative People's Republic of Yugoslavia ruled by partisans-communists, refused to obey Stalin.

In political and media terms, this had an effect greater than when the bomb was dropped on Hiroshima. At the same time, the Victors, the New Rulers of the World, were reminded of the ideological trenches they had dug out just ten years earlier, while the Molotov-Ribbentrop Pact was in effect and nobody believed a word Stalin said because he was staging show trials with the police and the courts which managed to kill not only all of Stalin's competitors—Trotsky, Zinoviev and Kamenev—but also the top brass of the Red Army, Marshals Tukhachevsky, Blyukher and others, which is why the first few months of Hitler's "faith-breaking aggression" on the Soviet Union went as smoothly as a knife through butter.

So, "dissidence against Stalinism" of the newly established regime in Yugoslavia was akin to a reformation movement against the omnipotence of the Vatican. It significantly reworked the established balance of dictatorships and I think that it offers to this day a model for how an exit was possible. This example made a not insignificant impression on the movements for liberation from colonialism, which erupted a few years after the break between Stalin and Tito.

With Stalin's death in 1953 and the formation of the political coterie around Khrushchev, a new dynamic emerged. It was acknowledged in front of Tito that "he had been in the right." This also signaled confirmation that socialism had to change. The Soviet Union underwent "the thaw" with waves of previously unimaginable freedoms in culture and release of hundreds of thousands of prisoners from the Gulag. These were the early 1960s that we remember as the years of optimism.

These openings and innovations created conflicts in the system, however. First at the social level: enterprises doing business abroad, building airports, roads and hydroelectric power plants in Africa and Asia, were doing business on the global market. "Ideological accord" was one thing, but the investments, market competition, semi-legalized graft, and managerial salaries were something else.

The Yugoslav self-managing companies did not pay "each according to their work" but exacerbated social disparities because each was making profit according to their "position in the global market." In Czechoslovakia, the government proclaimed it was building "socialism with a human face" and decided to use the Yugoslav model and go its own way. Czechoslovakia was invaded by the tank divisions of the Warsaw Pact which overthrew the party and government leadership and installed Moscow's pawns. Hundreds of thousands of refugees spilled over the borders because Czechoslovakia was situated in the heart of Europe. The West received refugees from Czechoslovakia and lamented the breach of their human rights, but everyone was minding their own business.

At that time, Tito's circle, we thought, felt like it was losing ground. Polemics about choosing between a market, self-managed, or state economy had no end. Dilemmas about whether young people were looking for "more socialism" or "more freedom" turned the group in power towards the old instruments of control.

Mass censoring began of youth newspapers, magazines and books. The films that had already been produced and praised were declared ideologically suspicious. There were changes in the make-up of the cadres: many who were capable were replaced by those who were obedient and toed the Party line. So, for me, all of the 1970s were a decade of re-Stalinization.

But it would be hard to say that the actual steps leading to Stalinization concerned the majority of the population, as long as they had jobs, healthcare, and free education, as well as the open space for economic initiatives and agriculture within the framework of the "self-management system." Already by the late 1970s, the language used by ideology committees and hare-brained Party officials was so thoroughly compromised that they talked about going back to "the old experiences." That's how the late 1970s and early 1980s, after Tito had already died, brought back some of the best of the climate of the 1960s.

Unexpectedly, I did most of my work on film in that kind of environment. And if I, being "marked" and outside the Party, could do that much, I can only imagine how much room there had to be for the "tractable" ones.

This is what was unusual: the film industry was controlled by a handful of monopolists who wasted huge budgets, while television, a far more communicative medium and more modest, practiced the cultural politics of "mature Titoism." The logic at work there I would formulate thus: after Tito, even more Titoism. But, the circumstances were completely different: Brezhnev's system was imploding and had neither the administrative nor the economic power to control half the world.

The newly liberated countries turned from socialist democracies into robbers' dictatorships, in which the political elites prioritized the depletion of resources and compliance with demands of the countries whose banks held their money. Margaret Thatcher eliminated the traditional British working class, redirected the economy towards banking and new technologies. Italy, Germany, and Spain went to war to the death of their radical youth rebels. The United States did that first, as soon as the early 1970s, when the Black Panther activists were assassinated and members of Students for a Democratic Society ended up in prison on decades-long sentences. In Germany, most members of the Rote Armee Fraktion were killed, and the few who remained were serving time at Stammheim.

The thing we have laconically named "Stalinism"—that is an incontestable dictatorship of the ruling group. It can be achieved in various forms, just like it can direct itself against a variety of "enemies." For example, what we elegantly call "liberal capitalism" or "the post-communist transition" today is not an option any more merciful than Stalinism. It has, to put it briefly, found its class enemy, those who disturb the technology of government itself, in the working people. These are the millions who took part in industrializing and urbanizing socialism. Liberal capitalism systematically destroys those millions of people through unemployment, lack of health care, starvation, by depriving their children of any idea of the future. And in former Yugoslavia, this has been achieved by re-fusing to recognize—by completely erasing—the roles of workers in the building of companies. Yet it was practically a general rule that those employed in a self-managed company would invest a portion of their earnings in the technological or other development of their factory. They would also buy, from their earnings, vacation resorts and build sports facilities.

All those investments that were documented in detail in the financial archives have been erased. The firms have been sold, but not for money but rather for "certificates"—practically certificates of membership in the new ruling class, among the war profiteers and the rich who share their profit with the party oligarchy. And for all the many nuances and laws of capitalism that exist in the newly made former Yugoslav states, the "brotherhood and unity of tycoons" is the norm everywhere, enabling the fully coordinated plunder of their own working classes and their socialist resources. It would be interesting to examine the makeup of the new ruling groups. When I think of just a few dozen names, I realize they all come from the party oligarchy of the "new storm troopers," the tractable ones from the early 1970s.

The design of that narrowing in the 1970s, didn't that eventu-ally open up a space for these, so to say, traditionalist sentiments, a path from nationalism to cultural traditionalism? And now, what can we see in those 1970s? We can see that artificial attempt at re-Stalinization and the pressure of re-Stalinization. It is curious that the nationalist discourse from the late 1970s and early 1980s was not designed by some chetnik-ustasha emigrants, as one might suppose it was looking back now. It was actually designed by a faction, we could say, by the mainstream of that intellectual and academic corps of that country.

BB
And that would be the classic bourgeois culture?

ŽŽ
Yes.

Well, the question is whether that classic bourgeois culture simply came from some people who reinterpreted it and who were actually communist officials at the same time, and some were the officials of that Yugoslav anti-Stalinist modernism, after the 1950s, as was the case with some members of the editorial board of the philosophy journal _Praxis_ in Belgrade, or someone like Dobrica Ćosić in Belgrade, and some others, and maybe it just came as a reaction to that iron belt of the recycled newspeak of the party, which I would say could be artificially imposed in that way.

But this is a subject that deserves longer-term reflection and even that would be hard-pressed to provide a more optimistic interpretation, because what happened was that things looked at first like a step towards some kind of return to the spaces of freedom, which later narrowed down to become the worst kind of—you could say a tribal slaughterhouse from some prehistoric time.

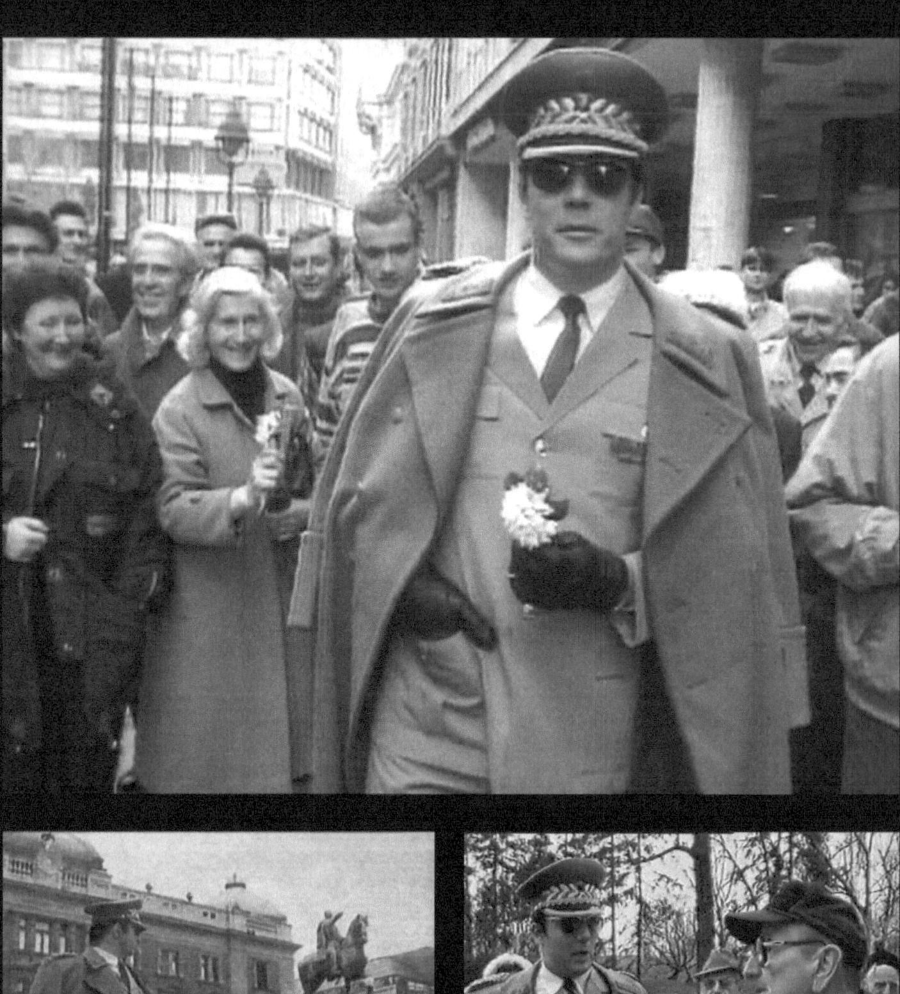

Tito (a dictator?)

To go beyond challenging this: The claim that Tito was a dictator is not just factually false. The factual aspect does not decide there at all. Discussions about the past which cleave to facts quasi-scientifically often resort to fruitless quantification of victims, like they would want to have a depravity contest: Who killed more people, Hitler, Stalin, or Mao? Whose record is bleaker, that of communism or that of fascism? And why not Catholicism, capitalism, nationalism, modernism, colonialism...?

The problem with the claim that Tito was a dictator is thus that it implies a view of the past that of necessity falsifies that past. Before us appears a picture of the evil individual, the dictator, on one side, and the innocent, benevolent people, that is, the freedom-loving dissidents on the other, a picture in black and white that clearly shows the distinction between good and evil, simplifies the past to the point of absurdity, and so fetishistically assuages the discomfort that accompanies our remembrance of it. What is more, it radically disrupts any causal relationships between the past and the present. One doesn't know what to believe, one's own eyes or the picture of one's past. What can one do when in the current reality those poor people who had been mercilessly trampled over by the boot of the dictatorship show themselves consumed by the flames of chauvinism, mindlessly destroying everything good that the past, even such a dictatorial one, had bequeathed to them, dragging not only their neighbors but themselves over the brink of catastrophe? Or when they find their ostensibly freedom-loving dissidents among murderers and criminals, the brazen barbaro-geniuses who will embarrass them when they show up on the benches of international crime tribunals? What was democratic freedom to them? A brief interlude between two jail sentences which they could use in full to multiply a hundredfold the evil they could do to their own society.

"Tito the dictator" is an empty phrase of the post-communist, and therefore also anti-communist, discourse that is not only a lie in itself, but first of all a lie for us, the lie that forces us not only to forget the past but also to deny the reality in which we live.

To say, by contrast, that Tito was the authoritarian master of former Yugoslavia opens up a completely different vista.

That claim is no stylistic trick designed to amnesty the dictator from his culpability. On the contrary, it situates his rule within a completely different tradition, that of authoritarian and occasionally absolutist rule of the pre-moderns, and so also of our pre-nationalist past, of those whose rule was admittedly extremely strict, often cruel and openly, viciously violent, but who fundamentally, and very conservatively, always managed to stabilize and preserve what their predecessors had bequeathed them. Let us recall: the multi-confessional, or as we would now say, the multi-ethnic core of the city of Sarajevo survived under sultans and kings, under the Kaiser and the Secretary General of the Communist Party, but it did not survive the post-communist democracy.

To claim that Tito was an authoritarian ruler is to recover still another, now completely suppressed dimension of Yugoslav communism, namely its traditionalist, conservative character which could from today's perspective be summarized in this question: Was not one of the historical truths of Yugoslav communism precisely its concurrent effort from 1941 on to stop the fascist self-destruction of Yugoslav nations, which effort, as we now know, failed miserably in the 1990s, such that the fascist project initiated in 1941 could finally be completed without interruption?

ŽŽ

Tito's career in power lasted a long time, plus he was promised tenure for life by the constitution.

He held a "leadership position" for many decades, but he practiced in different historical periods, so it could happen to him that being defeated or finding himself in mortal danger was part of the job description.

First there was the 1937 order from Moscow to "sort out" the Communist Party of Yugoslavia (CPY), which had brought several of his predecessors holding the same position in front of the firing squad made up of their communist comrades.

Then, he was living in the Kingdom of Yugoslavia in the capacity of the Secretary of the CPY, when any encounter with the police in the street presented the risk of arrest, torture, and imprisonment.

And even walking free was through a labyrinth: the prewar anxiety, while the Antifascist People's Front was organizing throughout Europe and Stalin was signing a pact with Hitler, figuring that fascism "would exhaust itself in the conflict with imperialist Britain and France." Tito's official assignment during this period was to implement the orders of the Comintern.

The next period of his life and leadership, after "Germany's faith-breaking attack on the USSR," so starting in late June 1941, was even more perilous and turbulent. He was organizing a guerilla war on the territory occupied on six sides by fascist armies which had divided the country and installed local quislings to assist in annihilating the fraction of the population that had decided to resist the occupation. Next to the thousands of friends and fellow fighters who died and facing his own risk of dying, in the four years of the war, Tito showed courage, resourcefulness, and broadmindedness, which ten years later brought him into the position where he was communicating with half the world and creating the Yugoslav model of socialism.

Partisan warfare managed to earn antifascist support from important intellectuals and experts from various regions: Antun Augustinčić, Pavle Savić, Vladimir Nazor, Edvard Kocbek, Priest Vlada Zečević, Ivan Ribar, Nurija Pozderac, Josip Smodlaka, Ivan Goran Kovačić... And then it earned the support of the Western allies.

From Prime Minister Churchill to Marshal Tito

JANUARY 8, 1944

I am resolved that the British Government will give no further military support to Mihailović and will only give help to you and we should be glad if the Royal Yugoslav Government would dismiss him from their councils. King Peter the Second however escaped as a boy from the treacherous clutches of the Regent Prince Paul and came to us as representative of Yugoslavia and as a young Prince in distress.

It would not be chivalrous or honourable for Great Britain to cast him aside. Nor can we ask him to cut all his existing contacts with his country. I hope therefore that you will understand that we shall in any case remain in official relations with him while at the same time giving you all possible military support. I hope also that there may be an end to polemics on either side, for these only help the Germans.

—from D. Biber (ed.), *Tito-Churchill: Strogo tajno*
(Zagreb: Globus, 1981), 75.

The uncompromising armed struggle against the occupiers adapted to the regional specificities is what made this possible. If you look at the testimony of Olga Humo, Tito's interpreter for English, who handled correspondence with the Allies:

> "I was present when Tito spoke to Churchill in Bari, in the summer of 1944. This was the height of my glory as an interpreter. Fitzroy Maclean was there, Churchill, me, and Tito, of course. Churchill asked Tito:
>
>> 'Do you intend to implement a Soviet system in Yugoslavia after the war?'
>
> I translated for Tito and he said:
>
>> 'We will take from them only what is compatible with the situation in our country. In principle, we will be independent.'
>
> Churchill then asked:
>
>> 'Are the Serbian farmers not supporting you, the partisans?!'

Tito answered that this was not accurate, that some of them were waffling, but that they were now all fully supporting us. As if. Although there was no resistance when we got to Serbia in 1944. Around the Central Headquarters it was all Serbs, and the attached battalion was made up of the partisans from Serbia. All on the command staff were Serbs.

Croatian partisans fought in Croatia, Slovenian partisans fought in Slovenia, and around Tito they were all Serbs. When it became known in the summer of 1944 that we would reach Serbia, everyone was ecstatic: Serbia, Serbia! You could feel the war was nearing its end. Churchill was extremely clever and had a great sense of humor. He was an anticommunist, of course, but this was never evident in the conversation, the focus was on the allyship.

There were also questions about the king. Churchill insinuated that the king might like to come back, that it would be nice if he were appointed the commander of some air force unit!

He didn't ask about it categorically, it was more of a diplomatic insinuation, a feeler. Tito replied,

'In our army the dynasty isn't held in very high regard— his return would have a negative effect on the military morale! We are in the thick of the struggle now and cannot take risks.'

He was a superb diplomat, and his goal was to form a joint government, without regard for the king. Churchill wasn't categorical on any one issue. He and Tito both knew exactly how far they could go.

'It would have a negative effect on the military morale' struck a chord with Churchill. He really was a practiced politician. Later Tito asked about the Western front, and we went into a small room where the maps were, and Churchill showed us where the Allies were advancing. They had a very simple conversation, without philosophizing, like children. Which, I've noticed, is the quality of exceptionally smart people."

The choice of the translator also suggests something about the method of working. Before the war, Olga had been a student and a communist, and her father was Momčilo Ninčić, a minister in several governments under King Alexander of Yugoslavia, who was during the war a member of the government in exile in London.

We get a different assessment from Olga Humo when she is asked about how the guerilla fighters "managed in their high-ranking positions."

> "All kinds of things happened after the war, all sorts of our Party nonsense. Those wretched villas in Dedinje... I said to the comrades:
>
> 'Why is this going on? The whole world is looking at us with suspicion, because of those villas and those cars! People are sick and tired of us!'

And they said:

> 'We gave him so much that he can use absolutely none of this against us.'
>
> That differentiation was unnecessary and bad, it left a negative impression. But our people were so oblivious to all this, so insensitive to such things! Tito was blind: he liked luxury and extravagantly rewarded those lieges around him with luxury. All of them were so brilliant during the war, and then did their best to make the people sick of them— pretending to be millionaires."

Tito's refusal to organize Yugoslavia on the model of other countries in the Warsaw Pact, and definitely all the above-mentioned luxuriating, and especially the recognition from Western Allies, these were all reasons for Stalin's criticism in 1948.

The struggle began, life or death. There was a call from Moscow to remove the leadership because they were "imperialist spies and nationalists," which deeply hurt the dignity of the party and state apparatus who convulsed in fears about their survival. This resulted in the harshest possible treatment of all who were not 100% on the side of Tito's leadership, anyone even remotely suspicious for supporting Stalin's "correct line."

It has been well established that nearly 20,000 communists, including dozens of ministers, generals, and pre-war underground activists were transported to Goli otok (Barren Island), where the regime of "reeducation" was more brutal than in a Soviet gulag. It is unlikely that anyone imprisoned there would have softened their descriptions of Tito's rule, to themselves, not out loud, rather than call it absolutist terror against anyone who would think differently.

The question you asked, whether everything that happened was organized at the hand of an evil and brutal dictator and directed against his naïve and benevolent subjects, is one of the large questions about the Goli otok prison. We have read hundreds of testimonies: the most brutal methods of psychological and physical torture were implemented by prisoners themselves, who divided themselves into "revisionists" who had "returned to the CPY path," and "the gangs" who still believed in Stalin. It goes without saying that no human-rights-watch-type organizations from the West were ever interested in the rights of these prisoners because these were supporters of Stalin, "our enemy's friends."

Under those circumstances, the military cooperation between Yugoslavia and NATO was restored, having been first established during the war.

So, Tito's military-state socialism showed it was able to sustain pressure and the threat of intervention from the USSR. In the internal, ideological-value-oriented context, it had won the propaganda war. Support from the West was unequivocal. Firm control and a clear hierarchy have been imposed because enemies threatened "from within and without." In the early 1950s, Tito's Yugoslavia was in a very knotty situation: it was trying to show what was different about it, more democratic than the USSR, that its communist project was more authentic than the Soviet project.

At the same time, in this "socialism with a human face," the typical Stalinist measures against those who think differently were in use.

These dramatic contradictions were the root of the systemic innovation happening in late 1949. The "Instruction on the founding and operation of workers' councils" was issued. An idea radically different from Soviet state socialism, it followed in the emancipatory footsteps of the Paris Commune and the anarchists' and social democrats' criticisms of Stalinism. Two years later, a constitutional law proclaimed the inalienable right of workers to participate in decision making processes. The property owned by state companies was renamed "social property." Companies did not receive production and marketing plans from a center but acted independently. This idea was being implemented against bureaucratic resistance, of course.

Today, when we sum up the results of the first two decades of the robbers' national-capitalism, we can see that the sense of ownership among the great majority of the population was stronger then than it is today. We can see that that first twenty years of socialism saw slogans like "Give land to farmers, factories to the workers" become reality, and that the number of newly established companies, newly employed workers and new housing construction was practically the same as the number of companies closed down, workers laid off, and living quarters destroyed in the period between 1991 and 2013. And the number of educated young people who left the space of former Yugoslavia is equal to the number of students from rural parts of the country who enrolled at universities in the first two decades of state socialism.

Don't leave, Koča, they'll forget you
the second you turn your back...

In the early 1950s, negotiations with the Pentagon began about cooperation and security. Huge military aid in tanks, airplanes, arms, and electronic equipment was received.

Chief negotiator was Koča Popović, Chief of Staff of the High Command of the Yugoslav People's Army. Having been the Commander of the First Proletarian Brigade during the war, then an army commander until liberation in the spring of 1945, Popović knew the American and British generals from their joint military operations which pushed the Germans out of the Balkans.

This was a man who had graduated with a degree in philosophy from the Sorbonne in 1932. He joined the Surrealists. He published a book he co-wrote with Marko Ristić, *An Outline for a Phenomenology of the Irrational*. He also published film criticism in *Paris Soir*. He joined the volunteers who fought against Franco's fascists in Spain. He got promoted to the officer rank serving in the artillery.

Koča Popović was Yugoslavia's minister of foreign affairs from 1953 to 1965, and one of Tito's closest collaborators. Those were the years when Yugoslavia established its very close friendly and economic ties with Africa and Asia, in addition to relations with the West, and even with the Soviet bloc after 1955, when the relations were repaired following the death of Stalin, after Nikita Khrushchev and Nikolai Bulganin had sent in their apologies to Yugoslavia.

I met Koča Popović when I visited my colleague Branko Baletić at home, and he lived in Dedinje, with his in-laws, and they were high-ranking officials from Tito's day. They were sitting in their garden drinking coffee with their neighbor Koča when Baletić and I came over. Branko's father-in-law, Puniša Perović, wanted to introduce us to Koča. He said we were film directors. Koča nodded and started to ask us questions in French. We were staring blankly because we couldn't speak French. Koča cut straight to the point:

> "How can you make films, you knuckleheads, and not know any French? Film was born there! It's like with philosophy students today—writing a thesis on Hegel without knowing a word of German."

I took his cue and spoke to him in German:

> "Comrade Koča, film was a kind of fairground entertainment in France. When Germans got into film, they made it into art. Murnau and Lang invented film directing. Asta Nielsen was the first movie star. Hollywood spoke German when it was founded by professionals from Budapest and Vienna."

Koča looked at us with his eyebrows raised, then offered us to sit. He said he wasn't watching any contemporary films because they were all bad.

About ten years earlier, a rumor was spreading that Koča Popović was there at the screening of *Early Works* for Tito. And that he didn't like the film. I wasn't comfortable asking. He didn't say anything. And the times were different. Koča had resigned in 1972, as Vice President of Yugoslavia. We wanted to know about that. In 1982, when we met, Tito had been dead for two years. Baletić plucked up the courage to ask,

> "Comrade Koča, when we think about the golden age of our foreign policy, was that all your thinking and leadership?

Koča snapped:

> "Don't talk nonsense! With Tito, I visited 290 heads of state, governments or sovereigns. 289 of them took notes of what Tito was saying. Only Churchill didn't have a pen in hand."

Our jaws dropped.

> "But Comrade Koča, Tito could hardly speak Serbo-Croatian, how could he communicate with foreigners?"

ПОЛИТИКА

ВЛАДИСЛАВ РИБНИКАР ОСНИВАЧ
рез. капетан, погинуо 1 септембра 1914 год.
ДАРКО РИБНИКАР УРЕДНИК
рез. капетан, погинуо 21 августа 1914 год.
ДР СЛОБОДАН РИБНИКАР ДИРЕКТОР
рез. потпуковник, умро 24 септембра 1914 год.

Директор: ВЛАДИСЛАВ СЛ. РИБНИКАР

ПРИМЕРАК 10 ДИН.

ТЕЛЕФОНИ: Централа 20-327, 20-328
Секретаријат: 25-668
Ревизорско одељење: 28-229
Администрација: 25-007

БЕОГРАД, ПЕТАК 27 МАЈ 1955
Број 15143 — Година LII

ЛИСТ НЕ ИЗЛАЗИ УТОРНИКОМ
РУКОПИСИ СЕ НЕ ВРАЋАЈУ
ПРЕТПЛАТА ЗА ЈЕДАН МЕСЕЦ
За нашу земљу 250, за стране земље 200 дин.

ПОЛИТИКА МАКЕДОНСКА 31

ЈУГОСЛОВЕНСКО-СОВЈЕТСКИ МЕЂУДРЖАВНИ РАЗГОВОРИ НА НАЈВИШЕМ НИВОУ

ДЕЛЕГАЦИЈА СОВЈЕТСКЕ ВЛАДЕ НА ЧЕЛУ С НИКИТОМ ХРУШЧОВОМ ДОПУТОВАЛА У БЕОГРАД

Претседник Републике и највиши југословенски руководиоци дочекали су на земунском аеродрому Хрушчова, Булгањина, Микојана, Шепилова, Громика и Кумкина

На аеродрому пре доласка делегације

Долазак Претседника Републике

Совјетска делегација ступа на југословенско тле

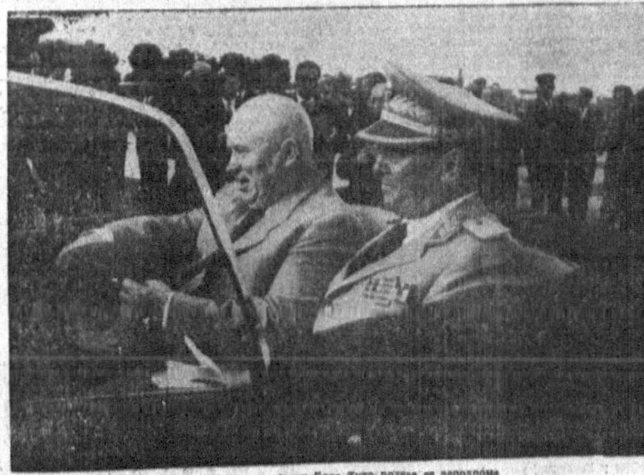

Никита Хрушчов и Јосип Броз Тито полазе са аеродрома

За време свирања химни на земунском аеродрому. С лева: Добривоје Видић, Анастас Микојан, Николај Булгањин, Јосип Броз Тито, Андреј Громико и, сасвим десно, Никита Хрушчов

Говор Никите Хрушчова

Драги друже Тито,

Драги другови, чланови владе и руководиоци Савеза комуниста Југославије,

Драги другови и грађани,

"Soviet Government delegation led by Nikita Khrushchev arrived in Belgrade," *Politika* (May 27, 1955)

Koča laughed:

> "Tito was bored here with us. He didn't have real
> interlocutors. And he could speak more foreign
> languages than I could. His grammar was far from
> perfect but converse he could. In Russian, German,
> English, Czech, French... And about his education
> you are also wrong. He was reading a lot and reading
> everything. He didn't care for modern art—paint-
> ing, music, and drama, that he didn't appreciate.
> He thought it was all a bunch of mystifiers making
> garbage. That's more or less what Krleža thought
> too. I'm not sure they were wrong."

We could see he was about to tear into us.

So Baletić went at it again,

> "Comrade Koča, but you clashed with Comrade Tito
> when you resigned. You were his deputy, as Vice
> President of Yugoslavia."

Koča sighed deeply.

> "What clash? What is this nonsense you are saying?
> First, I said that it was a mistake to remove the
> so-called liberal leadership of Serbia. Many young
> and competent people would end up pushed out
> of politics.
>
> I said it was no good because it was high time
> for our generation to step down. Tito replied that
> he knew that too. But the people remained ignorant,
> they were looking for authority, for a savior."

Tito had allegedly said,

> "If they remove my picture in the marshal's uniform
> from the wall, whose will they put up instead? Some
> new careerist? It is far more likely that they'll recover
> Franz Joseph, King Peter or Pavelić from the attic.
> Don't leave, Koča, they'll forget you the second you
> turn your back."

Koča Popović died ten years later. He was probably one of the most
brilliant Serbs of the twentieth century. Fewer than 50 people came
to his funeral. His last statement was,

> "The saddest bunch, the scum and sheep droppings of
> humanity have risen up to restore the empire of Emperor
> Dušan. Serbs will only ever oppose those who want to

make them a little smarter, but they will lionize anyone
who wants to make them dumber, more backward and
more miserable.

It is sad that Serbs in a civilizational and cultural sense
have occupied the same place for the past one hundred years.
They are not at odds with the world but with themselves,
and they are going back to the peasant hats and shoes they
had hardly abandoned. I have been and remain a Serb, but
I am not a sick moron or a Serbian chauvinist."

What's it these lunatics want?

BB

Tell me—I'm asking sincerely—it is commonplace
today to say that Tito was a dictator. But, to hear
you talk about it, I don't get that impression, of
course. Would you, on the basis of your personal
experience, say that Tito was, after all, a dictator?

ŽŽ

There was a moment in which Tito "expressed dissatisfaction" with
my work. He stopped the screening of *Early Works* and angrily asked:
"What's it these lunatics want?"
It was like this: on June 14, 1969, after three months of relatively
successful screenings of *Early Works* in cinemas around the country,
after much commentary and many polemics, director of Avala Film,
Dragiša Đurić, called me to come urgently to his office.

He was gloomy and waved his arm at Tito's photo above his
desk. These photos were a required item in any office. He said,
"The film was shown last night. The screening was
interrupted, and a discomfiting question was asked."
I said that I couldn't believe it, that these were just the tricks
played by our competitors, spurred by jealousy, because the film
was selected for the official competition at the Berlin Film Festival
which was starting in two weeks. Đurić said to his secretary to
call the employee who was working in the screening room. He had
been at Dedinje the night before, showing the movies. Tito's villa
was a ten-minute walk from the studios in Košutnjak Park. You
just go down the hill and then it's on a hill nearby, at number 15,
Užička Street.

The worker entered, and I knew him. He was gloomy as well. He said that after a half hour they were fed up with the film. Gile gave me a meaningful glance. The worker left. He offered me a seat and handed me a piece of paper. It was like a statement, and he and I were supposed to sign it, declaring that the film *Early Works* was still in the editing phase and unfinished, that it had been stolen from Avala Film and shown without our permission. The version of the film that was circulating we did not sign off on.

I got scared. I told Đurić that our colleagues, the press and the audience would know that we were lying. We had been showing the film at premieres, bragging about it in interviews and defending the film in polemics. I refused to sign the statement. Director asked his secretary to call the public prosecutor and explained on the phone that "the pretentious artist refused to cooperate."

When the conversation was over, he told me to go down to the bistro, get a coffee, and wait for the police car that was coming to pick up the copies of the film and to serve the subpoena.

I sat there for about twenty minutes. All kinds of situations I had heard and read about went through my head. I suspected the police patrol was coming to pick me up. In a rush I wrote a message I left with the bartender, for Branko Vučićević.

They called me again to come to the director's office. The police unit commander was there, signing the receipt for the copies they took, and delivered the "Court decision about a temporary ban on public screening of the film *Early Works*," file no. 31/69, signed by the district attorney Spasoje Milošev.

Gile Đurić jokingly asked the officer:

"Are you taking him in too?"

The officer answered:

"No, our orders are to deliver the decision and to pick up the copies of the film."

In a few days, the trial started. I was authorized by the co-producer, Neoplanta Film, to lead the defense. I attacked the prosecutor claiming that the accusation and the ban were typical Stalinist moves which would cause more harm to the dignity of our country than any artwork ever could. The court heard the argument between the prosecutor and the defense, watched the film, and accepted the argument of the defense. The film was released, and a week later it was shown at the Berlin Festival, which back then took place in early July. The film was well received by the critics, the audience, and the jury. The university students who were protesting were particularly interested in the film, and they gave to *Early Works* the Young Generation Award.

I wouldn't say that Tito was a dictator

I have heard in discussions among the right-wingers and among the leftists the same question you are asking. My answer was: I wouldn't say that Tito was a dictator.

Anyway, at that Berlinale, in addition to *Early Works*, which was in the competition, there was "A Week of New Yugoslav Film," very well received and which no one ever declared to be a bundle of films made under a dictatorial regime.

One should not forget, of course, that the Penal Code had an article in it concerning enemy propaganda and undermining of the constitutional order as criminal offenses. And that one was frequently abused. There has never been a thorough study of the number of critical films, books, magazines, and theater plays that managed to "pass," and still there were many indicted for crimes of speech and served prison terms. The sweeping claim is incorrect, that all who were visible in public and critically oriented had to be informants. That some of them were is best evidenced by the fact that, at least in Serbia, police files remain under lock and key more than twenty years later.

I remember several situations in which the State Security Administration tried to "clamp down." Here's one. In the winter of 1977, my friend Hans Angst, who had been my assistant director in Germany, called to say he was driving through Novi Sad on his way to Greece with a friend. I told him they should definitely stop by, get a good night's sleep, and then continue on their way. They arrived in the early evening. We went out for some stew and beers. Later that night we were sitting in my apartment, chatting. Peđa Vranešević, the composer, also came by. He's been another collaborator and friend. In Germany, he made the music for the film *Das Paradies*, and the year before we worked together at the Serbian National Theatre on the very successful play, *The Gastarbeiter Opera*.

At midnight, someone started knocking hard on the front door. Not ringing the bell but knocking. I opened the door and there were seven of them at the door. I recognized two or three of them, we had been in law school together. I asked them what was going on.

They showed me a warrant to search the apartment.

> "On what grounds?"
>
> "You broke the law—you didn't report the foreigners
> staying with you at home, and the law gives you six
> hours from their time of arrival."

At that point it was about six hours and fifteen minutes from the time they arrived. The seven of them entered, snooping around the apartment. Two of them started taking books off the shelves, shaking them out. One was "keeping watch" at the door. One took down personal information from Peđa Vranešević because he was going to become the "citizen witness to the search." A couple of the agents tried to talk to Hans and his friend in English. Who they are, why they came, where they were going. I said, it would be better if you spoke to them in German, that's their mother tongue.

I saw they were mumbling to each other, nobody could speak German. I took the opportunity to warn the guests to flush whatever down the toilet, if they had weed or some such. And they did it skillfully. The visit lasted half an hour to an hour. Then they told us to pick up our things, they were taking us to the police station to give our statements. It was 1:30 in the night. There was a police van in front of the building, engine running. They shoved us inside. Two of them stayed in the apartment to watch it, and Peđa was there as the witness. At the police station, there were two or three inspectors waiting for us. I asked them what they wanted; it was an oversight on my part, I didn't report my foreign guests, so "send me to the magistrate."

I told them not to bother these two foreigners, that it's going to be embarrassing. And they just shot back, with such cool:

> "Žilnik, man, you have no idea how many reports
> we get about you. And not only from Draško Ređep,
> who is the director of Neoplanta Film and also works
> for us, but from many of your colleagues. We were
> informed today that these two who were coming,
> were anarcho-terrorists, members of the Baader-
> Meinhof Gang. We have to check that out."

They sat the young men on chairs and then took out some poster with pictures of people wanted by the police, started to compare. When they checked their passports, there was a turnabout. Hans had a Swiss passport, not German, and I didn't even know that.

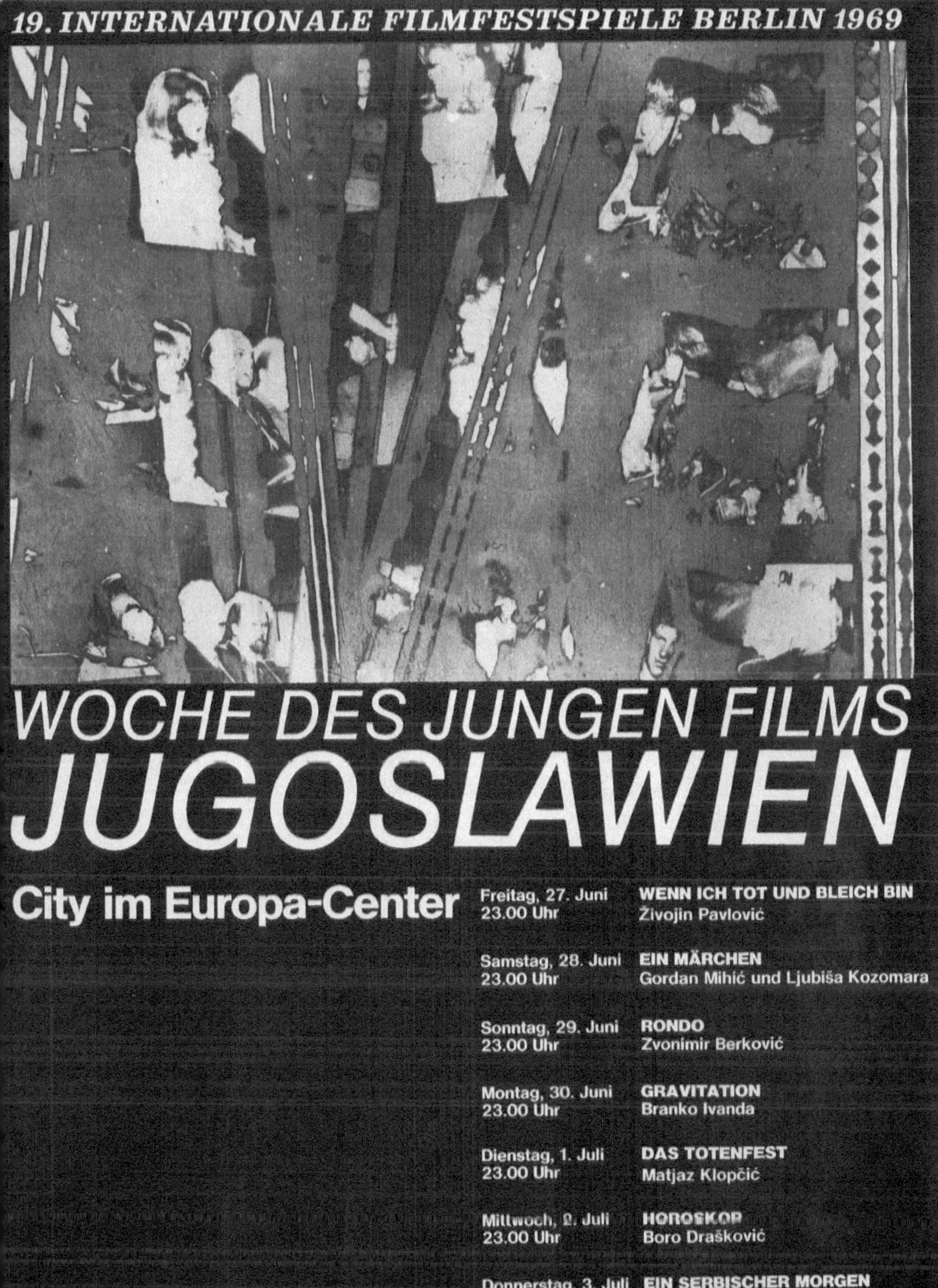

1969 Berlin Film Festival, *Week of Youth Film from Yugoslavia:
City in Central Europe*

Hans demanded to call the Swiss embassy immediately, even if it was three in the morning. He showed them the number that Swiss citizens had the right to call at any time of day or night. That seemed to cool the situation down. They drove us back to the apartment and politely asked us not to make noise about the whole thing. They had received a false denunciation.

Where to, Comrade Tito?

BB
So, you did not perceive Tito as a dictator, on the whole, to this day, after he died, Yugoslavia collapsed, and so on?

ŽŽ

How I perceive him is what I tried to show in the film *Tito among the Serbs the Second Time*, in early 1994. People needed Tito's authority, as much as Tito needed undisputed power.

In the winter of 1993-94, you could walk the streets of Belgrade and feel the fear, confusion, dejection among the people passing by. The rate of inflation was gigantic, the shops were empty, and the military police were picking up conscripts and refugees and sending them straight to the front line. People in uniforms bearing the insignia of quisling troops from WWII were strutting up and down the street. They were armed. They had long beards and greasy hair and wore big fur hats. I stopped to hear what the conversations were about in front of the stands selling alcohol and new heraldry. Everyone was calling upon some divine power for salvation.

One kind was sure that Russians were coming to help us, others said that Americans were already on their way. Like a refrain, every three or four minutes, someone would conclude,

"If he were alive, we wouldn't need anyone."

And again:

"If he were alive, these crooks would be hiding under
a rock."

Then the contrarians,

"He cooked it all up before he died."

I was surprised that Tito, whom the media and the politicians had ignored and sorted with the forgotten past, came to people's minds all the time.

The next day, the cameraman Miša Milošević and I put the crew together and organized a happening, in which everything unfolded spontaneously, except for the introductory sequence which I wrote:

Tito on an airplane flying through dark clouds. He lands in Belgrade.

He approaches in his marshal's uniform. The driver opens the door of the Mercedes.

Driver:

"Where to, Comrade Tito?"

Tito:

"Let's hear a bit of what people are thinking. So, you tell me, comrade, what happened to our beautiful country in this short while, while I was away?"

"The country fell apart, everything went to the dogs. There's war and poverty."

"Can it really be that bad?"

"Everything is bad. Incredibly bad."

"Okay, so you tell me, am I to blame for some of it? There is some talk up there that maybe I am to blame for what happened down here after me."

"Some will spit on you, some will bash you, and others will praise you...And it's your fault because you left your bureaucracy behind."

"What a minute, while I was down here they were all my little pioneers, my youth brigades. They fostered brotherhood and unity, as I always told them to do. What happened to the pioneers?"

"First, they threw out brotherhood and unity and called for mutual killing and then war. And then they tore down everything else."

"I have to look into this. Drive!"

"First they took your five-pointed star off of all the signage and insignia."

"Dear mother of god, this Belgrade has built up nicely. It's a beautiful city. Okay, so what do our friends and allies say? What say the surrounding countries, our neighbors?"

"The only one that helps us is Greece and nobody else."

"What is going on with the cadres? I did leave some hard-working, good cadres."

"I'd say you made one big mistake."

"What?"

"Are you going back again? Take with you all the
ones you left down here."

"The entire people?"

"No, not the entire people. The ones you left in power,
your successors."

The response to the 45-minute documentary was extraordinary.
It was sought after in all parts of former Yugoslavia, although the
distribution went through illegal channels. Tito was still a taboo
subject, for those who were in power at the time. And nearly all of
them had been officials in Tito's regime or careerists who spent
most of their lives singing, "Comrade Tito, to you we swear, from
your path not to stray."

The film was copied on VHS tapes, because this was before the
DVD times. We had the original on Betacam. If you use that kind
of tape for copying for two months, it will fade and the sound was
barely audible. We had it serviced, to see what was going on. They
said, "You must have made more than 100,000 copies from this tape,
since its emulsion is completely shot." We had to re-do the editing.

JNA, Yugoslav People's Army

Tanja Petrović, *Utopia of the Uniform. Affective Afterlives of the Yugoslav People's Army*, 2024

The Yugoslav People's Army can be understood in retrospect as a historically unique form of collective life, a kind of military barracks equivalent of the factory collective in the age of industrial modern and popular sovereignty—the endemic rarity, now extinct, that endures only in the memories with a certain expiration date. In some fifty years, all who served in it will have died. Still, it is difficult even today to imagine that the future and present generations will truly believe these memories.

That it was possible, in such relatively small quarters, in intense near-bodily contact, to keep together such a bunch of cultural, linguistic, ethnic, national, religious, and political differences, and at the same time, for that life together to maintain some form of normalcy and self-evidence, of a routine, almost of naturalness, without any great dramatic tensions, this from today's perspective appears completely improbable. Even to those who have experienced it, it will appear from the perspective of today's reality that their own past had been but a dream. As if it couldn't possibly have been possible.

Certainly, what we perceive to be reality is already ideologically mediated. "The real, that is, the necessary," is the ideological short circuit which leaves the past completely obscured and eventually absorbs all of memory, no matter how authentic. The reality of ethnically cleansed spaces of former Yugoslavia, the reality of cultural and linguistic segregation, the reality of complete political separation, automatically implies not only that there can be no other way, but that no other way was possible. So, what makes the past seem unreal is precisely the impossibility of imagining the reality in which we live otherwise.

A reality without an alternative is a reality without the past, and remembering can help with that. If Bosnian, Croatian, and Serbian children cannot speak a shared language, go to the same school, learn a shared history, the same math, then how could have their fathers served in the same army and the same units, communicate in a shared language, wear the same uniforms, eat at the same mess halls, take the same oath, and sleep in the same dormitories, bunk next to bunk, marching in step, day after day, from the Vardar river in Macedonia to the Triglav mountain in Slovenia?

"

This coexistence in the past has no name today. An enlightened liberal intellectual versed in hegemonic discourse, if at all
benevolent, would call this a multicultural experience. In the
same breath they could point to the still-ubiquitous nationalism,
the outpourings of hatred for all sorts of minorities, from sexual
to ethnic, as well as to the reality of segregation mentioned
earlier, and claim that these are the consequences of a lack of
multicultural tolerance and that it will take time for the treatment of cultural difference in the regions of former Yugoslavia
to reach the levels in the developed democratic societies of the
West. What people here need is cultural competence, that is,
as the definition puts it, the ability to interact effectively with
people from different cultures. Only with patient educational
activity with the public and in civil society will the people
acquire that ability over time and make it reality in the practice
of coexistence in tolerance. When?

In the future, the near future, we hope.

And what about that coexistence in the past? Were all those
soldiers and officers of the YPA, all those children and their
teachers and their parents, for whom their coexistence among
the cultural differences was a barely noticeable element of the
trivial everyday, were they culturally incompetent, some sort
of amateurs of multicultural tolerance? And did it all end in catastrophe precisely because of their incompetence and amateurism, a kind of catastrophe that surely would not happen again,
ideology suggests, once the scene is populated by the real, properly educated professionals of tolerant coexistence? No, first one
has to "study, study more, and study again," liberals will quote
Lenin. For how long? We are not children after all. And we were
not. We just forgot about something.

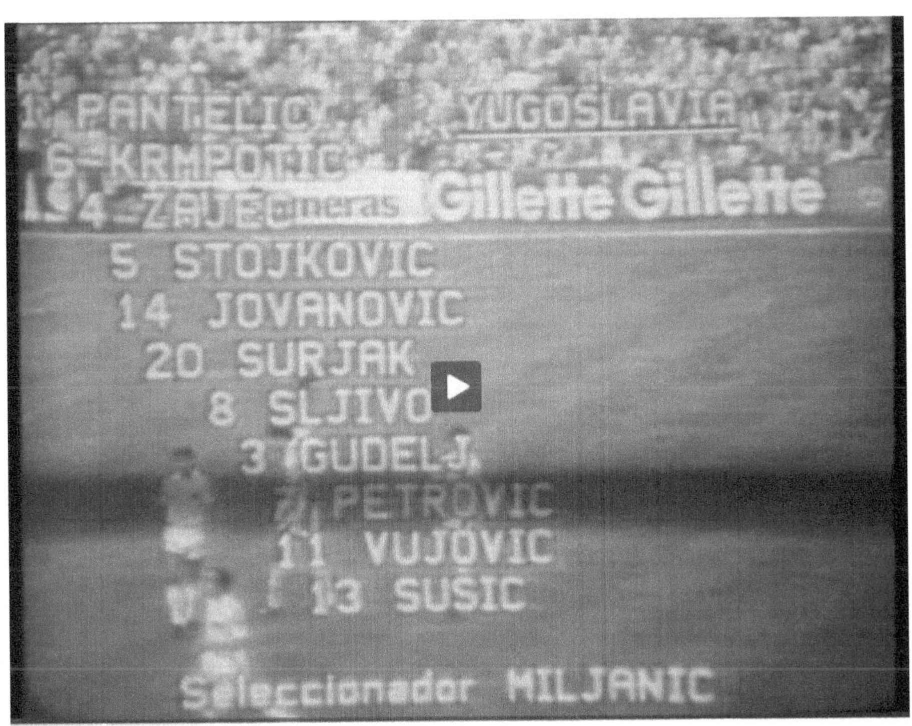

TV broadcast of a Yugoslav national team soccer match captured in
Pretty Women Walking through the City (1986)

And after that you joined the army, no?

Directly, five days after our films were shown in New York I was already enlisted in the armored brigade in Bjelovar. I had already turned twenty-seven, so when I joined the YPA I was one of the oldest soldiers. I immediately grew a mustache, and since most people around were kids between 18 and 20, I told them to call me "Old man."

This is how they addressed me for a couple of months until a question got asked at a staff meeting about "why the army washes in the snow." The winter was cold and there was a lot of snow. The pipes froze often. I would walk outside in the morning, and rub the snow all over, half naked. The officer asked why we were washing in the snow. He was probably worried we would get sick. A young soldier stood up and proudly said:

"The Old man leads by example. If he can stand the
snow at his old age, so can we."
The officer cut him off,

"You are not supposed to call anyone 'Old man.' He
is Private Žilnik and everyone must call him that."
I went to serve in the YPA wondering if I would receive any special treatment there, considering that the papers were still ringing with the "case of *Early Works*" in those months. But, as you described it, the barracks had a good statistical mix of population; a lot of young peasants we rarely saw in the cities, and laborers and artisans, while college students were a minority.

There was a large number of Albanians and Roma, because their birth rates were the highest. Most soldiers were satisfied with the technical standards and conditions of life. We had clean, practical, and warm uniforms. We had great shoes. We had comfortable bunks, and the toilet and bathrooms down the hall. Laundry was sent out for washing once a week. The meals were substantial and pretty tasty. You could eat as much bread as you wanted. You could even learn something in the morning classes.

In the afternoon, we had a few hours of free time. You could go to the library or join an activity group. In the evening we watched TV. On the weekends we had film screenings and shows. Half of them had it better there than at home. The soldiers who came from the cities were depressed at the beginning. But they also relaxed in the company of other soldiers, listening to various songs, stories, and dialects. If you could play an acoustic instrument—accordion, flute, or guitar—you could bring it with you. We always had small gatherings. Those of us who were older would bring cookies and juice from the commissary.

I have thought about how this culture of the recruit has persisted for thousands of years. From the ancient Greeks and Romans to today. I watched how quickly an esprit de corps developed, and it eliminated quarrels, fights, and divisions. I realized that the junior officers, who dealt with the practicalities and maintained a close daily contact with the soldiers, were outstanding psychologists.

In two minutes they could tell who was who. Who was lazy, hard-working, smart, dumb, crooked, honorable. And according to their assessments they would tactfully form groups, by dormitory rooms, by squads and platoons.

Second, I learned about the officer's stress: you hand arms to children and train them how to use them. You have to be careful they don't turn them around, first of all to aim them at you. There isn't much talking, but the possibility of getting killed oneself is factored in.

The unit in Bjelovar was a tank brigade, with Soviet tanks and related armored transporters. It was a lot of work to master the operation, and it required stamina, and good luck if you didn't want to get dented by the metal in these vehicles, especially when they were speeding over potholes and rocks.

We were driven in tanks along the bottom of the Drava river. The river runs above and the tank is like a submarine. It was a Soviet design, very modern at the time. The officers claimed that the Bjelovar brigade had enough "firepower" to defend the entire northern border of Yugoslavia. When we had to dig a trench for the tanks, such that "the enemy couldn't see it," we were sweaty and our hands were calloused. That was one ancient rule: keep the soldiers busy and tired. But, another rule was followed above all others: no spreading of ethnic hatred allowed, no insults, not even in jest. If there were any hints of anything of that sort, the initiator could be imprisoned and removed from the unit. But no one was prevented from declaring and identifying themselves any way they wanted or any way they felt.

I have heard the Albanians and others say: here I have more freedom to say who I am, what my father's name is, than anywhere else.

We also had a library, well supplied. Every day I read books for a couple of hours. Besides classic novels, by domestic and foreign authors, there were books published by Vojno delo (Military Works), the military publisher. I read all kinds of things, from Caesar to the memoirs by Guderian, Hitler's commander of the armored units.

It was the year 1970. The country entered a period of confusion, of contradictions: following student demonstrations in 1968 and the suppression of the Prague Spring by the Soviet intervention, our people took out of the freezer the "stronger role of the LCY on all fronts," "political compliance," and other such ideas used to encourage careerists and ignoramuses. Some student publications were banned. Activists from 1968 were expelled from the university. Vlada Mijanović, Pavluško Imširović and their friends were sentenced to prison terms.

From within the YPA, I don't remember that we could feel the "rumblings of civilian life." Newspapers, radio, and TV were all available, so we had the information.

After the military training was over, they took us to a karst desert, near Vojnić, where there were training grounds for armored vehicles. We stayed there for about three weeks for a shooting exercise, which was pretty risky, and the whole trip was an adventure because the terrain there was like in Afghanistan.

When they took us back to Bjelovar in August, they left us alone. I thought to myself: it all ended well. The YPA looked to me like it was the mainstay of that country, in which careerists and the petit bourgeois had begun to take the place of the working people. And the army showed very clearly who those "people" were and what they were like. I could see they were not so bad.

As I was strolling about and reading books at the library, an order came in.

> "Report to Colonel Vranić, in charge of the cultural
> work in our brigade."

I shaved, straightened up my uniform, and went to report. The Colonel blurted out,

> "You are that Žilnik, the filmmaker?"
> "That's me," I said.
> "You will shoot us a film about the history of the
> army in Bjelovar, because Bjelovar was founded as
> a military fortification."

I said:

"Okay. I need five soldiers, a camera, and rolls of film."

To which the officer said:

"So you can't do anything on your own! If I ask a cobbler to make the boots, we give him leather and soles and he does it by himself."

I answered:

"Filmmaking is a collective effort."

He dismissed me:

"I have to look into it. Come back tomorrow."

I came the next day and he said,

"You are right. You need six people. Make your selection according to appropriate ethnic and social categories: one Albanian, one Serb, one Slovenian, one Croat and so on."

"That's fine, but you would have to write the script."

"How come?" he asked. "I don't know how to write scripts!"

"Scripts are easy," I continued. "You just close your eyes and tell me what you would like to see in the film. I'll write it all down and at the end you'll sign off on it."

He closed his eyes and started to muse:

"Tank brigade charging." I was writing and asked how many tanks. He said, thirty-six. I asked: "What are you seeing next?"

"Tank brigade going through water."

"What kind of water?"

"Drava River."

"What is the third image?"

"Brigade headquarters."

"And fourth?"

"Commanding officer standing in the window giving a speech to soldiers in rows."

I wrote it all down and explained that we would also need a ladder, a microphone, and a tape recorder. He dictated to me about two hundred frames he saw. All of them were written down legibly. I gave it to him to sign. When he signed it, I said:

"Comrade Colonel, now we make our production plan."

He also signed off on the production schedule, which I laid out using his suggestions and added the necessary equipment for filming on 16mm. He gave me permission to go to Zagreb, to visit the camera operator Vladimir Petek who lent us a camera. I also had money for the negatives. For the next month, the six of us ran around Bjelovar shooting the film, sitting at bars, producing the colonel's script.

They gave me permission to go to Zagreb to do the editing, and we put together a 50-minute report, *Role of the Army in the History of Bjelovar*. We started from the Austrian fortress on the border, but most of the material was filmed using our unit and the young people who came to our events.

There was a big premiere. The credits said, "Screenplay by Lieutenant-Colonel Vranić," "Producer Colonel Zoraja" (he was the unit commander), "Logistics by Major Furčić," and so on. I mentioned all of us soldiers as "technical support."

After the screening, the audience in the hall was euphoric. And the officers were patting each other on the back. I was told to come to the commander's office first thing in the morning. It was the first time I spoke with the commander.

"Private Žilnik, civilians lie!"
What can I say, I wouldn't know. I responded:

"It does happen, some of them do like to lie."
Commander:

"They all lie, private Žilnik!"
I was uncomfortable, and wasn't sure what he was getting at. So I said,

"What do you mean?"
He took a thick folder out of the drawer and threw it on the desk.

"You see this? This is your file, which reached the army when you did. One hundred and fifty pages. They said you were dangerous, unreliable, that you work for the enemy. All lies! We checked you out. Give me your service booklet so I can write this all down."

I took out one of those green booklets. And he wrote "exemplary soldier" in it. He said:

"You deserve a reward. What do you suggest?"
And I said without hesitation,

"To let me go home."

He kept quiet and then asked someone how many days of service I had left. There were roughly five weeks until the end of my service term.

Colonel Zoraja shouted:

"At attention!"

I stood at attention. He said:

"I order you to return your gear and arms and to leave the barracks by tomorrow morning at 7am."

"Yes, Comrade Colonel!"

And so I left Bjelovar. Later I heard from several soldiers who served in Bjelovar in the 1970s that the film screened for the troops regularly and that the officers always bragged about it.

From what I'm telling you it's clear how surprised I was by the stupidity, the self-destructiveness, and the criminal projects undertaken by the YPA in the 1990s. None of the great devastation, deportations and imprisonments in the war zone could have happened without the YPA arms or its commanding officers.

This would be a subject for an entire book, but it isn't hard to draw parallels from history: only three years after the enlightened democratic promises of the Weimar Republic, with a social-democratic majority in the parliament, the brown shirts took over, and they didn't advertise Adolf the painter but created the atmosphere of retaliation and fear that led the majority to choose him in an election.

A Star is Born: a Brief Note on the Phenomenon of Cultural Initiation

Nothing reveals the true character of a culture as clearly as the way it prompts the drama of its own reproduction. The key element in this drama, the culmination of its plot and the symbolic summation of its meaning is the sight of cultural initiation, the moment in which the culture appropriates a creative individual as a creator of its own renewal. This scene is a genuine discursive test bed in which intersect a number of narratives great and small: the enigma of creation, eros and thanatos in their perpetual embrace, endlessly tested aesthetic judgment, autonomy of the cultural sphere or its economic-social causation, the political truth of culture, its universality or particularity, its decadence, its affirmative or critical character, culture as the battleground of emancipation, of utopia, of hegemony, of Hegelian struggle for recognition, culture as aura, as an industry, as entrainment, as idolatry...all that and more could be read into this relatively simple scene in which a human being, an individual, steps over the threshold beyond which the values they create acquire new, supra-individual, supra-temporal, sublime qualities to become the values of a culture which through them is constantly renewed. But who is the one to step over that threshold?

How is she chosen and why?

For starters, let us ask Hollywood. *A Star is Born*, George Cukor's 1954 musical, gives an instructive answer. The initiation happens in a rather dialectical contradiction between success and failure. The career of the elderly has-been famous actor Norman Maine, played by James Mason, is sadly on the wane. He comes to the studio drunk where they try to hide him from intrusive journalists and photographers. To no avail. Maine barges onto the stage where Judy Garland plays the young singer Esther Blodget. She immediately understands what's going on, takes him under her arm and includes him in the show so that it looks like his performance had always been part of the plan. At the end of it, Maine receives ecstatic applause from the audience. Grateful to her for saving him from humiliation, he gets to know her, falls in love, not just with her but also with her talent in which he sincerely believes.

By accident their paths diverge, and she again fades into anonymity, making ends meet by waiting tables and singing in television commercials. Also by chance, Maine discovers her again and persuades her to take a role in a movie, and uses his connections and influence to secure her a role in an important musical. Under a new name, Vicki Lester, given to her by the studio, she finally achieves enormous success. A star is born. But the story doesn't end there. While she climbs higher and higher up the ladder of recognition, fame, and fortune, Norman Maine, now already her husband, who so successfully engineered and executed the initiation of an anonymous, talented amateur as a cultural producer of the highest order, slowly loses the high and mighty status he once enjoyed in the film industry. In the downward spiral of failures punctuated by alcoholic outbursts, which are his attempt at suppressing the horrible truth of his cultural exhaustion, that is, his loss of any kind of use or market value, this former star sinks lower and lower until he is completely excluded from the process of cultural production and becomes a burden to his now famous and wealthy wife. Unable to withstand the humiliation, his own redundancy and rejection, he ends up committing suicide. The once-anonymous Esther Blodget, now star Vicki Lester, mourns him for a while and contemplates abandoning her career. In the end, she is talked into not wasting her talent which was discovered and mobilized precisely by her late husband. The show must go on and it does go on. Back on stage, now in a magnificent performance broadcast to the entire world, Vicki Lester is introduced as "Mrs. Norman Maine." Not only is the new star saved; the old one posthumously got to shine again.

So, all the stars are accounted for, and all the links in the canonical chain are connected by causal relationships. A previous, dead one, had initiated the next, still living, while the light of the one to come had already been sent out and it travels on to take up its designated place in the starry sky of (our) culture.

The cultural-pessimist critique of star worship is an old and well-established phenomenon. Early on, it was nothing more than a particular moment in the general critique of film as a decadent art. Walter Benjamin in his 1935 essay *The Work of Art in the Age of Mechanical Reproduction* (*Das Kunstwerk im Zeitalter seiner technischen Reproduzierbarkeit*) quotes French writer Georges Duhamel who "who detests film and knows nothing of its significance." Film for him is "a pastime for helots, a diversion (*Zerstreuung*, dissipation) for uneducated, wretched, worn-out creatures who are consumed by their worries…, a spectacle which requires no concentration and presupposes no intelligence…, which kindles no light in the heart and awakens no hope other than the ridiculous one of someday becoming a 'star' in Los Angeles."

For Benjamin, by contrast, the cult of the movie star has not only a rational explanation, but also a very specific function in the process of transformation of modern art. It is compensation for the loss of the aura, caused by the appearance of film, that is, by the mechanical reproducibility of the work made possible by the film technology. It is a symptom or the effect of a fundamentally progressive historical development. The cult of the movie star for Benjamin is "an artificial build-up of the 'personality' outside the studio. The cult of the movie star, fostered by the money of the film industry, preserves not the unique aura of the person but the 'spell of the personality,' the phony spell of a commodity."

To the degree that film capital directs film production, the only revolutionary contribution of film in the 1930s, as Benjamin claimed at the time, was its revolutionary critique of the traditional concept of art. The cult of the star, therefore, is itself an element of that critique.

But what is the meaning of this "outside the artist studio?" What does it mean that "personality"—Benjamin himself used the English word in his German text—is built up artificially outside the film artist's studio, that is, outside the narrowly defined framework of film production? Just that the authentic place of the personality cult or the cult of the movie star, the place where it achieves its strongest effect, is in the sphere of broader cultural reproduction. If the 1930s are the time when the cult of the star developed in the United States in the world of film, already in the 1950s it takes over the sphere of music production, growing with the accelerated development of the cultural and media infrastructure: radio and television, recording industry, concerts, illustrated magazines, and the mass proliferation of fan clubs.

In this context, Cukor's film—made, to reiterate, in the 1950s—was at conception already behind its time. It still makes its star from "within;" specifically, in this movie, and contrary to Benjamin's thesis, the star is born inside the movie studio. The work of initiating the new star, the task of selection and the responsibility for final decisions remain in the hands of the old, declining star. This is how the canon ensures its own continuity from itself, genealogically so to say, within the closed circuit of the star family within which the secret of the light passes from one generation to another.

Benjamin, on the contrary, would finish the last, fifteenth chapter of *The Work of Art* with the very significant sentence, "Das Publikum ist Examinator, doch ein zerstreuter." ("The public is an examiner, but an absent-minded one.") This goes first and foremost for film, which suppresses the value of the work of art by putting the audience in the position of an assessor, an arbiter, the position which at the movie theater does not imply any vigilance or alertness and concentration. For Benjamin, the final judgment about the value of the work of art in the age of its technical reproducibility is made by the dispersed, diffused, distracted masses (*zerstreute Masse*) having fun.

This certainly goes for the cult of the star. The task of selection is transferred onto the recipients, the audience. It is now the final examiner, the arbiter who decides who is going to be elevated among the stars and why. The modern cult of the movie star ultimately dethrones the once indisputable authority of aesthetic criticism, the devalued canonical standard of taste, the irretrievably compromised alleged competence of the bourgeois cultural elite, the insider knowledge of those "dedicated to the cause." Stardom is now decided by the laity, Benjamin's dispersed

masses who—while having fun—take on the leading role
in the drama of initiation.

This is at the same time about the qualitative transformation in the history of contemporary cultural canonization which was, in the progressive jargon of twentieth-
century modernism, identified with democratization:
opening of the canon to the masses, easing of access to its
creation, affirmation of the once despised popular culture,
a step towards later postmodern erasure of difference
between high and low culture. Canon, like its stars, in the
age of classical, that is, bourgeois culture, was constituted
from "within," not only, like in Cukor's movie, inside the
film studio, but "from within," in the sense of an autonomous art sphere or culture emancipated from the world
of economy, politics, and social life in general. Whether
it is about the art of some historically particular stylistic
formation, say the Renaissance or Baroque, or about the
supra-temporal, universalist concept of Goethe's world
literature, the canon was being experienced at the time
as the embodiment of transcendental aesthetic values
whose reproduction was made possible and guaranteed
by the massive infrastructure of cultural institutions of
the bourgeois period, from public education, academies,
museums and libraries, to theaters and opera houses,
concert halls, and so on. The ultimate responsibility for
the whole machinery of cultural production, and so for the
maintenance and reproduction of the ruling canons, fell
on the institution above all institutions, the nation state,
which legitimated itself by the canon of national history,
that is, of the national culture. Leaning on the untouch-
able authority of its canons, the cultural politics of a state
aimed for a historically specific telos—the cultivation of
its society-nation, its cultural refinement and education,
in short, for what the German Romantics called *Bildung*.
In cultivating the nation, canonization fulfilled its ultimate purpose.

Decay of the aura of the work of art that Benjamin
spoke about, the demise caused by mechanical development, that is by the newly mediated re-articulation of
art production, symbolizes the dissolution of the entire

autonomous sphere which sublimated bourgeois art and over which it could install like a royal canopy a starry sky full of its values and figures infinitely removed from the vulgarity of quotidian life, social labor, political struggle, and mass, popular, and trivial culture. The sublimity of its canons, which had served as the cause/effect for an endless perfecting of the masses under the command and control of the elites, now dispersed across a space that spilled not only over the boundaries of the autonomous cultural sphere and engulfed the entire society with its economy and politics, but also absorbed the undifferentiated space of economy, politics, and culture outside the framework of a particular nation, society, culture.

Canons are now out there...

The said processes of transformation could not be unequivocally set in a very particular epoch because they are present in their contradictions in multiple ones at the same time, regardless of how they get defined or located culturally, politically, or economically. Benjamin discovered them and conceptualized them in Europe of the 1930s, Hollywood could not reflect on them critically in the 1950s in the United States, and postmodernism, post-history and post-communism are still reckoning with their effects. It is no wonder that they were also present in the Yugoslav past. But in which one? Aiming to parse that past as epochs, although it clearly never was in any way, not politically or culturally or economically linear or totalizing in any sense, I introduced the vague notion a "mature Titoism," wanting to grasp the period of Yugoslav history from the late 1950s to the mid- 1970s. Unsure what exactly I meant by that notion, I asked Žilnik what "mature Titoism" meant for him. In his answer he never defined it politically or culturally or economically, but precisely in the sense of a specific form of cultural initiation, in the sense of his own becoming a producer of culture. This is his answer which, after all, brought on the topic addressed here.

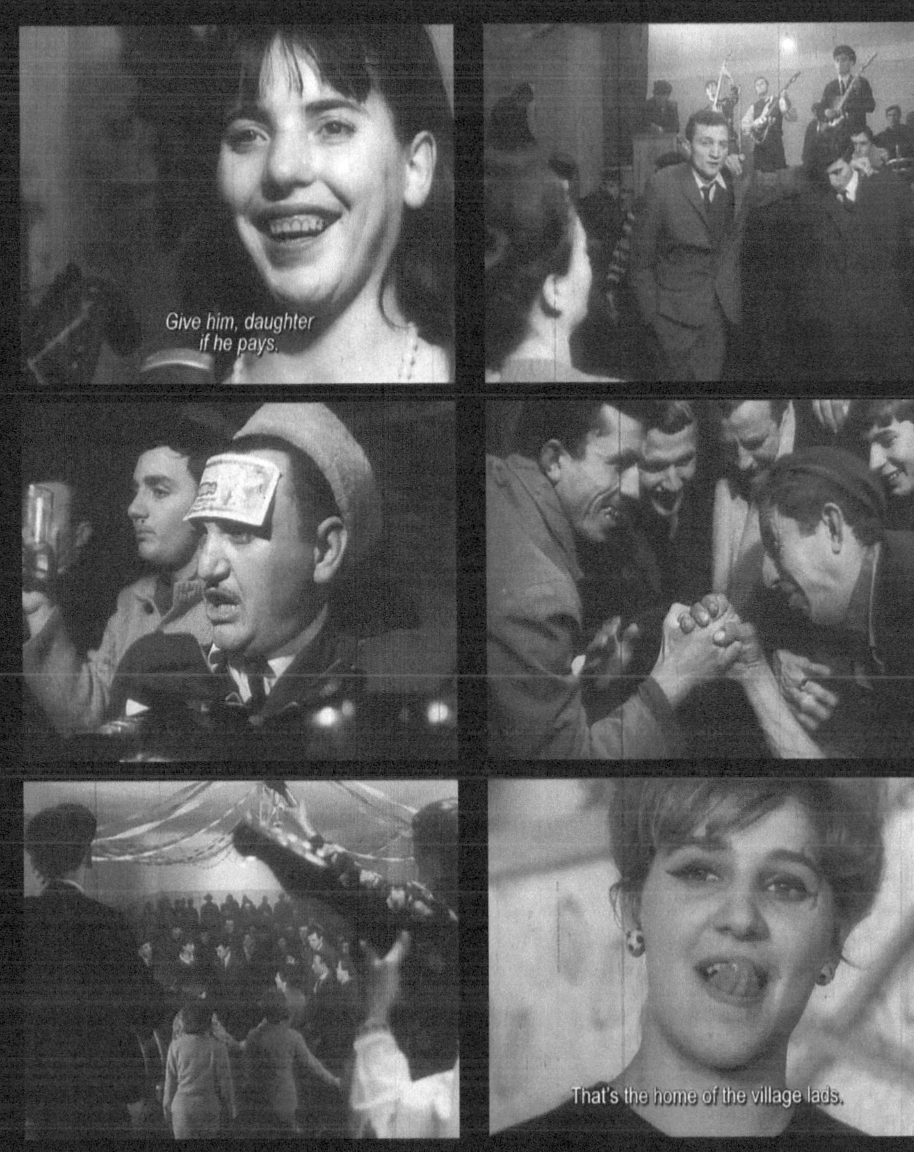

From *Newsreel on Village Youth, In Winter* (1967)

Entering the Sphere of Cultural Production in the Age of Mature Titoism

BB
What is a mature Titoism for you?

ŽŽ

We are in the year 1966. I wasn't yet 24. I already had some amateur filmmaking experience making narrow-gauge formats and listening in on the audience when they saw something you made on the screen. Also, reactions of festivals and juries, mostly to the great authors of the previous generation of alternative film authors: Hladnik, Makavejev, Pansini, Žika Pavlović. Knowing them helped me to get invited to Avala Film to sign my first "producer's" contract, as assistant director on the film *Love Affair, or the Case of the Missing Switchboard Operator.*

In previous years I had also had the experience of being the director of the Youth Forum (Tribina mladih), probably the most agile cultural center of early 1960s Yugoslavia. And I had just passed the final exams at the Law School in Novi Sad and was preparing for the first "real" job that would go on my employment record.

Avala Film was located in Košutnjak Park, on the outskirts of Belgrade. I have heard a story that after the war, one of the first tasks for the voluntary youth work groups was to clear that ground to make a film studio. The youth work brigades built those studios with bricks and mortar, as large as airplane hangars. This is where the film laboratory was located, the size of a large factory. Then the building with an audio recording studio which could fit a symphony orchestra and several choirs, the crucial link in the technological chain. Most films were shot "silently," and dialogue and other sounds were dubbed over later on. Music, composed especially for films, was played and recorded in the studio. There were large warehouses for floodlights, generators, costumes, props, armory, etc. There was a tailor shop and a wig shop; shops for production design and vehicle adaptation, from stage coaches to old automobiles and wartime gigs. Deep in the park, far from the passersby, was the pyrotechnics shop, for cannon blasts, fires, and explosive devices. In the middle of the huge yard, opposite the entrance, was the four-story management office building with

60 offices on each floor. Top managers were on the top floor, the bookkeepers below them, and the rest 100 or 150 rooms were for teams working on the different phases of filmmaking. Word on the street was that the place and the equipment were no different than in any other European studio. They had similar equipment and capabilities at Jadran Film in Zagreb, Viba Film in Ljubljana, and Bosna Film in Sarajevo.

The number of co-productions was greater in studios outside Belgrade, due to their fantastic locations, on the Adriatic Coast, on the islands, around the Plitvice lakes, in the wilderness of the mountains of Bosnia and Herzegovina. There was a bustle at Avala Film all day long. Editing, the lab, and sound studios worked through the night. Small crews at the time had thirty people of various professions, plus actors and extras. So a small crew would fill two buses when going to shoot on location. There were several hundred people in large crews. Trucks were used for transportation. For all of this to work, everyone had clearly defined tasks and their own field of operation.

The head of this "film factory" was Ratko Dražević, who looked like Humphrey Bogart and behaved like him also. Never to be seen without a cigarette and a glass of whiskey. They say he was a gambler in his free time. He made it to the end of the war a colonel of the State Security Administration. He was surrounded by art directors and screenwriters: Borislav Mihajlović Mihiz, Boba Selenić, and film director Aleksandar Petrović. All three of them were educated, talented, and highly esteemed artists. And they played cards. None of them had a "party reputation," I don't even think they were "organized."

In those years I was Makavejev's assistant. Our crew was small, around thirty craftsmen, professionals. Phenomenal actors: Eva Ras, Slobodan Aligrudić, Ružica Sokić, Miodrag Andrić a.k.a. Ljuba Moljac. We were filming in Belgrade. Chief of production, a position called "film manager," was a very experienced and serious, allegedly retired army major. As soon as we gathered, he gave us a suggestion-order,

> "So that we're not in the way of larger and more demanding projects, we should move to the basement.
> We can make do with three or four offices."

I was tracking down minor characters and extras and took them to the assistant director Branko Vučičević, who decided who would go in front of the director and the cameraman. Then I was gathering props with the prop master for a scene recorded in the storyboard, in the so-called development, where it clearly said:

> "Eva Ras is making cherry pie; one kilo of flour, yeast, half a kilo of cherries, two eggs. Bring three times the quantity for multiple takes. Two tablecloths, same color, rolling pin one. Stove one, wood-burning. Two cases of firewood and ignition paper. Box of matches, etc."

The work of the crew, the technical phases of production all ran like clockwork, because everyone was an expert in their field. The cameraman and his three assistants served the camera: they placed and changed lenses, one of them threading in a new reel and taking out the one that had been shot. The other one measured with the measuring tape the distance between actors and objects in the frame, wrote it down or remembered it, because he had to adjust the focus while the camera was moving and filming or an actor was moving. The third placed the tripod on the tracks, or the complicated carts, which then needed to be pushed along a predetermined path. The crew gathered early in the morning, especially if they were working in the field, because you couldn't work when the sun was at its peak. So, a workday lasted from 5 A.M. till 10:30 A.M., and from 3:30 P.M. until sunset. And in the studio, under floodlights, we usually worked until 10 P.M.

That year, in 1966, Avala Film made 11 movies on 35mm. One film would use about twenty kilometers of negatives and the same amount of transparencies, which means that the lab developed, just to meet the needs of Avala, around 200 kilometers of negatives and the same amount of transparencies for the working copies. When they made about ten copies of every movie for the theatrical release, the lab had to process 1000 kilometers of material on 35mm film, just for the Avala movies. They generally used Kodacolor film. So, just the blank film and the lab would cost five million dollars, which is nowadays the total amount with which the Serbian Ministry of Culture supports the production of all films in a year. In 1966 they figured the film stock and the lab made up about 10% of the amount invested in a film.

Domestic production filled movie theaters, so at least half of the films made recovered their investments. Avala Film made 11 feature films that year. What can this list tell us?

You could hardly call the programming or the human resource politics at Avala Film sectarian. Crews were made up of actors and collaborators from all constitutive socialist republics. Nearly all the authors who had declared themselves dissidents in the past two decades of post-communism had worked under the command of Colonel Ratko Dražević.

Most importantly, in the three years I'm talking about, more groundbreaking films were made than in the twenty years of "democracy:" *Dream* (*San*), *Warm Years* (*Tople godine*), *Return* (*Povratak*), *Man is no bird* (*Čovek nije 'tica*), *Girl* (*Devojka*), *I even met happy gypsies* (*Skupljači perja*), *Love Affair* (*Ljubavni slučaj*); and at Jadran Film, *Breza* (*Birch Tree*), directed by Babaja, and *Rondo* directed by Berković were also made. Of course, this was only one "face of Titoism." In 1947, when Avala Film was being established, times were very different, and also in 1974, at the peak of the campaign against "Black Cinema."

And Tito was alive this whole time and I believe that in someone's memory these other climates also resonate as a "mature Titoism." Not to mention the "historical progress" which only thirty years later, in the mid-1990s, transformed the grounds of Avala Film, its studio and its equipment, into a machine for nationalist propaganda and war propaganda, plus for turbofolk. Nearly everything

Films produced at Avala Film in 1966

1. *Bittere Kräuter* (*Gorke Trave; Bitter Herbs*), co-produced with Germany, directed by Žika Mitrović, known as "our John Ford," a fan of cowboy movies and publisher of comics since before the war. The movie plot: woman, former concentration camp inmate, refuses to testify against her torturer from the camp. Mostly foreign actors: Irene Papas, Daniel Gélin, Alice Treff. From today's ideological perspective the film could be accused of historical revisionism.

2. *Eagles Fly Early* (*Orlovi rano lete*), a children's spectacle, based on the novel by Branko Ćopić, about children who became outlaws to help the partisans. Directed by Soja Jovanović, activist in the women's movement. Actors are Ljubiša Samardžić, Miodrag Petrović Čkalja, Dragutin Dobričanin. Film contributes to the construction of new mythologies. A huge success in theatrical release.

3. *Swarm* (*Roj*), directed by Mića Popović, provocative visual artist, modernist and experimenter. The movie plot is set in 1804 during the First Serbian Uprising. The insurgents have put on trial the Serbian woman for turning her husband, a hero, over to the Turks. The real motives of this betrayal are revealed by the wise Turk, the beekeeper. Actors in it are Mira Stupica, Olivera Vučo-Katarina, Bekim Fehmiu, Rade Marković. The film is perceived as a shocking contribution to the deconstruction of a myth.

4. *The Protégé* (*Štićenik*), directed by Vladan Slijepčević, screenplay by Jovan Ćirilov. It's a story about a young careerist who will use any means to get what he wants. Cast: Špela Rozin,

Stanislava Pešić, Duša Počkaj, Ljubinka Bobić, Rade Marković, Ljubiša Samardžić. It's a film critical of social anomalies.

5. A *Time of Love* (*Vreme ljubavi*) omnibus, directed by Nikola Rajić and Vlada Petrić. Petrić later made a respectable career as a professor and film researcher in the US. He not only taught at Harvard but also started the Harvard Film Archive, the best in the US. One thing he said that wasn't true was that he had been persecuted as director in Tito's Yugoslavia. The cast was top tier: Neda Spasojević, Ružica Sokić, Pavle Vujisić, Danilo Bata Stojković, Bekim Fehmiu, Kole Angelovski.

6. *Return* (*Povratak*), directed by Živojin Pavlović. The film is about a criminal who leaves prison and tries to adapt to life in the city and ends tragically. Among the cast are Bata Živojinović, Snežana Lukić, Predrag Milinković. Pavlović made this film two years after his film *Grad* was banned in court in Sarajevo and burned.

7. *Dream* (*San*), directed by Puriša Đorđević. It's a film about two young people in love in the summer of 1941, in the liberated towns of Čačak and Užice, who dream about communism. Cast is Olivera Vučo-Katarina, Ljuba Tadić, Bata Živojinović, Ljubiša Samardžić, Mija Aleksić, Stojan Aranđelović.

8. *Before the War* (*Pre rata*), directed by Vuk Babić, a screen adaptation of two plays by Branislav Nušić, *The Dead Man* (*Pokojnik*) and *Bereaved Family* (*Ožalošćena porodica*). Cast is Mira Stupica, Sonja Hlebs, Snežana Nikšić, Branka Veselinović, Milan Ajvaz, Mija Aleksić, Slobodan Cica Perović, Milivoje Živanović, Nikola Simić.

was rented out or "colonized" by Pink TV and Komuna TV stations, and they have made and broadcast their programming from Košutnjak...

In the 1960s, however, there was another important segment of the "politics of the moving image" at work, although rarely mentioned now, which was the state-issued information journal newsreel, Filmske novosti, also a large company, located closer to the center of Belgrade, across the road from the Belgrade Fairgrounds.

Filmske novosti, in contrast to art film made by freelance authors and their collaborators who were contract workers, had several hundred employees: their film directors, camera operators, editors, and sound studios were fully prepared to send a ten-minute newsreel to theaters every Sunday, with a mandatory intro about Tito's activities. They were also brilliant professionals, and I reached out to them already in late 1966, when I was working on my first full-length documentary, *Newsreel on Village Youth, in Wintertime*.

I asked the producer to make my documentary "synchronous," in the field, and in those times that was like asking to use RMS Queen Mary. Why? Because there were only two huge movie cameras with the audio built in, each weighing a few hundred kilos: one was used by Filmske novosti to shoot sessions of Parliament, Party congresses, and

Comrade Tito, and the other one at Avala Film for co-productions.

My producer, the director of Neoplanta Film Udovički, happened to be the best man at the wedding of Vaso Tobdžić, the technical director of Filmske novosti, so a truck full of equipment and a crew from Filmske novosti showed up on the set for me. From them I heard that half of their colleagues were constantly filming in the newly liberated countries: Algeria, Tanzania, Mali, Congo, and Mozambique.

In some they were following the activities of their liberation fronts and giving filmmaking seminars at the same time. They knew the Algerian leaders—Ahmed Ben Bella, Abdelaziz Bouteflika, Houario Boumédienne—better than the local "comrades." They talked about the delicacies at the court of Emperor Haile Selassie. Their adventures in the jungles of Mozambique with the Frelimo movement. That was another face of "mature Titoism."

9. *The Warm Years* (*Tople godine*), directed by Dragoslav Lazić, a film about two young people who come to Belgrade to begin their new life there. The young man works at a steel mill, the young woman works at the workers' canteen. It's a film about young people and everyday life in socialism. The cast is Dušica Žegarac, Bekim Fehmiu, Stevo Žigon. The script was written by Ljubiša Kozomara i Gordan Mihić, who wrote the scripts of many films that were challenged in the later years.

10. *Soldier* (*Vojnik*), directed by George Breakstone, co-produced with the US. The film memorializes the boy fighters in the People's Liberation Struggle. The cast are domestic and foreign actors.

11. *How Romeo and Juliet loved each other* (*Kako su se voleli Romeo i Julia*), directed by Jovan Živanović. It's a love story about characters from two social classes which ends tragically. Cast is Lidija Pilipenko, Rade Marković, Sjeverin Bijelić. At Avala film that year they were preparing for *I Even Met Happy Gypsies* (*Skupljači perja*), directed by Aleksandar Petrović; and *Soledad*, directed by Jacqueline Audry, co-produced with France. In that one are Emmanuella Riva, Laurent Terzieff, Rick Battaglia... And only a year earlier, Avala film produced *Three* (*Tri*) by Saša Petrović, *Man is no Bird* (*Čovek nije 'tica*) by Dušan Makavejev, and *To come and to stay* (*Doći i ostati*) by Branko Bauer.

BB
You said that before "joining the film industry"
you were in charge of the Youth Forum. How
did one get to that position?

ŽŽ
I graduated from the Moša Pijade High School in 1961, and we were
supposed to write a capstone essay. My topic was, "The concept
of alienation in the early works of Karl Marx." A collection of the
early works of KM was published already in the 1950s, clearly on
the heels of the dramatic debate with the Soviets, following the
Resolution of the Cominform in 1948. It was pushed aside when
Milovan Đilas mentioned in a series of articles the option that the
Communist Party may "self-dissolve" because class consciousness
can accomplish its historical mission also without the help from
the professional apparatus.

So, the first corollary of this thesis was tested by Milovan Đilas
himself, because he was expelled from the apparatus and ended
up convicted and in prison. This polemic was renewed in 1958, in
the context of the new program of the LCY which adopted some of
the romantic proclamations and promises—about freedom, about
"perpetually going beyond what had been achieved," about "humanism without borders." This also brushed up against the philosophy classes in schools and our free time activities: we organized a
big "show" at the end of the school year, full of quotations from
modern art—poetry, drama, visual arts, but also original satirical
sketches. City youth officials came to this show, and they called
in my school mate László Végel and me for a meeting, where we
were offered to direct the Youth Forum. The Forum's leadership
would be "rejuvenated" every four years...

So I was promoted to executive director of the Forum, and
Végel was editor-in-chief for the Hungarian language editorial board. Both of us can remember that we worked harder there than
ever before in our entire lives. We learned a lot in the process, and
daily programming created a lot of pressure: exhibitions, guest
performances, literary evenings, sociological debates, and guest
screenings. For the first time we saw domestic, amateur, and alternative films when we invited Vladimir Petek and Mihovil Pansini
from the Zagreb Cinema Club, and Marko Babac and Aleksandar
Petković from the Belgrade Cinema Club. They brought us moving

pictures that were unlike anything that was showing in regular theaters. And in Yugoslavia, the theater repertory was among the richest and freshest in the world, because films were imported freely from the East and the West, and our market even served as a kind of "testing ground" for large global distributors.

It helped that the Youth Forum was already held in high regard and had an established group of collaborators. In Novi Sad, we received brilliant advice and assistance from the editorial board of the art magazine *Polja* (Fields), mostly from Dejan and Bogdanka Poznanović, and from Ervin Šinko, literary writer and professor at the Faculty of Philosophy. We invited guests from all over Yugoslavia, especially those whose work was innovative and polemical. For example, before the philosophy journal *Praxis* was being published, we had a series of debates held by the future editors of *Praxis* that entire spring. We also invited the editor of the future journal *Perspektive* from Ljubljana, who was being watched by the domestic "ideological movers and shakers." Then a brilliant younger group of essayists and polemicists from the biweekly culture magazine *Danas* (Today).

BB
These people were invited, they gave lectures?

ŽŽ
Yes, people came to the Forum like they were going on a pilgrimage. I remember Ljerka Krelius, the Belgrade correspondent for the Zagreb daily *Vjesnik*, who came to Novi Sad and took notes in shorthand, when the "objectionable" thinkers came from Zagreb to speak, and then she published her commentary.

We noticed and used the fact that cultural politics were different in different regions. Vojvodina was a very open region until the very late 1960s.

There were cultural initiatives of national significance happening there: Sterijino Pozorje, the most important theater festival; meetings of young intellectuals at Stražilovo, on the Fruška Gora mountain; the codification of Serbo-Croatian grammar in the collaboration of Serbian and Croat cultural institutions, Matica srpska and Matica hrvatska.

Today some read this as just a part of Tito's "divide and rule" politics. Others say this was designed to "weaken Serbia." The

OTVORENA PITANJA NAŠE SAVREMENOSTI

**DISKUSIJE SE ODRŽAVAJU
OD 26. FEBRUARA DO 13. MAJA 1964. GODINE
SVAKE SREDE U 18 ČASOVA
U AMFITEATRU POLJOPRIVREDNOG FAKULTETA**

RAZLOZI I CILJ DISKUSIJA

Revolucionarno izmenjena društvena sredina i situacija u kojoj se vaspitava i idejno formira današnja generacija mladih i dalje postavlja pitanje društvene angažovanosti, konformizma i niz drugih pitanja. Ako se naglasi činjenica da su najprogresivnije, i ujedno dominantne, snage našeg društva za svoj moralno-politički kredo izabrale kritičko i samokritičko, antimitsko nezadovoljstvo ostvarenim, a u ime onoga što je još naprednije, još humanije — onda se čini opravdanim potreba da prema savremenosti, prema stvarnosti u kojoj egzistiramo uspostavimo kritički, nikako apologetski ili pak negatorski odnos.

Međutim, svojom praksom manifestujemo i posve drugačiji odnos: umesto otvorenog suočavanja sa postojećom realnošću, umesto angažovanja akcijom, mišlju i maštom, u cilju prevazilaženja dostignutog i sputavajućeg, mi često otkrivamo svoju neodlučnost, svoje prizemne ambicije i svoje kratkovide programe, pravdajući sebe uzdahom da su bitke za realizaciju snova dobijene i da je socijalizam postao školski predmet. Revoluciju često shvatamo kao dnevno-političku taktiku, kao zbir kompromisa u ime takozvanih viših ciljeva koje ti kompromisi očigledno samo udaljuju.

Ovakav odnos u suštini onemogućuje svaku argumentovanu kritiku, i ne govori ni o čemu drugom do o nesposobnosti da se vidi dalje od ostvarenog stupnja materijalno-duhovnog progresa. Ovakav odnos je takođe izraz prikrivanja sopstvenih mrakova, zabluda, nezadovoljstva i neostvarenosti. On jeste strah od obračuna sa pojavama savremenih-nesavremenih mistifikacija, podčinjenosti i malograđanskog samozadovoljstva, klišetiranih odgovora na sva pitanja, strah od obračunavanja sa pojavama hijerarhijske kritike, karijerističko-birokratskog angažovanja, zakulisne tehnike upravljanja, strah od obračuna sa antisamoupravnim i antidemokratskim branjenjem fetiša i takozvanih opštih interesa.

U težnji da doprinesu dubljem i potpunijem kritičkom osvetljavanju savremenosti, traženju i nalaženju odgovora na otvorena pitanja razvitka, redakcije Tribine mladih i „Symposiona" organizuju ovaj ciklus OTVORENIH DISKUSIJA o pitanjima naše savremenosti.

The Open Questions of Our Time, Youth Forum program notes (1964)

PROGRAM
DISKUSIJA

26. II   **SLOBODA, INDIVIDUA, ZAJEDNICA**
Uvodno izlaganje: DR RUDI SUPEK

4. III   **MARKSISTIČKA MISAO DANAS**
Uvodno izlaganje: DR PREDRAG VRANICKI

11. III   **PROBLEMI RASPODELE U NAŠEM PRIVREDNOM SISTEMU**
Uvodno izlaganje: DR MILOŠ SAMARDŽIJA

18. III   **SOCIJALIZAM I KULTURA**
Uvodno izlaganje: ERVIN ŠINKO

25. III   **DIJALEKTIKA USMERAVANJA DRUŠTVA**
Uvodno izlaganje: DR MIHAILO MARKOVIĆ

1. IV   **TEŠKOĆE I IZGLEDI SOCIJALIZACIJE POLITIKE I KULTURE**
Uvodno izlaganje: VELJKO RUS i PRIMOŽ KOZAK

8. IV   **RAZLOZI I SMISAO DANAŠNJEG ANGAŽOVANJA**
Uvodno izlaganje: DOBRICA ĆOSIĆ

PERSPEKTIVE NAŠEG PRIVREDNOG RAZVOJA
Uvodno izlaganje: DR KOSTA MIHAILOVIĆ

22. IV   **SOCIJALISTIČKA DEMOKRATIJA DANAS I SUTRA**
Uvodno izlaganje: DR SVETOZAR STOJANOVIĆ

12. V   **SOCIJALIZAM I POLITIKA**
Uvodno izlaganje: DR LJUBOMIR TADIĆ

6. V   **MOĆ I NEMOĆ NAŠE UMETNIČKE KRITIKE**
Uvodno izlaganje: SVETA LUKIĆ I SVETOZAR PETROVIĆ

13. V   **ZAVRŠNI RAZGOVOR**

The Open Questions of Our Time, Youth Forum program notes (1964)

response to which I am more sympathetic would be the one that says that the Yugoslav model had become respected and productive. It was not only supported by the West because it "broke through the Iron Curtain," but we were also perceived in the East as a country of greater freedoms and higher living standards. The multiethnicity of Vojvodina was the reason to start strong publishing houses in Hungarian, Romanian, Rusyn, and Slovak languages. There was also the powerful Radio Novi Sad, part of the national public network, whose programming in the languages of the minorities could be heard outside our borders. There was theater and other artistic practices by all ethnic minorities living in Vojvodina. You could meet intellectuals from Budapest, Bucharest, Prague, and other cities on the streets of Novi Sad.

We at the Youth Forum were under the impression that the only boundary of intellectual freedom was determined by creativity and talent. And that the socialist system would be able to "humanize itself further." Just look for example at the program for "The open questions of our time."

BB
This means you had the freedom and the funding to invite whomever you wanted?

ŽŽ
We made all decisions independently, me and my editors. On the Hungarian editorial board, they had a dozen talented and courageous poets, painters, and musicians.

Besides Végel, there were Ottó Tolnai, István Brasnyó and István Bosnyák, painters and graphic artists László Kapitány, Ferenc Maurits, and our first performance artist, Katalin Ladik; a brilliant team. They launched, with great effort and many polemics, the journal *Új Symposion*, the most important culture journal in the Hungarian language anywhere. It was read abroad more than inside the country.

What were the political reactions to our work? There was support, and there were repudiations, especially in the press. The strongest resistance came from the Novi Sad daily *Dnevnik*, whose culture pages were edited by conservatives. One "blast" we got from a politician that I can remember was this: Joca Lukić, the curator of an art salon, told me that an art group had appeared in

Belgrade, and they were not interested in abstract or *informelle* painting, the mainstream in those days. Let's go meet them. We went to meet them in the old pavilions of the Fairgrounds on the Sava riverbanks in New Belgrade, which had been turned into a prison and a camp during the war. In those wrecked spaces, with window frames that had no window panes in them, we found Dado Đurić, Uroš Tošković, Ljuba Popović, Peđa Ristić nicknamed Jesus, Kosta Bradić, Siniša Vuković, and the young, lanky Olja Ivanjicki. They were sitting there immersed in their canvases and painting "Leonardo"-style.

We were fascinated by them, like they had appeared from another world. We asked them if they were interested in having a show. What do you mean a show? They were puzzled because their colleague, Leonid Šejka, had been taken to prison a few days earlier.

We went to see poet Maria Čudina, Leonid's wife, who was sitting in their apartment with some Russian guy, drinking vodka. The Russian said:

> "No big worry. He is in prison, he is safe. Prison is
> for humans."

Maria sent us to Miro Glavurtić, a brilliant draftsman, who was working at the Yugoslav Institute of Cartography. Miro was the leader of Mediala, which is what the art group was called, now that Leonid was locked up. Glavurtić, who was looking like a mad preacher from a drawing by Albrecht Dürer, got in our faces:

> "We want to unite the world. East and West! We
> agree to a show, but only if it's going to be opened
> by the Roman Pope and the Ecumenical Patriarch
> of Constantinople together!"

Joca Lukić and I were dumbstruck, and laughed our heads off when we got out on the street. Finally we met the artists, the lunatics! This is it! We started preparations for the exhibition and printed the invitations Glavurtić designed. The invitations had already been sent out when the phone rang, someone calling from the County Committee of the LCY. It was Comrade Duško Draginić, chairman of the committee for the questions of ideology. We should come in for a meeting immediately. When we came to his office, he asked,

> "Did you inform the Cabinet of the President of the
> Republic that you have invited the Pope?"

We said we didn't. He started shouting,

"You are a bunch of amateurs! The Pope is also a
head of state. If that guy from Jerusalem comes,
that's on you, you find him accommodation. But
the Pope, that's a state-level visit, and Tito has to
agree to receive him before he can open your show!"
We were petrified, because none of this had ever crossed our minds.
We said we had never really sent an invitation to the Vatican. Comrade Duško threatened us:
"If the Pope arrives, you're both out of the Party!"
The show was held, a spectacle, a wonder. Today Mediala is seen
as a body of ethnocentric, nationalist mythomaniac work. But then
again who has not fallen into that hole...

BB
Listen, let's go back to film again. I'm interested in something specific: How did you become a film director and how did that entire generation of film directors come to be?

ŽŽ

We came up like the previous generation, through the cinema club scene. Among jury members in the early 1960s we had people better than those on the jury of the Pula Film Festival. Because "new film" had just begun its conquest of the big studios. Our role models were Pavlović, Makavejev, cameraman Petković, Marko Babac, Rakonjac, Pansini, the most significant film theorist Dušan Stojanović, all recently emerged from the amateur filmmaking culture.

We became confident when the amateurs of my generation—Zafranović, Karpo Godina, Rakidžić, Srđan Karanović, Radoslav Vladić—started getting awards for their work on 8mm from those very "studios." Cinema clubs were formed within the framework of the organization called People's Technology (Narodna tehnika).[01] They had all kinds of equipment, one had photography, one had audio and radio equipment, another one had filmmaking.

The clubs drew crafts professionals and hobbyists, the enthusiasts who shared with young people their knowledge about how to use the tools. People's Technology was not part of the dominant culture and ideology, so the question of subject matter was not a priority so much as it was important to figure out how to complete the technical tasks: shooting, camera movements, lighting, photochemistry for film processing, film editing, etc. This created space for the subject matter to be completely personal

---

01 People's Technology of Yugoslavia (Narodna Tehnika) was a network of state-funded organizations established in 1948 to improve public access to technology. Under the motto "Technology to the People," the network offered free programs that cultivated "technological literacy" throughout Yugoslavia, encompassing school clubs of young (children) technologists and independent youth Photo and Cinema Clubs. It published the magazine *Technology to the People.*

and an alternative to the "official cinematography." And film festivals were basically a competition in visual experimentation and provocations.

We learned very early on that the technical part was relatively easy to learn, but the question of style and creativity was individual and could not be shared. There were clubs in all parts of the country, as well as film festivals, and all those colleagues and I remain friends to this day.

"We can't promise to do more than experiment!"*
On Yugoslav experimental film
and cine clubs in the sixties and seventies

What **Jan-Christopher Horak** wrote about the US tradition—that 'in the earliest phases the American avant-garde movement cannot be separated from the history of amateur film (Harak J-C (ed.): "Lovers of Cinema: The First American Film Avant-Garde, 1919- 1945", Madison University of Wisconsin Press, 1995, p.18." quoted in Stevan Vuković, "Notes on Paradigms in Experimental Film in Socialist Yugoslavia" in the catalogue *This is All Movie: Experimental Film in Yugoslavia 1951-1991*, exhibition curated by Bojana Piškur, Ana Janevski, Jurij Meden and Stevan Vuković, Museum of Modern Art Ljubljana, 2010.) —holds true also for the Yugoslavian experimental tradition. Namely, in the former Yugoslavia experimental film almost consistently derived from the tradition of so-called amateur film, whose base consisted in the numerous cinema clubs (*kinoklub*) that developed in all major cities of the former federation, especially in the sixties and seventies.

According to the official system—socialist self-management of the time—self-organization was also present in the field of culture. Even more so, cinema clubs were part of the socialist project to bring technical culture and achievements closer to all citizens, and not only professionals; thus, the formation of amateur societies (amateur film, amateur photography, visual amateur groups and 'colonies', etc.) was systematically encouraged. In 1946, a special institution was established: Narodna Tehnika (Popular Engineering Society) with the aim of organizing, sponsoring and promoting different amateur activities. Even though they were under the 'political' control of the centre and were hierarchically organized, they were mostly left to their own devices as peripheral

* Reply of the KÔD Group, a group of visual artists from Novi Sad, Serbia, to Dušan Makavejev when he invited them, as selector of the special program at the newly established Belgrade Film Festival in 1971, to present a performative piece.

BB
And you started going to these clubs in high school or…?

ŽŽ

No, a little later. I learned about the initial programs and authors at the Youth Forum in 1962 and 1963. In high school, I was interested in the practice of visual arts. Following Gauguin, for example. In 1959 I won an award at the exhibition of the young painters of Vojvodina. They declared that I was working in the style of fauvism. This I understood to be an indirect claim about my lack of talent for precise drawing, so I resorted to broad strokes and thick paint to cover up badly done figures and portraits.

BB
So, as a kid, a teenager really, you were already a fauvist?

ŽŽ

That's what I was told. But soon, as I said, I dove into the work of cultural managerialism at the Youth Forum. That's where I met a few film directors in person: Puriša Đorđević, Živojin Pavlović, Dušan Makavejev.

BB
They also came to Novi Sad and that's how you met them?

ŽŽ

I went to Belgrade to meet them. By the early 1960s they were just beginning to make their first professional short films, on 35mm.

BB
Makavejev is a little older than you?

ŽŽ

Ten years older. Makavejev made the film *Smile 61 (Osmeh 61)* as part of a youth voluntary work drive of 1961. That summer, I volunteered for the construction drive to build the highway named *Brotherhood and Unity (Bratstvo-jedinstvo)* in the Grdelica Gorge. I was working on the concrete mixer. The hair and heads of my group were completely cemented from sweat, we were white from the dust, like ghosts. Makavejev came over with his cameraman and said,

> "You look silly with those helmets on your heads. Why don't you strike each other with hammers, smash the concrete, it's going to look great in the film."

That's how my group got into the film *Smile 61*. We are on that tape to this day. When I looked for him that fall in Belgrade, he was in a circus wagon.

BB
Who was?

žž
Makavejev.

BB
In a circus wagon?

žž
He was living in it, in a ditch where the Mostar highway loop now is as you enter Belgrade. And Žika Pavlović lived in the workers' temporary housing barracks, in the neighborhood of Zvezdara. When I first went looking for Žika Pavlović, he was outside washing his face out of a washbowl. And it was freezing outside.

BB
Just like the beginning of the film *When I Am Dead and Gone* (*Kad budem mrtav i beo*), when Slobodan Aligrudić washes his face in front of a shack...

žž
Yes.

BB
Living in what sense?

žž
They didn't have apartments. They were just starting to build

apartments for workers and artists. Žika Pavlović came from the village of Vratarnica near Zaječar, and Makavejev is from Sremska Mitrovica and Novi Sad. I came in contact with the practice of filmmaking through the Youth Forum.

BB
And you knew immediately that you wanted to make films?

ŽŽ

I joined the cinema club because I was also a passionate filmgoer. I regularly followed the new directions in movies at the time. You could see Chabrol, Godard, Buñuel and Bergman on the regular program, and all of Italian neorealism.

I remember that in 1959 (I was still in high school) I heard of the Cannes Film Festival for the first time, because they were showing at Cinema Jadran a whole series of films from the festival: *Black Orpheus* by Marcel Camus, *400 Blows* by Truffaut, *Hiroshima, Mon Amour* by Resnais. I was watching all that and thinking, film is the most powerful medium which reflects life with more complexity than any other.

BB
So, this was their regular programming?

ŽŽ

Yes, at the theaters, the regular programming all over the country.

> The participants at film evenings in cinema clubs in the former Socialist Yugoslavia were frequent visitors of commercial cinemas, regular readers of film studies and possessed vast knowledge about cinema; one of the major impetuses came also from the modernist models of other arts: visual arts, literature and theatre. Yet, film as a medium was becoming more and more widespread; it was the only medium that allowed for an intertwining of visual arts, literature of (anti) narrative, music and film references; it allowed the choice of different subjects and the employment of various techniques.

BB

How did the transition happen from amateur to professional filmmaking?

ŽŽ

We are probably idealizing, like everyone does, the years of my youth. But these are the facts: the old filmmaking technology, because of its complexity at every stage, required collective work. What a fifteen-year-old can make today with a digital camera and edit on the computer in a day, back then had to be done and coordinated with difficulty among at least five people for two weeks.

Filmmaking spontaneously spread out and motivated various kinds of people, professions, genres. There were a thousand times or a hundred thousand times fewer moving pictures in circulation than today. A screening outside a theater was a miracle. Not to mention making your own films. Festivals were meeting places and competitions. Films had their place in newspapers, in their culture sections, as did the people who kept up with all of it. There was ten times more film criticism and polemic than today. Some names were given already in their amateur days the status of a "discovery" or even a "star." This gave you legitimacy to show up in front of professional producers who had already heard about you. This was the basis on which, a few years later, starting from the mid-1950s to the early 1960s, filmmaking created its own cadre, its structure, the production infrastructure, and the market.

Kids today don't stand a chance. When you ask what their next move is, they say, to join a political campaign of one of the parties, to make a video clip, to follow the leader, a guy far inferior to the crew that's there to shoot him, or they throw themselves into commercials for music and into sales. And there you have it…

Owing to constant demands for professionalization in all social systems, especially in the art world, from today's perspective it is almost impossible to read correctly the meaning of the terms 'amateur film' and 'amateurism' as related to film buffs active in the cinema clubs in the sixties and beginning of the seventies all over socialist Yugoslavia. Yet members of cine clubs were amateurs, most of them adhering to the meanings **Maya Deren** stressed in her 1959 essay 'Amateur Versus Professional,'

in particular her consideration of the Latin roots of the term 'amateur.' It designates one's practice as being 'for the love of the thing rather than for economic reasons and necessity.'
(Maya Deren, "Amateur Versus Professional," *Film Culture*, 39 (1965), 46.)

Or as **Jonas Mekas** pointed out when referring to the role of the independent filmmaker:
'You will make movies, you will record and celebrate life, but you will not make any money.'
(**Jonas Mekas** on underground film, Whitney Museum, New York, 1992)

Regarding the former Yugoslavia, the term 'amateur' mainly designates production conditions, while 'experimental' indicates the procedures, aspiration and effects of a specific cinematic expression. Thus the separation between the two is unstable and unclear. This creative confusion in classification can be attributed in part to most of the filmmakers whose works can, in retrospect, be described as experimental. Either they soon exchanged amateur filmmaking for professional work in the cinema (e.g., **Dušan Makavejev**) or in the visual arts (e.g., **Mladen Stilinović**), or they went down in (or out of) history as film amateurs when the mid seventies saw the decline of cine clubs.
(**Bojana Piškur** and **Jurij Meden** "A brief Introduction to Slovenian Experimental Flm" in the catalogue *This is All Movie: Experimental Film in Yugoslavia 1951–1991*, exhibition curated by **Bojana Piškur, Ana Janevski, Jurij Meden** and **Stevan Vuković**, Museum of Modern Art Ljubljana, 2010.)

The Serbian filmmaker **Lazar Stojanović**, writing about American underground film, associates it with freedom and rebellion, rather than with a cinematic genre, where underground equals amateurism, directness, imperfection and resistance. Moreover, an (independent) film director is supposed to have above all a good knowledge of film and a strong personality. This praise of amateurism, in combination with a militant attitude of the director, can

also be observed, albeit in a more apolitical version, in **Mihovil Pansini** and his GEFF (the biennial Genre Experimental Film Festival).
(**Sezgin Boynik**, "Contributions to a Better Apprehension and Appreciation of *Plastic Jesus* by Lazar Stojanović," *Život umjetnosti*, no. 83, Zagreb, 2008)

The main tendencies of GEFF are: to fight against conventional film, and especially against conventional work in amateur film. To draw our amateur film from the narrow frameworks of the amateurish... we want to tear down the borders that exist between amateur and professional film. Film is one. ...Someone makes a film as an amateur but works as a professional. On the other hand, an amateur film can be sold subsequently. Therefore it is not possible to say what amateur, or what professional film is. If we cannot determine this, then there is no point in dividing films into amateur and professional.
(Mihovil Pansini, "Prvi dan 19.12.1963," in *Prva knjiga GEFFA 63*, Mihovil Pansini, Vladimir Petek, Zlatko Sudović, Kruno Hajdler, Milan Šamec (eds), GEFF Komitet, Zagreb, 1967)

The most political stance in experimental film in the former Socialist Yugoslavia is definitely in the activity of the Belgrade cine club circle. From the Cinema Club Belgrade founded in 1951 and the Academic Club Belgrade founded in 1958, as opposed to the Split School and Zagreb antifilm tendencies, emerged films of symbolic and expressive cinematography. Under the influence of Russian Expressionism, the Polish Black Series and French New Wave, the first Belgrade film from the end of the fifties reflected human anxiety in search of the surreal and the absurd. Variations on the theme of innocence in flight from reality is a frequent subject of Belgrade film lovers of the time, as seen in the films *The Wall* (1960) by **Kokan Rakonjac**, *Triptych of Matter and Death* (1960) by **Živojin Pavlović**, on the failure to escape and on existential anxiety, or in *Hands of Purple Distances* (1962) of **Sava Trifković**, about a girl's flight through a deserted and bizarre landscape. The Cinema Club Belgrade mainly gathered a group of film connoisseurs organizing for the members practical and theoretical classes. It was necessary to pass exams to enter the club as well as to propose the script to the judgment of the rest of the members to get the necessary equipment for filming. The participation in the film projects of other members was also required.

The first antagonism in particular with the Zagreb circle already started during the first GEFF discussions, when Belgrade cinema makers like **Makavejev**, stressed their interest in researching reality and distancing themselves from pure experimentation. Moreover, they started to have their films produced by the national production companies, switched filming to 35mm, while the Zagreb based filmmakers still filmed in 16mm or even 8mm, without being remunerated: some of them, being unable to professionalize, turned to visual arts, like **Mladen Stilinović**, or like **Gotovac** who developed his very specific practice.

Hence we already see in the sixties the journey, as **Stevan Vuković** defines it, from the 'amateur paradigm' to the 'author paradigm'. (Stevan Vuković, op. cit., 53.) The Cinema Club Belgrade gave rise to the new major film paradigm of the sixties and seventies, what would later be denoted as the New Yugoslav Film. Namely, the cine club activity was a useful framework for the production of professional filmmakers, like **Dušan Makavejev, Želimir Žilnik, Živojin Pavlović, Aleksandar Petrović**, (and **Karpo Aćimović-Godina** in Slovenia), as the disruptions that occurred in 'amateur' films flow into the mainstream or in this case, professional film.

Yet, for those directors the cine-club activity was a sort of matériel d'apprentissage. **Želimir Žilnik**, active in the Cinema Club Novi Sad, very quickly saw film as a tool of criticism, and he said this about the advantages of 'amateur' film: 'Very early I was forced to use all the

methods of movement of amateur film. This environment of amateur film enabled me to rid myself of administrative labyrinths, which were the only way of acquiring money to make a film. It was a form of freedom.'
(Marina Gržinić and Hito Steyerl, "Firm Embrace of Socialism, an interview with Želimir Žilnik', *Zarez*, nos. 134–135, Zagreb, 2007.

Žilnik's film *Early Works* was made in 18 days and obtained the Golden Bear at the Berlin Film Festival in 1969. Anyway many of the "Black Wave" films have been shown during foreign festivals, mainly at the Oberhausen film festival.

While the amateur films in Zagreb are characterized by experimentation with the medium, and while in Split a unique film expression is developing, Belgrade film amateurism makes a step forward and turns towards open criticism of the present and the alienation of the modern socialist man, pointing to class and social contradictions of socialism in contemporary Yugoslavia, breaking through the rarely disputed boundaries of state-socialist values. (Among the first films that were locked away in a vault between 1958 and 1971, were **Dušan Makavejev**'s *Don't Believe in Monuments* (1958) and *The Parade* (1962) while the amateur omnibus *The City* (1963), by **Marko Babac**, **Kokan Rakonjac** and **Živojin Pavlović**, is one of the officially forbidden films in the history of Yugoslav cinema.) They later pointed the finger at a specific phenomenon: the thriving of capitalism under the guise of a socialist revolution, and depicted the reality of precarious lives, mass unemployment, failed strikes, crises, etc.

As a consequence of an ideological campaign led by the cultural-political establishment, those films became known as the Black Wave. The article that introduced the term Black Wave was published in the newspaper *Borba* in 1969. A journalist stated that the Black Wave in Yugoslav films presents a 'systematic distortion of the present, in which everything is viewed through a monochromatic lens. Its themes are obscure and present improper visions and images of violence, moral degeneracy, misery, lasciviousness and triviality.' Thus started the process in the course of which **Makavejev**'s, **Žilnik**'s, **Godina**'s films were prohibited from local screenings while **Lazar Stojanović** got a prison sentence for his film *Plastic Jesus* with **Tomislav Gotovac** in the main role.

from **Ana Janevski**, "On Yugoslav experimental film and cine clubs in the sixties and seventies" | MACBA Museum of Contemporary Art of Barcelona. *Quaderns Portàtils*, March 2012, 1–16.
+
from Ana Janevski, "We Cannot Promise To Do More than Experiment! On Yugoslav Experimental Film and Cine Clubs in the 60s and 70s." In Gal Kirn, Dubravka Sekulić (eds.) *Surfing the Black: Yugoslav Black Wave Cinema and Its Transgressive Moments* (Maastricht: Jan van Eyck Academy, 2011), 46–77.

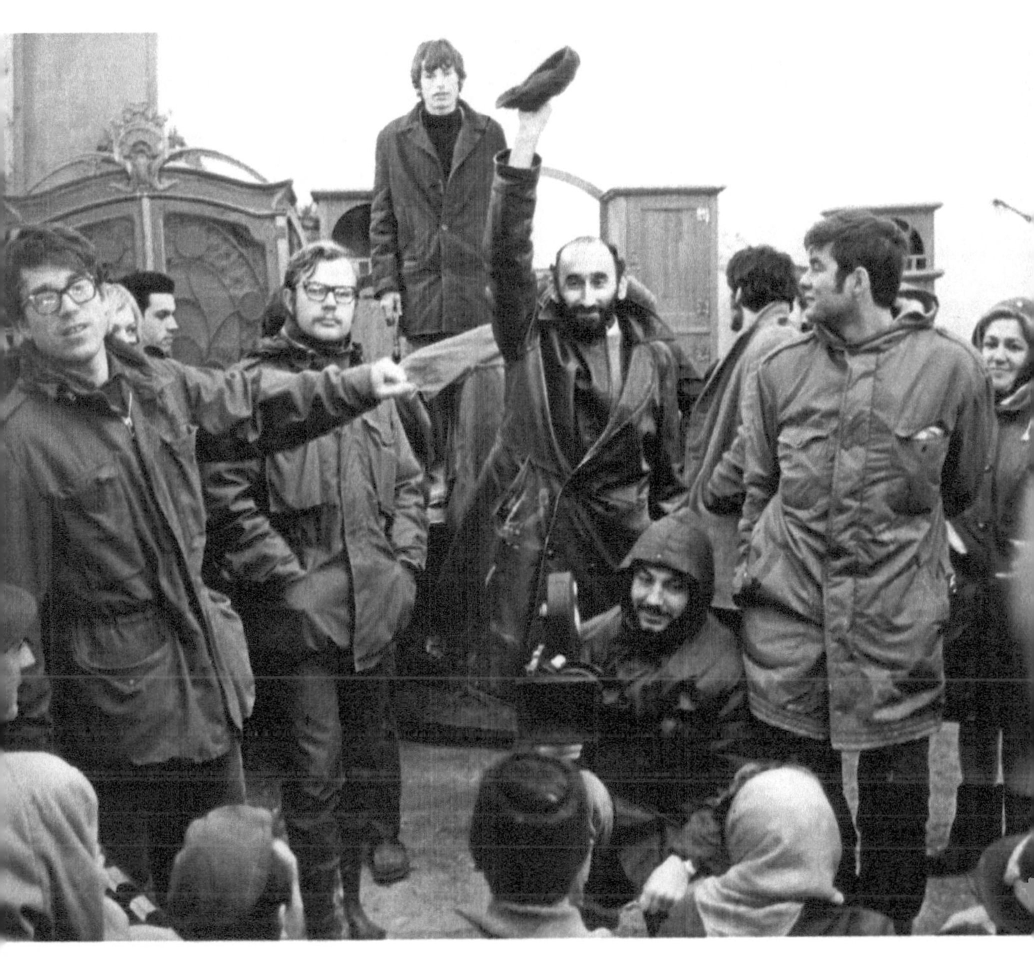

On the set of *Early Works* (1968). Branko Vučićević in the middle, Karpo Aćimović Godina with camera. • PHOTO ANDREJ POPOVIĆ

Yugoslav idol:
Back to the Present
in Three Images

IMAGE ONE: and it's just one side of us

There is an iconic image that sums up in a surprisingly or, better yet, frighteningly precise way the ideological truth of the time in which we live: Susan Boyle's performance on the cult TV show *Britain's Got Talent* in April 2009. The YouTube video, which has since been seen more than a hundred million times, shows a modestly dressed, plump, unpretty, middle-aged woman stepping confidently onto the stage. What's your name, darling?, we hear the voice of one of the members of the jury. She replies eagerly and decisively, explaining that she comes from Scotland, from... One member of the jury asks if it's a bigger city. No, she replies, it's a collection of villages, and here we hear the audience begin to laugh. How old are you, Susan? Forty-seven—and again we hear thunderous laughter. She comes back coquettishly—And it's just one side of me!—and swings her hips lasciviously. The audience breaks into an ovation, having a great time while the camera catches the same member of the jury rolling his eyes while the one next to him nervously and skeptically looks at what is happening on the stage. The camera shows the exhilaration of the staff backstage who are also having a great time. Susan then explains how she wanted to become a professional singer. Here the camera zooms over to the face of a girl in the audience who is also rolling her eyes in disbelief and sneering. The next question is about her role model, or, to be precise, the role model for success—Who would you like to be as successful as? Elaine Page, she responds as the audience is jeering at her again. What are you gonna sing tonight? "I Dreamed a Dream" from *Les Misérables*. With the first measures of the song, Susan got serious, as did the members of the jury and the audience. Tense anticipation. The moment her voice is heard, in the lower left-hand corner of the screen, the text appears against the outlines of a Union Jack: "SUSAN BOYLE, UNEMPLOYED, 47." And the dream becomes reality, becomes success and a standing ovation, a best-selling album on the world charts, and a joint performance with her role model for success Elaine Paige—in short, full satisfaction in defiance of all the inadequacies of a social loser.

The case of Susan Boyle perfectly sums up the hegemonic narrative of our time: the destiny of an individual is in the hands of the individual, contingent only upon their abilities and talents, that is on their willingness to put those abilities and talents to the test—to enter the competition. The act of evaluation or selection is ultimately left to the audience, an obscure subject of decision-making, which in the reality television show format makes itself heard from the anonymity of the masses, constructed on the principles of voluntary participation and generated exclusively by the media, by phone, text messaging, or the internet.

Although it actually parodies the practice of democratic decision-making, this mechanism strategically takes up space lit up by the aura of the democratic process, embellishing its parasitic position with the worn out feather of democratic legitimacy. Even in its most ragged edition, the aura of democracy still flawlessly does its job—the forgetting of reality. The disproportion between the individual winner in the spotlight and the great collective of losers who disappear into the media blackout goes completely unnoticed. In the end, that's what the people wanted. In any case, democracy expects us to identify without hesitation with the free will of the people, that is, with the winner. As far as social reality is concerned, is this winner, no matter how far in the minority, not the living proof nonetheless of what the language of sociology calls vertical mobility? It does move after all!

The very story of Susan Boyle and the TV format that produced her for the media seem to be quintessentially of our age, the age of global neoliberal capitalism. The motif of amateur wannabe competitions in this or that form of musical, film or stage production, and the motif of the so-called audition, are the cliché of popular culture. We can find it in various ideological-political layers of the past and in different cultural locations, but what is new in this case is the global visibility and legibility of this competitive format, that is of the idol being produced. What is also new is the relationship of power on which the global character of the format rests. Today it lays claim to originality which it never had before, originality whose articulation is twofold. A motif without cultural or media specificity is first set unambiguously, culturally, as a British, that is Western media format, and then the format itself gets patented through the media as an *interactive reality talent show*, which has an author with a first and last name, its production company, its logo, which is in short its own brand. This is therefore a move of cultural and media expropriation of a motif that was once a banal element of popular culture and media practice throughout the world. And that is the novelty—to have this theme appear to us today as if coming from the West as "the place from which it originates" (as

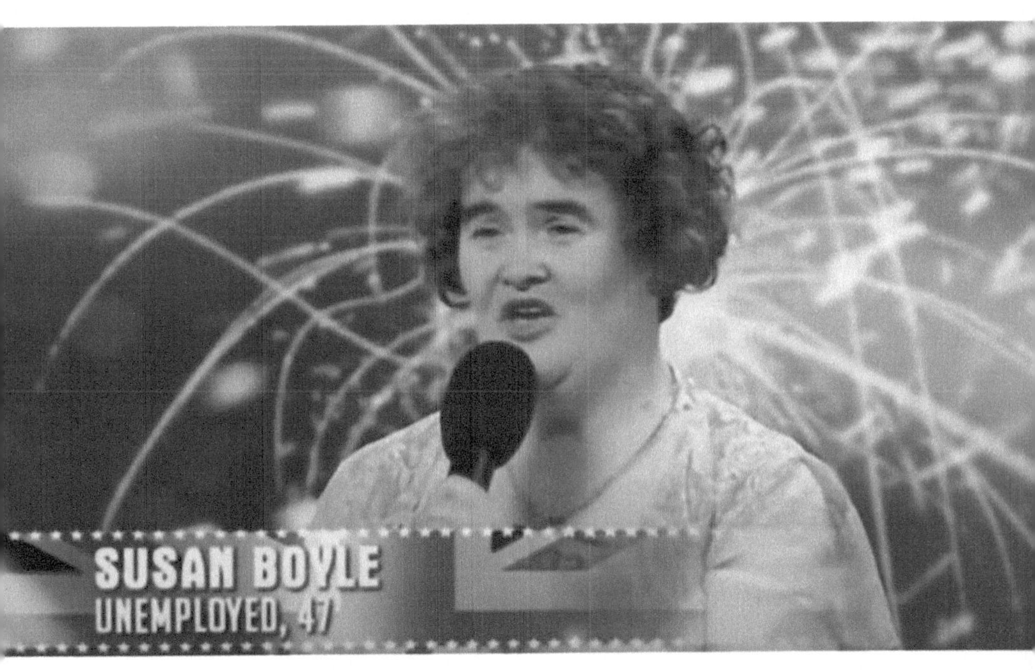

Susan Boyle performing on *Britain's Got Talent* (YouTube, 2009)

the English phrase would have it). That it comes from the West means not only that it comes from a different place but also from another time. To all that is not the West, first of all to that which is called the East, the West appears as if from the future. In other words, relative to the West, everywhere else runs behind, culturally behind most of all, which means in the relationship of perpetual catching up which takes on various forms of emulation, repetition, copying, quotation—in short, of translation. The West is the original, everything else is a translation... or a franchise. The British television show *Pop Idol*, another *real-life soap opera* in which the talent hungry for pop idol fame compete, has been transferred since it first appeared in 2001 into a dozen countries throughout the world as *American Idol, Arab Idol, Indian, Japanese* and *Nigerian Idol*, as well as *Croatian Idol*, and *Idols* in Serbia, North Macedonia, Montenegro...

One of the consequences of the cultural and media transfer of this television format, that is of its cultural dislocation and dissemination, is that its theme, the talent contest, now appears in the local context as something that has come from the outside, something that had never existed there before. The sensibility or the associations it evokes in the context of reception, along with the cultural, political and ideological meanings it acquires in that context, now appear as novelties which had also never previously existed in that place and have no original reference or precedent in its cultural history. The original is always elsewhere, and what you get here is merely its translation, or, as traditional translating would understand it, its secondary production. This secondary quality of the experience of reception, its delay, and so its second-rate status with respect to the original experience, has a devastating effect on the production of local historical experience. It ruptures the bonds of association, decontextualizes it socially, culturally, politically, degrades it normatively. If Susan Boyle could reply to, "Who would you like to be as successful as?" by saying, "Elaine Page," a local idol, Croatian, Serbian, Indian, Indonesian or any other, would respond to the same question by saying, "Susan Boyle." If in the former instance the idol-object of identification was embodied in an actually existing pop star, in the latter instance the object was idolatry itself embodied in the actually existing wannabe. Susan Boyle imitates Elaine Page, and everybody else imitates Susan Boyle, as if they had never seen anything like her before.

To the degree that one's own (historical) experience cannot provide an original reference for association, there is really no translation. All that remains is sheer imitation. Moreover, the experience that has nothing to say to the reality that succeeds it will of necessity lose all meaning. Much like the reality which pays no mind to experience loses all sense of direction. No strategy of caretaking or conserving the experience will help with this. Memory can still be deposited in archives, packaged in canons, and carefully cultivated as cultural heritage, or turned into museums as a transtemporal aesthetic value, but for experience, this spells death. Experience either lives outside, in the street among people from whom it constantly learns and from which they constantly learn through their struggle, their work, through various forms of their cultural practice, and through the practice of real history, or it will perish. Memory, no matter how well taken care of culturally, if it loses contact with experience itself becomes a form of forgetting. And a very dangerous one because it presents itself as its own antipode. It's like poison proffered to us as a remedy.

IMAGE TWO: Culture will save us

At the end of Mark Herman's *Brassed off*, a British film from 1996, a brass band made up of Yorkshire miners plays at the national competition of amateur brass bands at Royal Albert Hall. They play the Overture to Rossini's *William Tell* in front of a packed hall. Members of their families are in the audience, their wives and children eagerly anticipating the finale. There's excitement, exchange of glances between the audience and the players, occasional amateur clumsiness, but then an excellent performance. It's a triumph. Needless to say, they win, they are the best.

Still, they were losers at first, social losers like Susan Boyle. All unemployed. The film is based in fact on the story about the traumatic consequences of one of the most important historical turning points in modern British history. In the late 1970s, the Tory Margaret Thatcher came to power and introduced radical neoliberal reforms. The goal was to relieve the state of the numerous social obligations it had taken on under pressure from strong labor unions and the political influence of social democratic parties following WWII. The dismantling of the social welfare state works toward the ideal of the neoliberal state whose primary function is to facilitate, simplify, accelerate, and stimulate profitable capital

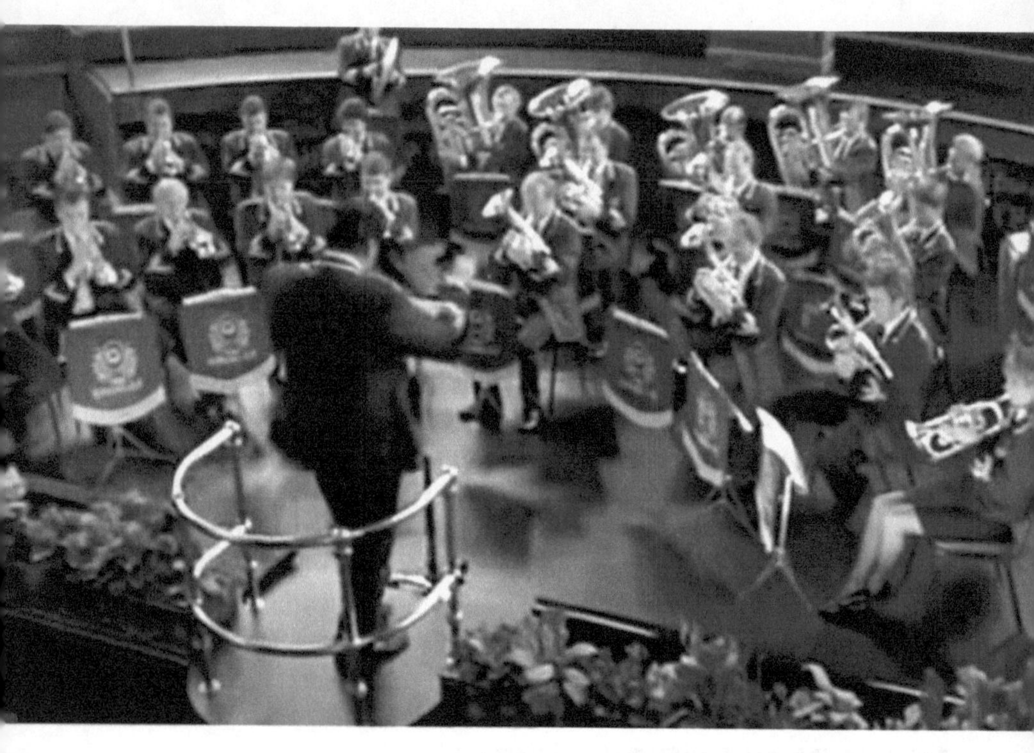

Miners performing at Royal Albert Hall in *Brassed Off* (1996)

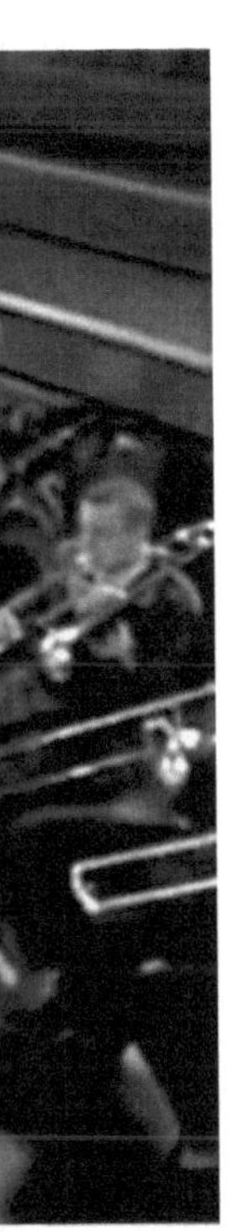

accumulation. The state apparatus no longer serves the interests of the broad masses of workers and middle-class citizens who see the state as the guarantor of social security, free healthcare, and education accessible to all, in short, as a social service in the public interest. At this moment, by contrast, another set of interests are served, or the interests of others are, of private property, business, multinational corporations, financial capital... The radical intervention in the social fabric of society, that deep and painful cut—as this magical remedy for all symptoms of the crisis of capitalism is called to this day—would cut, piece by piece, the entire society off of its institutional frame, the state, to such a degree that about ten years after she came to power, Margaret Thatcher could coolly proclaim that "there is no such thing as society." This was of course a proclamation made in the name of freedom, that is, the individual freedoms secured, according to neoliberal ideology, primarily in the freedom of the market whose worst enemies become all sorts of state interventionism it ultimately equates with dictatorship, whether communist or fascist in character.

We should not forget that the neoliberal turn in those years was not a British peculiarity. Only a year before Thatcher came to power, in 1978, Deng Xiaoping changed the course of communist China toward economic liberalization, which would secure in the coming decades the economic growth in China that was without historical precedent. A few months after Margaret Thatcher became British Prime Minister in May, one Paul Volcker, whom David Harvey has described as "a relatively obscure figure," took over the Federal Reserve in the United States and in a short time managed drastically to change its monetary policy. One year later, he would receive full support for his reforms from Ronald Reagan, the newly elected president of the most powerful country in the world. So, it is no wonder that above-mentioned David Harvey begins his book *A Brief History of Neoliberalism* (2005) with the sentence that says, "Future historians may well look upon the years 1978-80 as a revolutionary turning-point in the world's social and economic history." This is definitely something that comes to mind when we come yet again across the dominant cliché describing the epochal historical turn called "the great democratic revolutions of 1989-90" that toppled communism. Inflating the historical meaning of this event serves to repress awareness of its continuity with another historical turning point, or "revolution" as Harvey explicitly called it, launched two decades earlier. Or even earlier than that. Harvey also warns that the first successful implementation of neoliberal economic philosophy came following one clearly undemocratic turn, Pinochet's coup in Chile, which took place on September 11, 1973, and now gets called, not without irony, "the little September 11." On that day, let's recall, the democratically elected president of Chile, Salvador Allende, was deposed and murdered. The coup d'état was instigated by the local entrepreneurial elite and supported by the CIA, U.S. corporations, and Henry Kissinger, then U.S. Secretary of State. After the violent elimination of leftist social and political organizations, neutralization of unions, and liberalization of the labor market, into this deregulated economic space entered a group of neoliberal economists known as the "Chicago boys," for the fact that most of them had studied under their theoretical guru Milton Friedman at the University of Chicago. The ensuing economic growth was short-lived. By the early 1980s, Chile was facing a new crisis. Despite all this, the implementation of neoliberal doctrine in the Chilean economic and social reality, made possible by the violent suppression of social and democratic rights of Chileans, achieved its goal. As Harvey points out, the brutal experiment conducted on the periphery again became the model for politics in the center. In other words, we are back in Britain of the early 1980s, in Yorkshire to be precise.

The dismantling of the welfare state did not go without resistance. The strongest resistance came from the powerful British unions, that is, from their striking force, the miners. Still, the Iron Lady broke them too. The final act in this drama happened in June 1984 during the great miners' strike, the largest in Britain since the general strike of 1926, which went down in history as the Battle of Orgreave. This is now also the title of the canonized artistic re-enactment of the events of 1984, made by Jeremy Deller seventeen years later, in 2001, in the same location with some 800 participants. Deller didn't mince his words in emphasizing the importance of this event:

"It would not be an exaggeration to say that the strike, like a civil war, had a traumatically divisive effect on all levels of life in the UK."

Families fell apart, divided by mutually exclusive loyalties, unions divided on the question of support for the miners, and the media contributed to polarization to the point where neutrality was no longer possible.

"So in all but name it became an ideological and industrial battle between the two sections of British society."

Herman's *Brassed off* directly refers to this event, thematizing its long-term consequences on the lives of politically divided and morally humiliated miners. Specifically, the film depicts the hopeless situation in which the miners found themselves after the closure of the pits in a small Yorkshire town, ten years after they had lost the battle of Orgreave. They sought salvation, and the film ultimately suggests they found it, in culture, specifically in starting a brass band, in their own improvement as musicians, and the socializing made possible in joint rehearsals and the eventual trip to London, performance at Royal Albert Hall, and victory in the talent competition.

The trope of miraculous transformation of defeat into victory, of loser becoming winner, follows the same logic in both cases, in the case of Susan Boyle and in the case of the Yorkshire miners' brass band: what has been lost in society is repaid manifold in culture. The ship named society, sunk by neoliberal politics in the 1980s, didn't drag all its passengers to the bottom. Those among them who were capable, those talented, diligent, and courageous, those expected to survive, and therefore those who deserve to survive any shipwreck, jumped to the ship named culture in a timely fashion, and on it they now are, happy and sailing to a better future. This is not just about the compensatory character of culture which pays people back for the misery of their actual lives, a property through which culture could once trace its kinship with religion. This is also not much about what Marcuse called the alternative character of the culture in the late 1930s, its ability to emancipate itself in its bourgeois stage of development in the form of a unique spiritual world, to rise as a sui generis realm of values above the world of reality, and as such to take on the function of affirming and supporting unconditionally a better and more precious world, infinitely different from the world of actual daily struggle for naked existence. This is culture which has turned into a mechanism of affirmation for the world which any individual, using their inner resources, could realize for themselves, while not changing a thing in the reality in which they live. In the year 1937, when Marcuse published this essay, fascism was still on its unstoppable rise, and the author, conscious of defeat, bitterly laments the fate of bourgeois culture which renounces all social critique and in place of resistance to social injustice glorifies retreating into inner life and adaptation to what exists.

This is certainly not the case with the culture in which Herman's characters, those victims of neoliberal destruction of society, took refuge. This culture not only refuses to renounce its socially-critical function but, on the contrary, becomes itself the recognized topos of resistance, the medium of social critique, and the space of alternative political articulation. It is precisely because it is political in nature, and not because it renounces politics, that it becomes the refuge of the socially defeated and devalued.

After the winners are announced at Royal Albert Hall, onto the stage comes Danny, the miners' band leader, and in a dramatic address to the audience refuses to accept the trophy. People are important, he points out defiantly, not the music or the trophies, and then goes on to criticize the government openly: "...this bloody government has systematically destroyed an entire industry. Our industry. And not just our industry—our communities, our homes, our lives. All in the name of 'progress.' And for a few lousy peanuts."

How different from Susan Boyle, who in her triumph is no longer capable of reflecting on the miserable social reality from which she came onto the stage. In her case, the case of her cultural triumph, that reality is completely expunged, banished from that imaginary circle drawn by the stage lights, the circle in which Susan Boyle in narcissistic ecstasy celebrates her triumph, her salvation from the world of social poverty and political defeat. That same circle, the place of public visibility, the imaginary outlined by stage lights, becomes for the Yorkshire miners the stage for political resistance and struggle, a battleground on which the Battle of Orgreave once was lost and now gets reanimated, only now in the field of culture, not in the field of social struggle. The struggle once lost in society now gets continued in culture. But not with the same drama and suspense.

The winners' trophy Danny refused to accept is taken by another member of the miners' band. It all ends with a passionate kiss on the upper deck of a London double-decker bus while the band plays Elgar's "Pomp and Circumstance March No. 1," famous for its chorus from *Land of Hope and Glory*. It's the happiness of a successful love to the sounds of a patriotic march. This is what one could call a happy ending. On the other side of it, the side which sets the mood for the entire film, there is nostalgia, nostalgia for the spirit of the workers' collective, for the solidarity that permeated equally the permanently collapsed plants of industrial modernity and the lost battles of the social justice warriors. In the end, it is nostalgia for society as such, society that was irretrievably lost to the historical transformations of post-industrial capitalism. Nostalgia is, of course, more than a feeling. It is a cultural phenomenon, one of the effects and manifestations of cultural memory. As such, it has its material existence, but also its market value, because it is itself a product of the cultural industry of late capitalism, a medium of its perpetual reproduction in which a culturalized past inhibits the present in the endless recurrence of the same.

Brassed off invokes culture as the place for rebirth of utopia from the ashes of industrial society. This utopia did not only replace society by culture as its proper medium of historical articulation. Instead of the future, it now faces the past, the only temporal dimension in which it could still reach its telos. Nostalgia, much like the enormous obsession with cultural memory or cultural heritage, is a secondary derivative of this retro-utopia. There is no future. There is nothing we can do with the present. Let us then change the past, the only remaining dimension of free creation.

Herman's film feeds on the already dominant faith in the emancipatory potential of culture, augmenting this faith by giving it new retro-utopian properties: artistic expression or cultural creation now enables the resurrection of that historically actually decayed society, in this case the society violently dismantled in postindustrial transformation, long overtaken and steered by the conservative politics of neoliberalism. What is more, cultural creation promises real political effects. The working class, which definitely lost the war over the material conditions of its social existence, which could not prevent the closure of the pits and industrial halls, or as Danny says in his desperate lament over the workers' defeat, the "systematic destruction of an entire industry. OUR industry. And not just our industry—our communities, our homes, our lives," now succeeds at scoring an important victory on the stage for amateur musicians, the symbolic re-appropriation of cultural heritage previously alienated from the working class. The music which, often patriotically, warmed the hearts and souls of the national cultural elite, now echoes from their amateur, lowbrow trumpets.

Culture will therefore save us more than it will provide the appropriate recompense for a political defeat or the loss of the social. More than that, culture is the future finally showing itself from the perspective of a subversively captured, emancipated and therefore better past.

It is precisely in the motif of competition of amateurs in culture and art, of the political losers and social outsiders, that Mark Herman's *Brassed off* manages to articulate a critique of the actual relations of domination, in a word, the political critique of which the future, embodied in the triumph of Susan Boyle, would prove itself incapable. Here, then, the past is still one step ahead of its future.

IMAGE THREE: If you crash, you blow

In one of the final scenes of *When I Am Dead and Gone* by Živojin Pavlović, the protagonist Jimmy the Boat (Barka) joins the competition of amateur pop singers in Belgrade. On the stage before him appear young talents to greater or lesser success, and most receive loud applause from the audience and good scores from the jury. The program features international hits from the 1960s, "Memphis Tennessee" by Chuck Berry, "I'm a Believer" by The Monkees, "Cuore Matto" by Little Tony, and so on, and the competitors sing backed by the band Black Pearls (Crni biseri). Jimmy sings a local hit, "Going out on the town" ("Izlazak u grad"), a ditty dedicated to the recruits serving in the Yugoslav People's Army. He is tone deaf, however, and can't sing. His performance is a disaster, and the audience runs him off the stage with their hoots, boos, and whistles. At the end of the film, this loser meets a tragic end, killed in an outhouse.

He also started out as a loser, that is a social loser, *unemployed*. The first few frames of the film reveal in an ingeniously succinct way, in two or three scenes or dialogues, the social, economic, and political situation of Yugoslav socialism in the mid-1960s. On a collective farm the workers arrive at the manager's office on a tractor trailer. Jimmy approaches the supervisor, who would shoot him at the film's end, and asks clearly on behalf of all the workers,

"Where are we to go, Milutin? You know that..."
The supervisor replies brusquely, "The work is over, you got your money, fend for yourself."

Jimmy, more out of desperation than out of protest, mutters a "but..." but the manager cuts him off, "There's no but! Go to the factory, go to the town, I'm not your nanny from the cooperative."

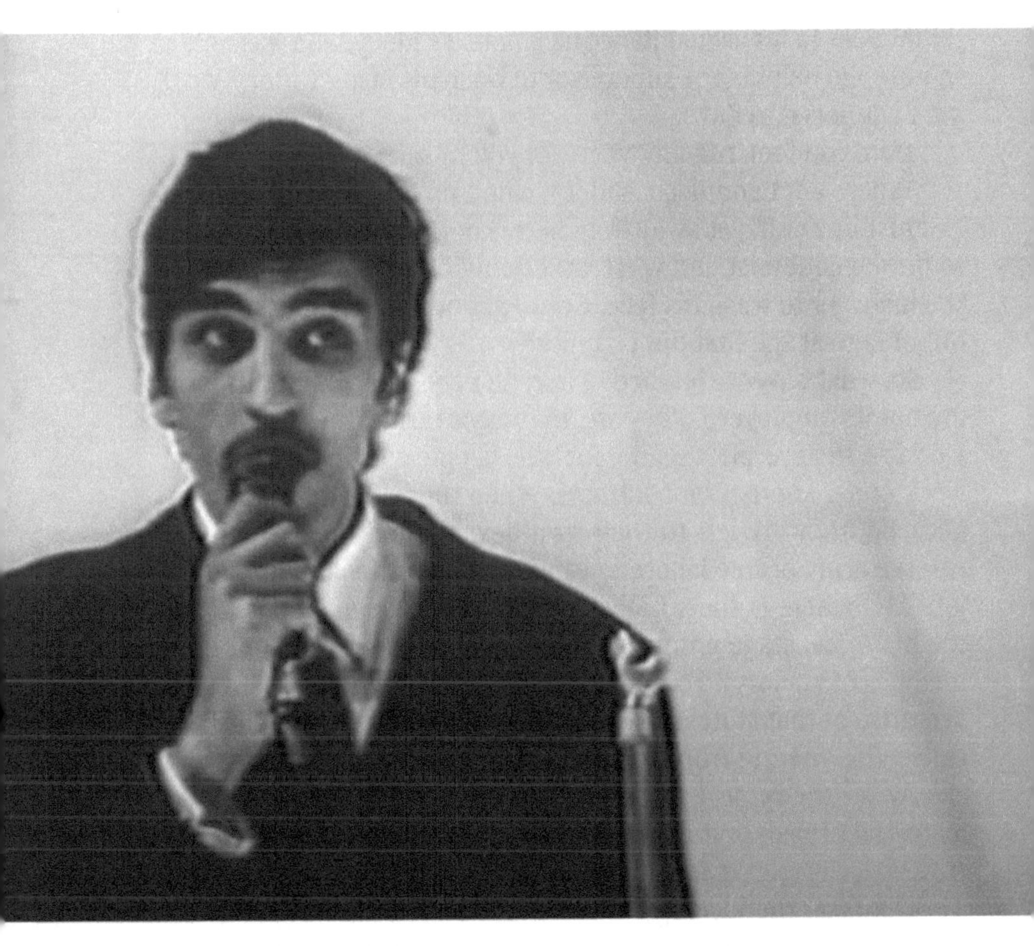

Jimmy the Boat performs at a talent contest in *When I Am Dead and Gone* (1987)

Jimmy goes to his acquaintance nicknamed Kidney, who was until a minute ago helping the supervisor to wash his face. "Kidney, what am I supposed to do?"

"Run, you fool, run anywhere, or you're screwed."

"Where am I gonna go, Kidney, climb up the tree and chirp?"

"Just buzz off, get away from here. Look at me. I was educated to be an economist and what am I doing now? Pouring water for the manager to wash his face. Got to get out of here, I have to get out of here at the first opportunity."

So, what have we learned? First, that the workers on this farm are not its employees. They are, in today's terms, the casual wage workers, the precarious labor for hire, people who in the best case work under short-term contracts. When the job is done and they get paid, they are left to their own devices, and they re-join the reserve army of free laborers wandering about looking for a new job. And where is the socialist welfare state which stepped onto the historical stage promising full employment and care for each member of society? To quote the supervisor, who plays a representative of that state in the film, this social socialist state is here called the "nanny from the cooperative." Here already we can clearly see the cynical attitude of the government toward its own historical project or its own ideological legitimacy. What ideology authentically speaks from his mouth, if not, even at the level of a worn phrase, the ideology of communism or of the Yugoslav socialist self-management? This is the ideology we know well from our bright global capitalist neoliberal democratic present, not from the darkness of our totalitarian communist past, the ideology that can repeat today the words of the socialist supervisor—"No buts! Go to the factory, go to the town, fend for yourself"—as its own.

But how did our protagonist end up going, instead of to the factory and the town to live hand to mouth, into the culture industry, while also remaining in the boondocks? How did this social loser become a producer of culture in the next part of the film? This transition, which paradigmatically summarizes and symbolically announces the epochal twilight of industrial capitalism, the emergence of new, post-Fordist forms of production, and the migration of capital into a new field of expansion, the sphere of culture, has often been interpreted psychologically, with a special emphasis on the protagonist's relationship to women. Indeed, the unemployed Jimmy the Boat is initiated into the work in the culture industry by a woman, Duška the folk chanteuse, a star of small-town bars and country fairs. Her motivation could be erotic or maternal, or erotic and maternal in equal measure, but the way she pulled it off far exceeds personal motivation as well as the reality of a backwards socialist backwater. Her way is called media manipulation.

At a fair, where she performs together with Jimmy, Duška runs into an old acquaintance, a journalist from a big city. The guy clearly represents the bourgeoisie, that is the urban cultural and intellectual elite that through his mouth speaks of itself with self-pity and strong resentment for the communist government. "This backwater is killing me, I can speak three foreign languages but who am I supposed to talk to here? My editor was a shepherd until yesterday, but what can you do, he's a Party member so he's on his way up..." At the same time, this self-professed victim of the allegedly primitive communist regime, which prevented him from acquiring the appropriate social status and blocked his access to executive power, which he believes he deserves in light of his abilities and superior bourgeois education, is very much aware of the power he has as a journalist. Duška is no less conscious of his power to make a social outsider and untalented loser such as her protégé Jimmy into a pop singer or a media star. "Help him, publish his picture, a comment, something like that, and put in the headline, 'Famous all over the country,'" Duška asks him. And this is not a favor for a friend, but a business deal, a morally bankrupt quid-pro-quo arrangement. The journalist, an aging fop, asks to be paid back for doing the favor in sex with Duška. She agrees right away and soon an article appears in the newspaper: "Young singer wins over audience." A star is born.

This scene is not a mere rehearsal of the tired slogan about the suppression of media freedoms under the boot of communist totalitarianism, the commonplace of anti-communist discourse that dominates unchallenged the opinions held about the so-called Yugoslav-communist past. On the contrary, it reveals another, parallel register of power which had already set itself free of communist government power, which in no way lags behind and possibly far exceeds the corruption potential of the government itself. This power is generated precisely by the freedom of the media, whose absence at the time—the "repression"—gets lamented in heart-rending terms to this day, and which remains inseparable from the actual market articulation of the ideologies concerning the "freedom of public discourse." It matters not whether we describe this power as "the power of tabloid journalism" or as power indistinguishable from the freedom of the media under the conditions of market reproducibility. On the contrary, it is important to ask, What is Pavlović's film actually about? Is it about the dark past, Tito's communist dictatorship, totalitarian suppression of the freedom of the media? Or is it about the bleak truth of the present, about Rupert Murdoch's global empire and the unscrupulous manipulation of the "freedom of public speech?" Of course, we must not forget the enormous difference. Socialist yellow journalism, saturated with corruptible journalists and run by incompetent party members, the ex-shepherds, had the power to transform an untalented nobody into a star of the local entertainment industry. The global yellow journalism in today's post-industrial, neoliberal capitalism, whose corruption scandals are shaking up the public spheres of the oldest democracies, revealing its collusion with corporate interests and political elites, has the power of filling the most powerful political offices, up to the rank of ministers or prime ministers. Even when we are completely conscious of its corruption, we still rarely question the competence of the characters who run it. This is naive. The British Commission which investigated the circumstances of the so-called phone hacking scandal (*hackgate*), when the employees of Murdoch's News Corporation bribed the police and hacked not only into the phones of celebrities, politicians and members of the royal family, but also the phones of crime victims, victims of terrorist attacks, including the phone of a girl who had been murdered, found that the big boss himself, Rupert Murdoch, was "not a fit person to exercise the stewardship of a major international company."

But let's go back to Pavlović's film. Just like the Yorkshire miners in Herman's *Brassed off* who were to come to London thirty years later to join the brass band competition, Jimmy the Boat at the end of the film comes to Belgrade with his new lover to join the young talents' singing contest. As soon as he gets there, he runs into the acquaintance we know from the beginning of the film, Kidney, a fellow loser who, although he was educated to be an economist, never managed to find a better job, and had to "pour the water for the supervisor to wash his face." At that time Kidney advised Jimmy to get away, go anywhere, and that he would himself "get out as soon as possible."

Kidney really did get out and—he succeeded! In response to Jimmy's plea to help him with the contest, Kidney says, "Of course I'm the best manager in the Balkans, but the thing that works now is hard-hitting dance music. What am I supposed to do with you?" It's a fact that Jimmy's repertoire consists of cheesy folk songs, and he doesn't stand a chance in the capital that had already been taken over by international pop songs and rock'n'roll.

Isn't Kidney another living proof (on film) that culture will eventually save us? He was once an unemployed economist and now he is the most successful manager in the Balkans. Is that Žika Pavlović, trying from the darkness of Yugoslav communist totalitarianism to give us the momentous formula that will put us on the shortest path to a bright future: there is no business like show business; there is no industry like the culture industry? Is *When I Am Dead and Gone* not the precursor of Herman's saga about unemployed Yorkshire miners who have survived the postindustrial turning point and the neoliberal dismantling of society thanks to becoming cultural producers? Isn't this film a marvelous work of socialist anticipation of a solution for the crisis that capitalism hadn't even encountered at the time? Isn't that its political message and its social and critical meaning?

Once the hero of Pavlović's film takes the stage he will not do like Danny in *Brassed off* and use this opportunity for political agitation. Jimmy won't even be allowed to finish his song, let alone give a political speech. The stage is not a platform that gives back the voice to those whose protest had been repressed and who had been silenced in the political sphere. There are no miracles happening on the stage: those paralyzed did not walk again on it, the blind didn't get their sight back, the mute did not speak. Why would we believe then that it would put a cultural happy ending on a social tragedy and have a beneficial emancipatory effect? The stage, or what it stands for in both of these films—the autonomous sphere of culture—is a place of work, and therefore, especially under the conditions of post-industrial capitalism, is the space of exploitation, merciless competition and struggle for survival which has no mercy for losers.

In his specific historical situation, Jimmy the Boat found himself face-to-face with the capitalist truth of the reformed Yugoslav socialism—and he lost. But the film that tells his story is not just a critique of that socialism whose reality ended when it did, and which is valued today about as much as the quasi-timeless aesthetic form in which it found its cultural expression. The thing we had just deposited in the past in the form of aesthetically canonized cultural heritage, as worn-out critique of a historically wasted utopia, now suggests itself to us as a critique of the utopia in which we find ourselves living—not simply a utopia of a better capitalist future but, on the contrary, the utopia of a facile promise of emancipation.

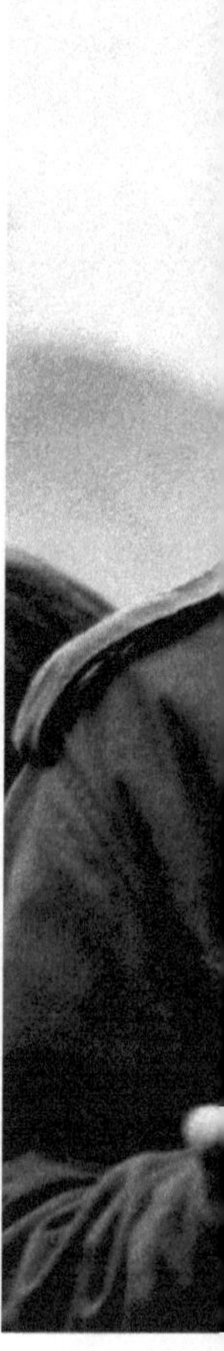

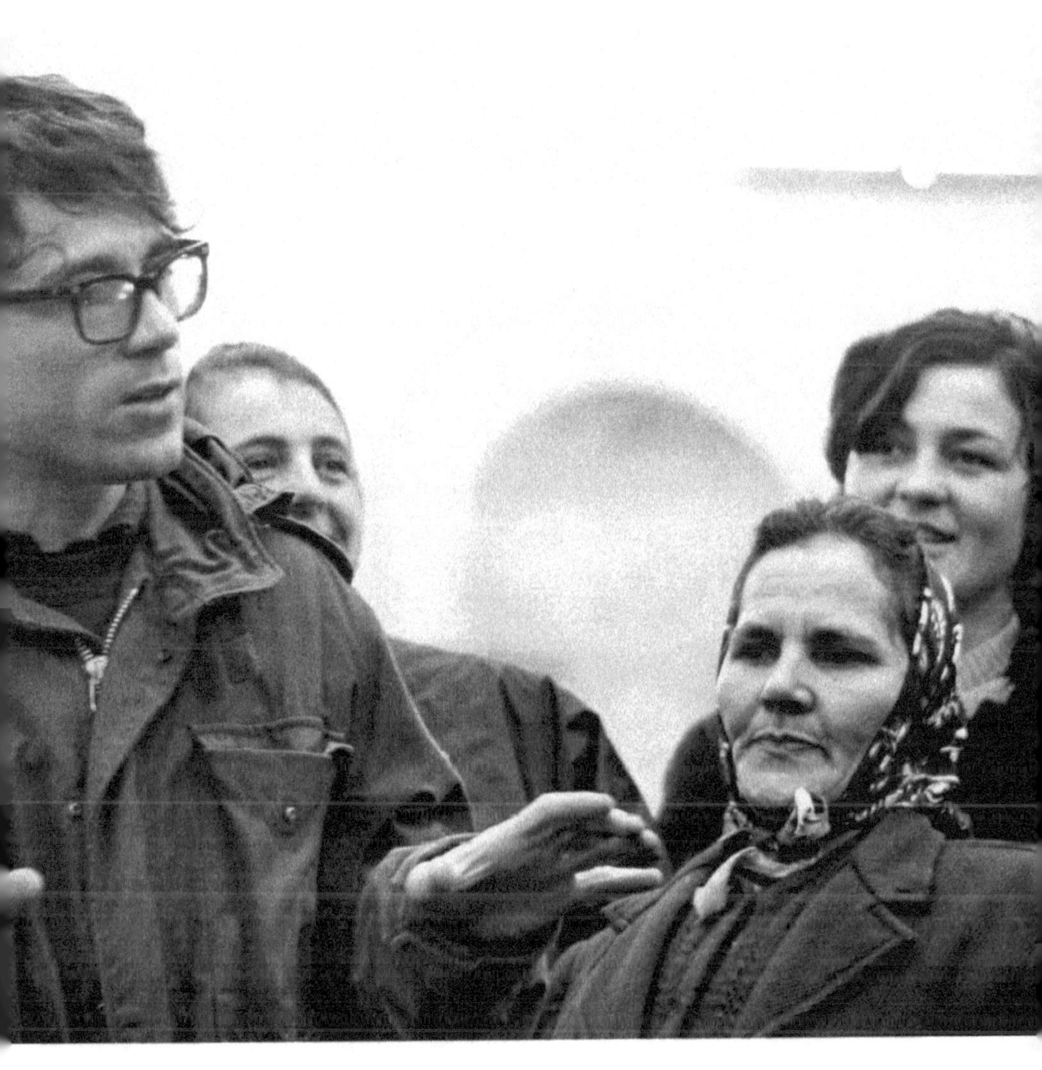

Želimir Žilnik on the set of *Early Works* (1968)
• PHOTO ANDREJ POPOVIĆ

Shoot It Black! What is Black in the "Black Wave?"

This chapter is a slightly revised version of Boris Buden's "Shoot it Black! An Introduction to Želimir Žilnik," published in Boris Buden, *Transition to Nowhere: Art in History after 1989* (Berlin: Archive Books, 2020), 177–187. The essay first appeared in *Afterall* 25 (2010), 41–48.

*It's not easy facing up when your whole world
is black.*
The Rolling Stones, "Paint It Black," 1966

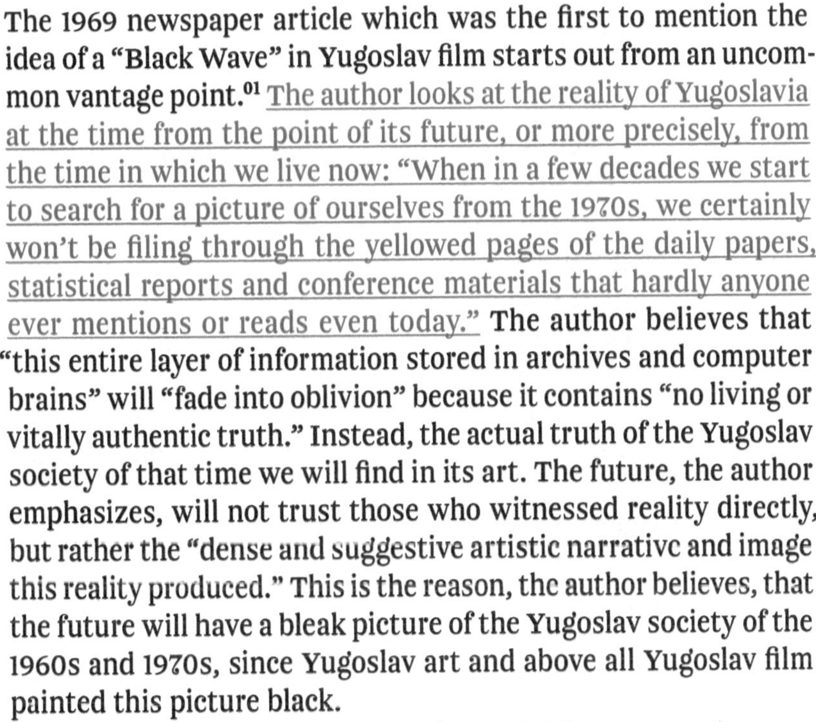

The 1969 newspaper article which was the first to mention the idea of a "Black Wave" in Yugoslav film starts out from an uncommon vantage point.[01] The author looks at the reality of Yugoslavia at the time from the point of its future, or more precisely, from the time in which we live now: "When in a few decades we start to search for a picture of ourselves from the 1970s, we certainly won't be filing through the yellowed pages of the daily papers, statistical reports and conference materials that hardly anyone ever mentions or reads even today." The author believes that "this entire layer of information stored in archives and computer brains" will "fade into oblivion" because it contains "no living or vitally authentic truth." Instead, the actual truth of the Yugoslav society of that time we will find in its art. The future, the author emphasizes, will not trust those who witnessed reality directly, but rather the "dense and suggestive artistic narrative and image this reality produced." This is the reason, the author believes, that the future will have a bleak picture of the Yugoslav society of the 1960s and 1970s, since Yugoslav art and above all Yugoslav film painted this picture black.

Isn't that interesting? In a society ruled by Communists one would expect the voice of the Party—and the newspaper *Borba* (*Struggle*) in which this article was published certainly was that—to be the voice of history, and not to tremble helplessly before this history in anticipation of its final judgment. "What will the future think of us?" is not a question asked by those presumed to know the course of history and legitimize their power precisely from the point of that future. Moreover, there is no law of historical materialism, no Marxist concept, however undogmatic and creatively enlightened, that would make art, that phenomenon of the superstructure, into the only "true" picture of society and even give it the last word on history. And yet exactly this is the logic of the argument made against filmmakers of the Black Wave. *Borba*'s critic accuses them of treason. What have they betrayed? Not reality first of all: he is

---

01 Vladimir Jovičić, "'Crni val' u našem filmu," *Borba*, 3 August 1969, 17–24.

not accusing them primarily of using their films to misrepresent reality, for example for showing it to be bleaker than it really is. Their actual "crime" is misrepresenting the society of which they are part. When the critic uses the phrase "the true picture of our society," for instance, it is not so much the "truth" as a realistic representation of social life that concerns him, but "the picture of society." Very specifically, he complains that the society in the films of the Black Wave "dresses up in rags to have its picture taken." By this he clearly does not mean that it should take all its clothes off and show itself naked, the way it really is.

This seemingly slight shift in emphasis from "truth" to "picture" has far-reaching consequences. The real conflict between the critic and the "traitors" happens not where it is usually projected to have happened from the post- and anti-communist perspective, namely between communist ideology on one side and "autonomous" art on the other. The case of Yugoslav "Black Wave" is definitely not a case of that well-worn story about the ideologically unbending communist apparatchiks who will try to impose the dogma of (socialist) realism on freedom-loving artists. Moreover, what the critic insists on is not a matter of socialism. The familiar discourse about the social function of art, about its programmatic role in the building of the new society, about its pedagogical and edifying functions, in boosting optimism for example, the classic doctrine of socialist realism is completely absent from this polemical text.[02] The critic argues instead that the problem with pessimism of which he, and in his voice the Party itself, accuses the Black Wave filmmakers is not that it spreads defeatism and so incapacitates the progressive forces of society, but rather that it spreads an unflattering picture of the Yugoslav society. This is what the whole drama is about:

---

02 The author explicitly distances himself from the "hedonist and educational purpose for the existence of art." He is prepared to accept the thesis that "it is pedagogically old-fashioned to ascribe to art any functional attributes." The idea that a work of art should deliver some sort of message he also dismisses as "Zhdanovism," referring to the party doctrine of Soviet arts and culture developed by the Central Committee Secretary Andrei Zhdanov in 1946. He openly writes that he could have sympathy for the "blackness" of these films had they at least given some pleasure in the "artificiality of art for art's sake and its polish." Ibid., 19.

how the society represents itself to the Other, whether the Other abroad or the Other of posterity. Specifically, the authors of "black films" are accused of "clowning up the nation and the society for the love of threepenny ephemeral world fame." In the eyes of the critic they are responsible for kowtowing to the fashionable tastes of the international market.

To support his criticism, the author must refer to authoritative sources. These are not, however, Marx or Engels or Lenin, and it isn't Tito, or any of the Yugoslav Marxists or leading party intellectuals. Instead, it is Bosley Crowther, the legendary film critic for *The New York Times* and art director of Columbia Pictures at the time, quoted from an interview he gave to a Yugoslav weekly:

> "You Yugoslavs [...] you are so vital [...] you know how to look at women, you laugh from the heart, you are open, there is genuine joy of life in you. Why then are your films so bitter, so dark? [...] What is the truth? You as I have seen you, or the way you present yourselves in the films? [...] Or is this in your film a temporary fashion for pessimism which reaches your authors from abroad with a certain delay?"[03]

Thus the official position of the Party on cultural issues at the time aligned its arguments with a Western-Orientalist gaze that imagined Yugoslavia as an exotic realm of authentic enjoyment of life and natural vitality.

But the question of representation becomes even more dramatic from the perspective of the future, or with regard to the relation to posterity. Again, it's about the picture of society whose works of art will outlive it. According to the author, we should not be indifferent to "this sort of recognition," e.g., to the question about which picture of us would be bequeathed to the future, for if art paints this picture black now, the future will have a black picture of us as well.

Writing from a contemporary perspective, this is all to suggest that we must abandon our post-communist perspective if we really want to understand what that "blackness" was about that gets ascribed to a great deal of Yugoslav film production in the late 1960s. This isn't just because of all those insufferable clichés about the communist past whose actual ideological effect is not so much to

---

03　Ibid., 20.

blacken the utopia of the past which has since foundered, as it is to glamorize the actually existing one, the utopia of liberal democracy and capitalism as the final resolution of world history. There is another, better reason: the very concept of the "Black Wave" was conceived from a post-communist perspective.

"Black Wave" is a concept clearly forged in struggle, and suggests a certain way of instrumentalizing art for that struggle. But what kind of struggle is this? Not one for a better society, say, one more just, in short, classless, communist. Here we are surely not dealing with a story about art dragged (unjustly) into the social struggle. From the point of view of the critic who introduced the slogan "Black Wave," the social struggle was already obsolete, or, to be precise, its social cause was gone. The struggle continued, however, but in another form, on another battlefield and for another cause: it was now the struggle for recognition fought exclusively in the field of culture. What was at stake in this struggle was now identity.

It sounds paradoxical, but the position from which the voice of the Party pronounces its j'accuse against the Black Wave filmmakers was the position of a society that was already dead, one that had exhausted all of its utopian potential and had reached the limits of its further expansion in terms of social justice and broad social prosperity. It was a society facing its historical end, a society without a future. It literally could no longer see itself in that future, or better yet, it could see in it only an alienated picture of itself, a picture already appropriated by art, by the films of the Black Wave. This is why our understanding of the Black Wave cannot be reduced to the post-communist cliché about art struggling for freedom against a society under communist totalitarianism. On the contrary, this is a society that's fighting art over its "true" picture, a society in terminal struggle for its one remaining way to survive, surviving culturally. Launching this struggle in 1969, the communist critics of the Black Wave proved to be post-communist long before all of those "democrats" who would succeed them in power. They already knew very well that they could no longer command history, but they were still able to anticipate its development. Moreover, by occupying themselves exclusively with the question of cultural representations they had already accomplished that notorious cultural turn which would be later ascribed to postmodernism as one of its main features. Moreover, by taking on just the question of their cultural representation, they had already completed the notorious turnabout that would later be attributed to postmodernism as one of its central features. Yugoslav communists of that era were already looking at the society they ruled from the position of its posthumous life in the sphere of cultural representation.

Of course, politically the Party was still jubilantly identifying with its historic mission, namely, radically to change society for the better, still believing itself capable of achieving that goal. But this was, to use the Lacanian term, only the imaginary level of their identification. In short, this was the way Yugoslav communists identified with the ideal image of themselves, with their ideal-ego. Yet at the same time, but on the symbolic level, they identified with the view of history itself, i.e., with their ego-ideal, in which they saw the society they had created surviving only in a form of cultural translation that was completely escaping their control. There was no doubt they had the undisputed rule of society, but again only in the imaginary sense. Symbolically they had already lost it, having surrendered it to culture. In 1969 the challenge for them was no longer how to build a new, better society, but rather how to correctly represent the one already dead. So a true picture of social reality still seemed possible, but only in the anticipated cultural retrospect. This is reflected in a shift in realism itself: from its socially prospective dimension (concept of socialist realism employed in the service of society as a utopian project) to a culturally retrospective realism. The latter is no less ideologically dogmatic than the former. But the name of that dogma is now "cultural memory," the only form that remains in which to articulate social experience today, in retrospect of course. The Party knew this as early as 1969.

Now we could probably answer the introductory question: to what does "black" refer in the notion of the "Black Wave" of Yugoslav cinema? It refers primarily to the end of society, to the experience of the abyss that gapes open at that ending, to that boundless contingency to which we get exposed after the social experiment has been completed once and for all, or better yet, after the potential of human experimentation with society historically has been exhausted. It is the blackness that absorbed all utopian light that had until then illuminated society's path to the future. In its subjective dimension, it is the darkness of fear that consumes us in the existential encounter with the finitude of society as such, that is, in becoming conscious of the possibility of its total absence—a social fear in the ontological sense.[04] This has been perhaps best expressed by one of the best known actors of the Yugoslav Black Wave who also acted in European and Hollywood productions, Bekim Fehmiu, who is quoted in the article, "We have never lived better, and yet everything is black before our eyes."[05]

To allay this fear or quell this ambivalence, a fetish was introduced: the fetish of cultural identity that also implied, folded within the political concept of sovereignty, a national identity. At that time, in the late 1960s and early 1970s in former Yugoslavia, there was a key change in the way Yugoslav Communists legitimized their rule. The narrative of class struggle was fundamentally abandoned. The Party ceased to imagine itself as the vanguard of a universal history that would guide that history to its classless end, to communism. Instead, it began to legitimize its rule within the framework of the particular history of its own nation, identifying itself with its political elite. Having completed the struggle for national liberation and achieved full national sovereignty, the elite would lead its society (framed by a nation) into progress under received historical conditions, the conditions of the regulated socialist market economy and open participation in international *Realpolitik*, that is, in what was already taking the shape of the order we now call global capitalism. In short, the communist leaders of this moment would no longer try to alter society so it becomes more like the communist utopia. Instead, they would adapt the communist utopia to the society they had fully conflated with the nation. This of course fundamentally changed the situation on the so-called cultural front. Communists were no longer fighting the trench war against traditional bourgeois culture whose primary preoccupation was still creating essentialist identities for each one of the Yugoslav nations— Serbs, Croats, Slovenes, Bosnians, Macedonians, Montenegrins, Albanians, etc. They reached a truce with it instead, to say: "you leave politics to us, and we'll leave national culture to you," with a few clearly defined exceptions, and so further strengthened their identitarian, that is, national legitimation. To remain in the driver's seat, they swapped

---

04 In terms of Heideggerian *Angst* that makes a subject experience society's being-toward-death.

05 Ibid., 20.

vehicles, got into the identity politics car, and sped recklessly into the catastrophe of the 1990s.[06]

To sum up: what opened up a perspective on life after the end of society was identity, or in a somewhat broader sense, cultural identification. No wonder then that nearly all grasped for it. But not all did, and some preferred not to.

The most prominent among those who entered the darkness at the end of society with their eyes—and the lenses of their cameras—wide open was and still is Želimir Žilnik, whose entire oeuvre on film, spanning more than half a century, represents the most radical and the most consistent expression of its "blackness".

Moreover, Žilnik is the only one of the Black Wave film-makers who explicitly responded to the official accusation: "You are blaming me for making black films. So be it, then." In 1971 he shot a documentary titled literally *Black Film*.[07] Žilnik picked up six homeless people from the street and brought them to his home, not only to share the warmth of a middle-class family's apartment (it was January), but also to participate actively in the making of a film about their problem. (This would become typical of Žilnik's docu-drama: he made it possible for amateur actors about whom the film was being made to participate consciously in its making, that is, to play themselves.)[08] The next day on the streets of Novi

---

06 The Constitution of 1974 tacitly made multiculturalism the official ideology of the Yugoslav state. The discourse of social justice did not simply disappear from Yugoslav politics. It was translated into a new language of the politics of identity which came to rule the political discourse of those years, not of course as a trans-social but as an international problem. The question of (un)just redistribution was now posed not in relation of one class of society to another, but rather in relation of one republic—one nation—of Yugoslav (con)federation to another. This was a clear departure from the "socialist political imaginary in which the central problem of justice was the question of redistribution, to the 'postsocialist' imaginary for which the central problem of justice is the question of recognition." Nancy Fraser, *Justice Interruptus: Critical Reflections on the 'Postsocialist' Condition* (New York and London, Routledge, 1997), 2.

07 *Black Film* recently featured on the film program of documenta 12 curated by Alexander Horwath.

08 "I do not hide from the people I am shooting the fact that I am making a film. On the contrary. I help them to recognise their

Sad he brought random passers-by in front of his camera to ask them about how to solve the problem of homelessness in the city. None of the passers-by, and also none of the officials responsible for this problem, had an answer to this question. The filmmaker himself did not have one either because "these people who stink," as he explicitly says in the film, could not stay in his flat forever. Eventually, after he told them that no solution for their problem had been found and that he was running out of film, Žilnik asked these people to leave his home.

Again: what is black in this *Black Film*? The reality it depicts? The failure of communists to solve social problems? The gaping abyss between the utopian promise and reality? No! It is the film itself, the very idea of art, especially the art of film which claims the power to change social reality—that is what is truly black in *Black Film*. In fact, it starts off with the author saying to the camera that he used to make films like that two years ago, but such people [the homeless], are still here. The film is a radically sincere self-reflexive critique of the idea and practice of the so-called socially engaged cinema. Žilnik openly thinks of *Black Film* as his own tomb. In the manifesto published on the occasion of the 1971 film festival where the film premiered, he calls the whole festival a "graveyard."[09] "Black" here refers to the "poverty of abstract humanism"[10] and the "socially engaged film which has become the dominant fashion in our bourgeois cinematography;"[11] it refers to its false avant-gardism, social demagoguery and left-wing phraseology; its abuse of socially marginalized people for the purposes of filming; to the

own situation and to express their position to it as efficiently as they can, and they help me to create a film about them in the best possible way." Želimir Žilnik, interviewed in the daily *Dnevnik*, Novi Sad, 14 April 1968. Quoted in Dominika Prejdová, "Socially Engaged Cinema According to Želimir Žilnik," in Branislav Dimitrijević et al. (eds.), *For an Idea—Against the Status Quo*, (Novi Sad: Playground Produkcija, 2009), 164.

09 Želimir Žilnik, "This Festival Is a Graveyard. Manifesto to the 18th Yugoslav Festival of Short Film, Belgrade, 1971," in Will Wehling (ed.), XVII. *Westdeutsche Kurzfilmtage Oberhausen* (Oberhausen: Westdeutsche Kurzfilmtage Oberhausen, 1971), 24–25.

10 Želimir Žilnik, quoted in Heinz Klunker, "Soziale Experimente," in Wehling, ibid., 23.

11 Želimir Žilnik, "This Festival Is a Graveyard," ibid. 24.

filmmakers' exploitation of social misery, etc.[12] Even more importantly, "black" does not refer at all to a "lack of freedom," usually presented from today's post-communist perspective as the worst "blackness" of the communist past. Žilnik explicitly claims, "Those at the top are preoccupied with their own problems. They gave us our freedom. We have been freed, but ineffectual."[13] "Black" refers to the chasm that no freedom can bridge, one that will survive the fall of communism.

For Žilnik, film and culture more broadly, no matter how liberated from totalitarian oppression, will never provide a remedy for social misery. For him the emancipatory promise of culture is a bluff. In mocking the authors of socially engaged films in 1971, who search "for the most picturesque wretch prepared to suffer convincingly,"[14] he already makes fun of liberal inclusivism that would impose twenty years later, after the fall of communism, its normative dogmatism on the cultural producers of the new (and old) democracies. We know that story very well: somewhere on the fringes of society we discover the victims of exclusion, the pathetic subaltern creatures with no face and no voice. But luckily there is some artist nearby who will help them, in the language of the new hegemony, to "show their faces" and "make their voices heard." How nice: whatever the bad society has excluded, good art will include again. Because, as widely believed, what has been socially marginalized can always become culturally central, that is, brought to light—to the transparency of the public sphere from the dark corners of society. The rest is democratic routine: a benevolent civil society, sympathetic to the suffering of the poor and excluded, makes a political case out of social darkness; once party politics are involved, a political solution is sought and ultimately found, a law is changed, and democracy is reborn, more inclusive than ever.

---

12 Cf. Želimir Žilnik, in Heinz Klunker, ibid., 23.

13 Ibid. Reporting from the festival in Belgrade the same German critic, Heinz Klunker, criticizes Žilnik for seeing the situation "too darkly" and for underestimating the freedom that filmmakers in Yugoslavia have been granted, a freedom that Žilnik, as Klunke writes, "equates with sheer complacency." From H. Klunke, "Leute, Filme und Politik in Belgrad," *Deutsches Allgemeine Sonntagsblatt*, 28 March 1971.

14 Želimir Žilnik, "This Festival Is a Graveyard," ibid., 24.

Not for me, answers Želimir Žilnik, as early as 1971. He, who has been working his entire life with different kinds of so-called marginalized people, from street children, unemployed, trans, and homeless people, illegal migrants, Roma, etc., knows very well what their "blackness" is about. It is about the absence of society and about what politics, however democratic, cannot represent: a "blackness" swallowing ever faster the light around which we have historically gathered.

From *Black
Film* (1971)

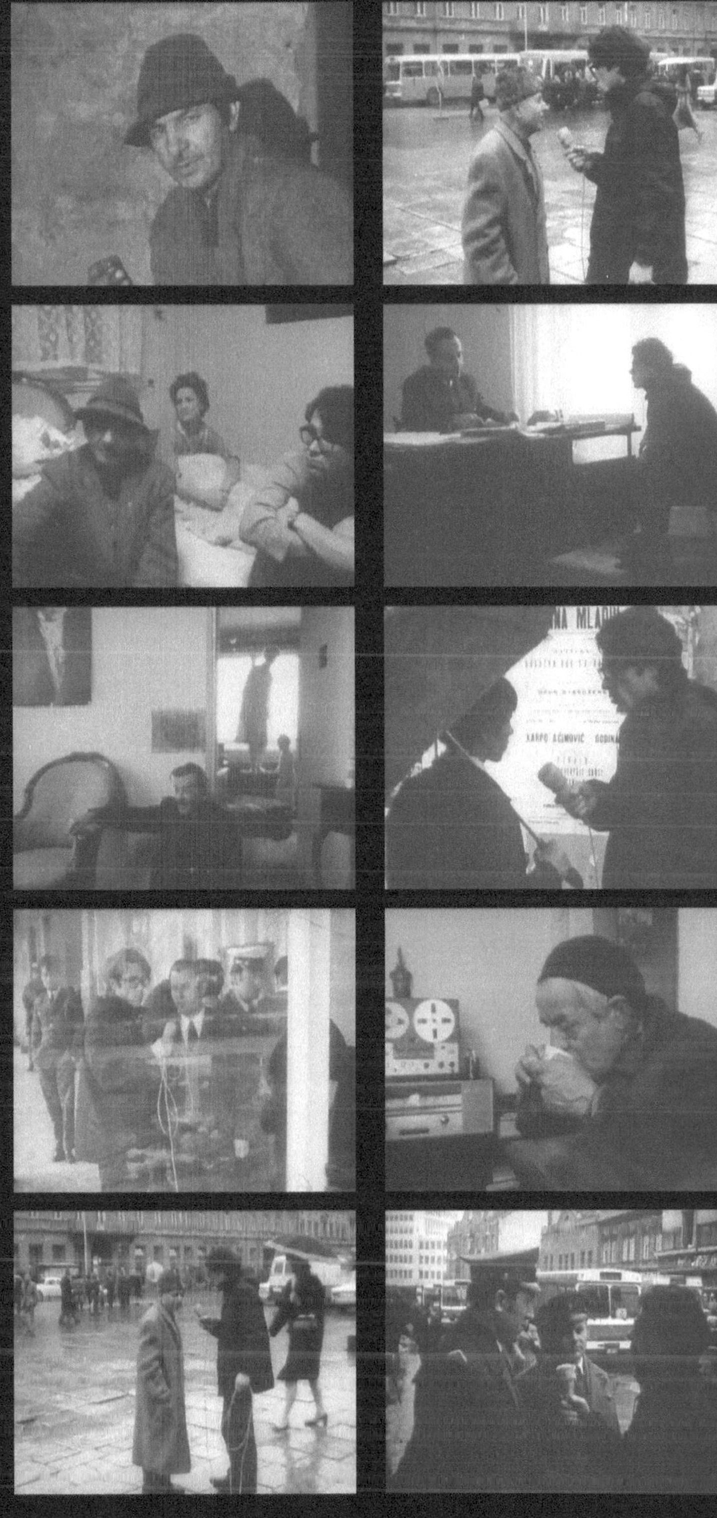

In Place of an Epilogue: Revolution, or the Marble Ass of History

For Vjeran Miladinović Merlinka (1960–2003),
lost between two revolutions,
one forgotten and one missing

Shame parade

A work of video art by Igor Grubić bears an interesting title, *East Side Story*. Its subject—pride parades—is familiar to the public of former Yugoslavia. The film depicts the violence that attended these events in Zagreb and Belgrade, the peaceful marches of various sexual minorities as well as those who support their right to be recognized in their difference. We see them surrounded by an angry mob which hurls insults at them, then blocks their way, and finally attacks them and beats them up. We also see the police, reluctant to protect them, as they get pulled into the violence and eventually even become its victims. We also see the helplessness of event participants exposed to the murderous assaults from groups that are greater in force and numbers, but also witness their courage, defiance, and resolve not to back down before the violent mob. The scenes in this film leave one sick to the stomach, not only because of the intensity of violence and the expressivity of hatred we witness, because of the indecision and incompetence of the otherwise arrogantly repressive state apparatus, because of the failure of civic courage among the silent majority... There is another thing that heightens our discomfort manifold and more than anything else creates in us the feeling of humiliation—the "East" mentioned in the title of Grubić's work. It is unlikely that anyone would be unaware of the contrast in these pictures, the western contrast implied directly in the title: the *West Side Story*

We all know that parades of the LGBTQ communities in the past few decades became an integral part of the urban metropolis in the West. From San Francisco to Chicago and New York, from London to Cologne and Berlin, hundreds of thousands of people, sometimes more than a million, as in Madrid, many of them not members of those so-called sexual minorities, participate in these big city festivals enjoying what we now call the culture of tolerance. The situation in Eastern Europe is completely different, of course. If a pride parade takes place at all, despite enormous obstacles and more or less deliberate obstruction from the authorities, we will see more police and security in the streets than participants. In some cases, as Grubić's work suggests, there will be clashes between the police and the opponents of these marches or severe beatings of the participants and even of the police. Farther out East, pride parades are not taking place at all. They are prohibited for so-called security reasons, as in Belgrade, or, as in Moscow, where they have been banned for the next one hundred years. Prohibited by law!

How much longer for the love of god

Is this not clear proof of a deep cultural difference between the East and the West, proof supported by the statistics which make it clear as day that homophobia gradually grows stronger as you go from West to East? And in the ex-Yugoslav regions, while you can safely hold a parade in Zagreb today, in Split it is already "a security risk of high degree," while in Belgrade there is no parade anymore. Does this not also demonstrate the need for an even more intense westernization of the East: even more "schools for tolerance," more care for minorities, more support for the cultural projects dealing with human rights, in short, a better developed civil society which will one day become strong enough to put pressure on the state, and by doing that, positively to affect legislation, political decision-making processes, as well as the entire public, broadly advancing the still-lacking culture of tolerance?

But how far is it possible to speed up the process of westernization and the process of post-communist transition in general? How long does it take for it to complete? When will the East catch up with the West? When will we finally see a joyous city party in the center of Belgrade or a million people in the Red Square waving rainbow flags? That is the wrong question, reasonable liberals will have us know. Forecasting the future is the bankrupt business of communist utopia (or a totally lucrative one, for psychics), not the sort of thing that enlightened democrats do. But who ever said this was about the future at all?

Better forget it

In the provocatively titled text, "Will the East's past be the West's future?," Rastko Močnik warns that the Cold War division between the East and the West managed to survive the collapse of communism to this day largely because of its ideological function, which is to deprive both sides, the East and the West, of their history. This is how today the West appears to us free not only of its own history, but of history as such. Exactly this is the reason that it can be imposed on us as something general, universal, or, as Močnik writes, "canonical."

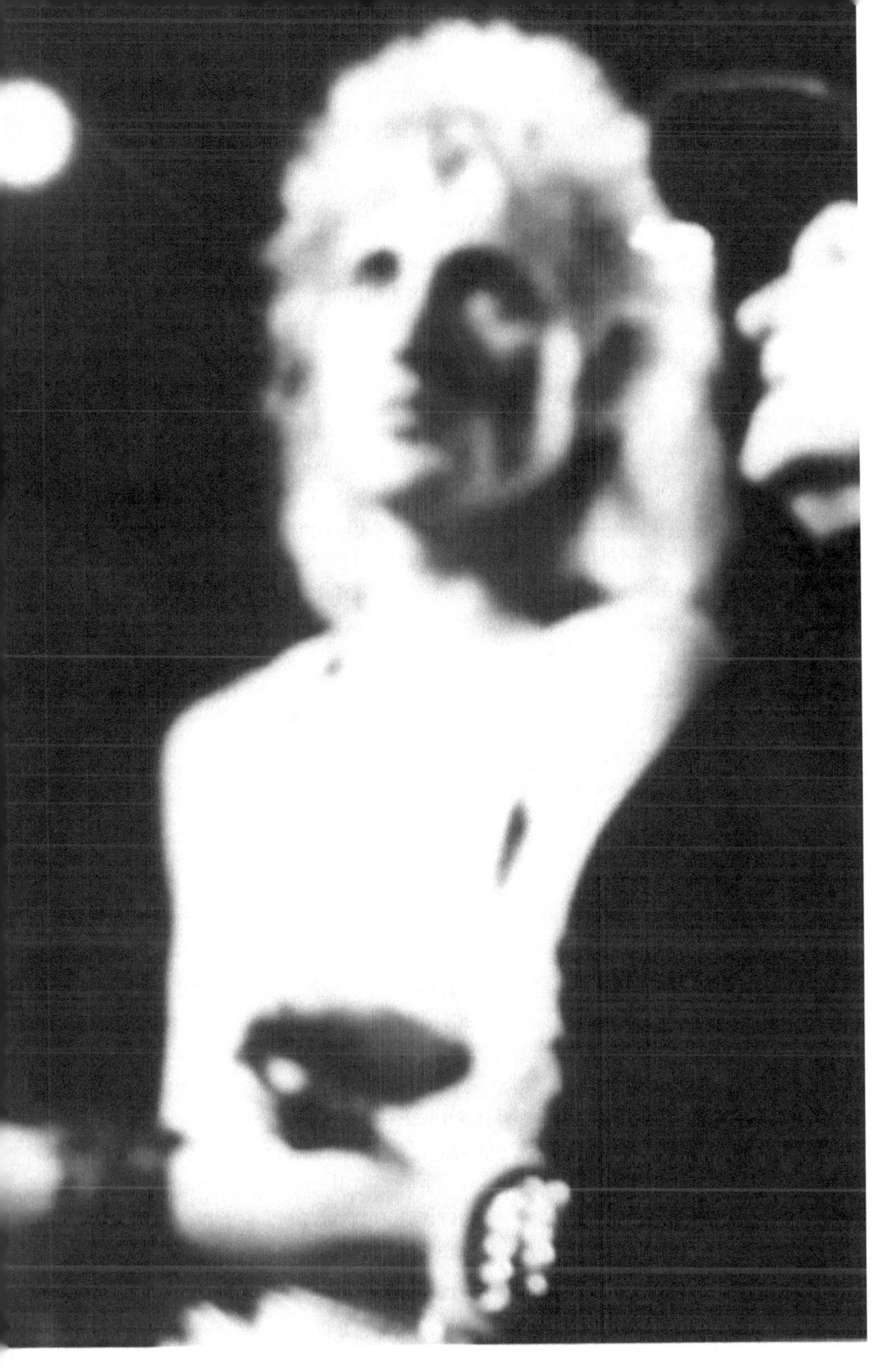

From *Pretty Women Walking Through the City* (1986)

By contrast, the notion of the East, claims the author, functions as a form of amnesia whose aim is to be relieved (get rid) of history, and so to become an a-historical non-space like the West. Its own history makes the East peripheral and provincial. So it has a past, but the past that had, as Močnik writes, "better be forgotten." Habermas would here use the word "rewind" (*rückspülen*), whereas Boris Groys in a similar context talks about "musealization of the East." No matter what we call this phenomenon, it boils down to how the notion of the East presupposes, as its condition of possibility, a kind of forgetting of history. The East can be (re)constructed as a museum only after it has been turned into a junkyard, or even better, into the dustbin of history where one throws failed ideologies and spent political concepts, and where the past is finally stripped of all historical experience. Only the past that has nothing to tell us, from which there are no lessons to learn, once culturally fetishized, can be deposited in a museum, for instance as national history, or very broadly, as cultural heritage. Močnik will therefore also claim not just that the East-West division has robbed both sides of their shared past, but also prevents them from having that shared history in their future:

> "It freezes them into an eternal unequal couple, one
> part of which is forever doomed to struggle to get
> rid of its phantom past, while the other is bound
> to an everlasting autistic celebration of its idiocy."

Pants, hair, cigarettes, revolvers, divorce, revolution, the West...

So then, rather than speculate about the unpredictable future, we had better turn back to the forgotten past. The question is simple: is it really true that sexual emancipation and its corollary, the changed relations between the sexes, are exclusively Western phenomena, a liberal step forward in the development of Western modernity which can be reduced historically to the general process of modernization, or very specifically, to the so-called sexual revolution of the 1960s? Is it true that formerly "communist" societies of the East never experienced anything of the sort?

For political theorist and historian Bini Adamczak,[01] the fact that the Russian Revolution began on March 8, 1917, the sixth anniversary of the Working Women's Day, was more than a coincidence.[02] "People who until then had been considered women, put their pants on, cut their hair off, grabbed their cigarettes and revolvers. Shortly thereafter they got divorced—a handwritten statement on a piece of paper was all it took." Adamczak points out that the Russian Revolution introduced the most progressive marriage and divorce legislation the modern world had ever seen. It abolished the draconian Tsarist punishments for homosexuality and legalized abortion. In 1922, a Soviet court ruled that the marriage between a cis-gendered woman[03] and a trans man was legal, regardless of whether it was a same-sex or a trans marriage. It was enough that the marriage was entered into by mutual consent. Adamczak concludes, "The Russian Revolution was not only ahead of its time, but ahead of ours. It was, in part, a queer-feminist revolution."

This certainly provides no evidence for the conception of the East as culturally, civilizationally, historically backwards relative to the West. Even less does it support the responsibility of the communists for that setback, for the historical "delay" of Eastern modernity. On the contrary!

Adamczak reminds us of the fact that Bolshevik delegates were euphorically welcomed at the conference of the World League for Sexual Reform established by Magnus Hirschfeld among others. The reason for this was ironic in a way, as the author writes: it was precisely the Bolshevik Revolution that brought the liberal bourgeois discourse on sexuality to Russia, where categories like homosexuality, pseudohermaphroditism, and transvestism did not exist at all before the Revolution. In fact, those notions were first developed and institutionalized in the context of Western

---

01 What follows draws on Bini Adamczak's talk at the Institute for Cultural Inquiry in Berlin, "The Feeling of Revolution. Queer Questions of 1917," at *Utopia. Wreckage* conference on June 16, 2011.

02 The revolution is called "February Revolution" because the Gregorian calendar was still in use in Russia at the time.

03 The term cis-gendered is used in cases where the sexual identity of the person coincides with their gender, and with the traditional gender role or behavior associated with that gender. This term replaces the ideological notion of "normal."

biomedical sciences and psychiatry. Tsarist Russia only recognized different forms of non-reproductive sexuality which it persecuted using so-called sodomy laws. After the Revolution, the abolition of these sodomy laws was justified by the argument that homosexuality was neither a sin nor a crime, but a biological aberration. Another example: in the spring of 1929, public health commissar Nikolai Semaschko summoned a committee of "experts"—forensic gynecologists, clinical psychiatrists, biologists, etc.—to help the Commissariat of Justice make a decision in the request by (woman) citizen Kamenev for a surgical and legal change of sex. Adamczak explicitly points out that this was the Western bourgeois model that was imported into Russia by the Bolsheviks.

More Western than the West—Revolution

So, the communist revolution not only did not block the westernization of the East, that is, the expansion of modernity to the East, but facilitated it to an extent that could transform the East into a West that was more western than the West itself. We know of course that just a decade later all this emancipatory progress was completely reversed. In Stalin's Soviet Union, abortion was banned again, sodomy laws were reintroduced, and the family was brought back as the elementary cell of society and the state. Maxim Gorki, who supported this oppression, equated homosexuals with fascists in the early 1930s. This regressive turn would not have been possible had the very experience of the revolution not been destroyed first, the experience that held open the horizon of possibility on which "male" and "female" could articulate their fundamentally queer character, and each moment of emancipatory struggle could be "eastern" and "western" at once.

If East really is the name for forgetting, then it is first of all the forgetting of the revolution. ●

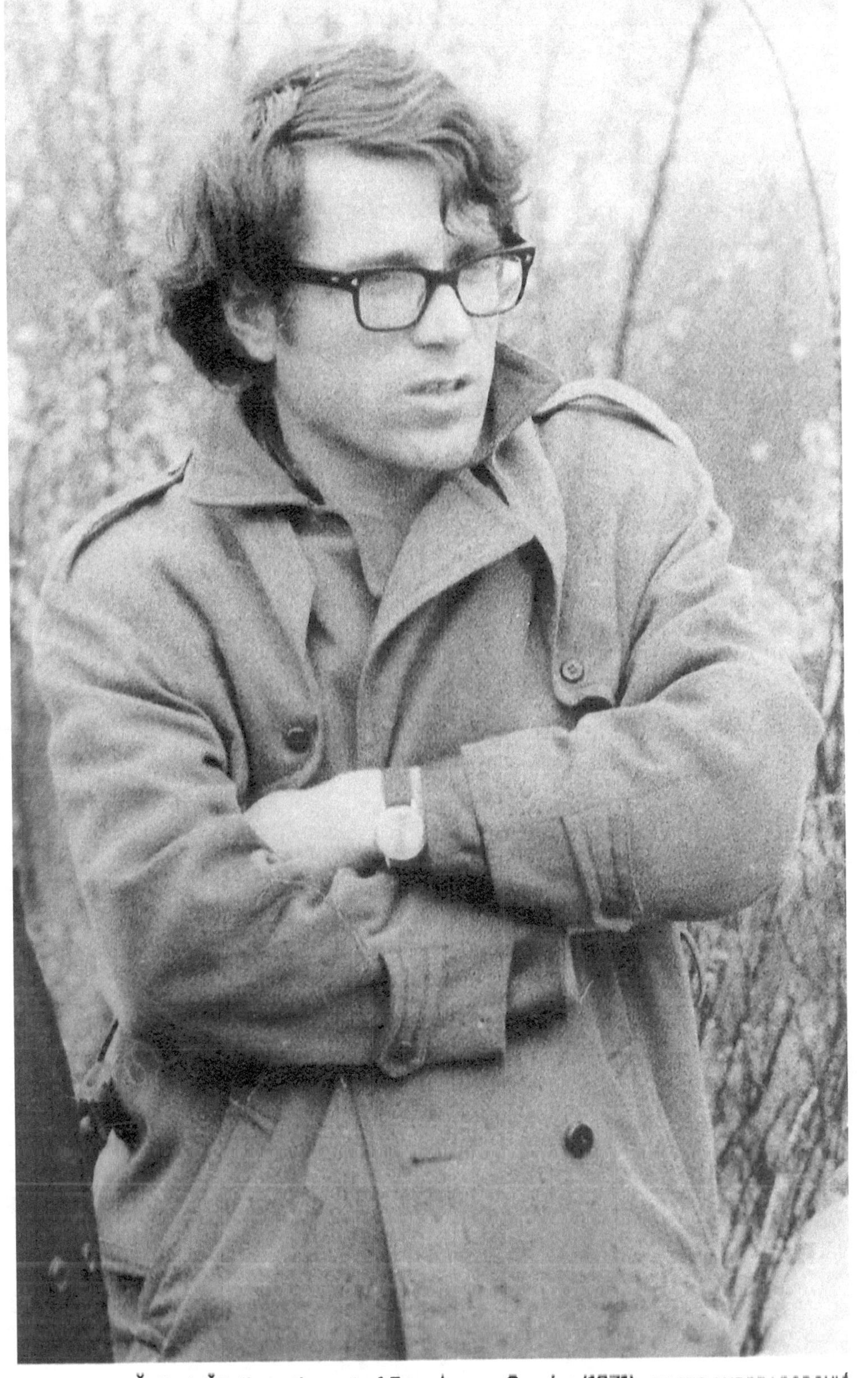

Želimir Žilnik on the set of *Freedom or Comics* (1971) • PHOTO ANDREJ POPOVIĆ

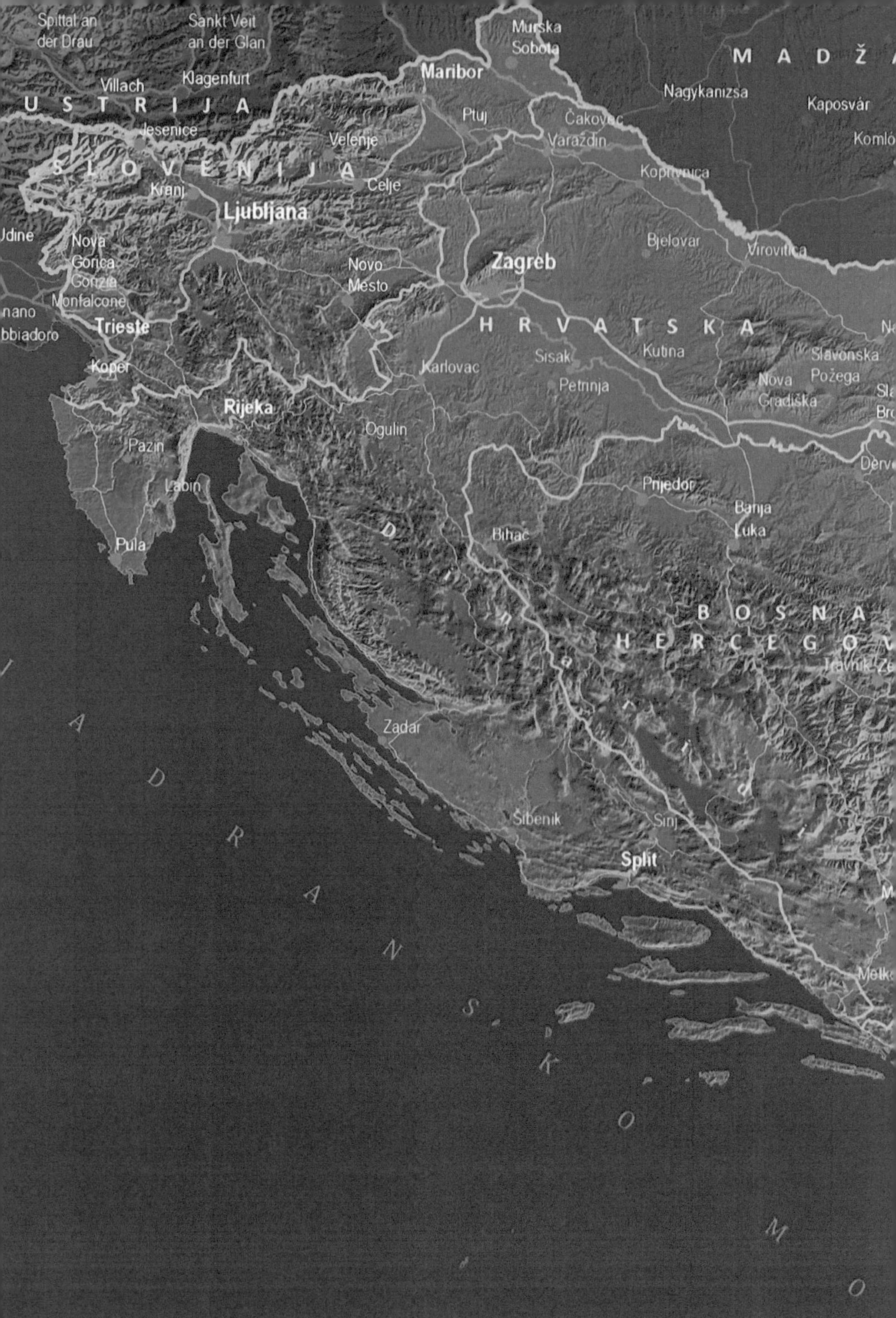

Media Landscape of SFRJ

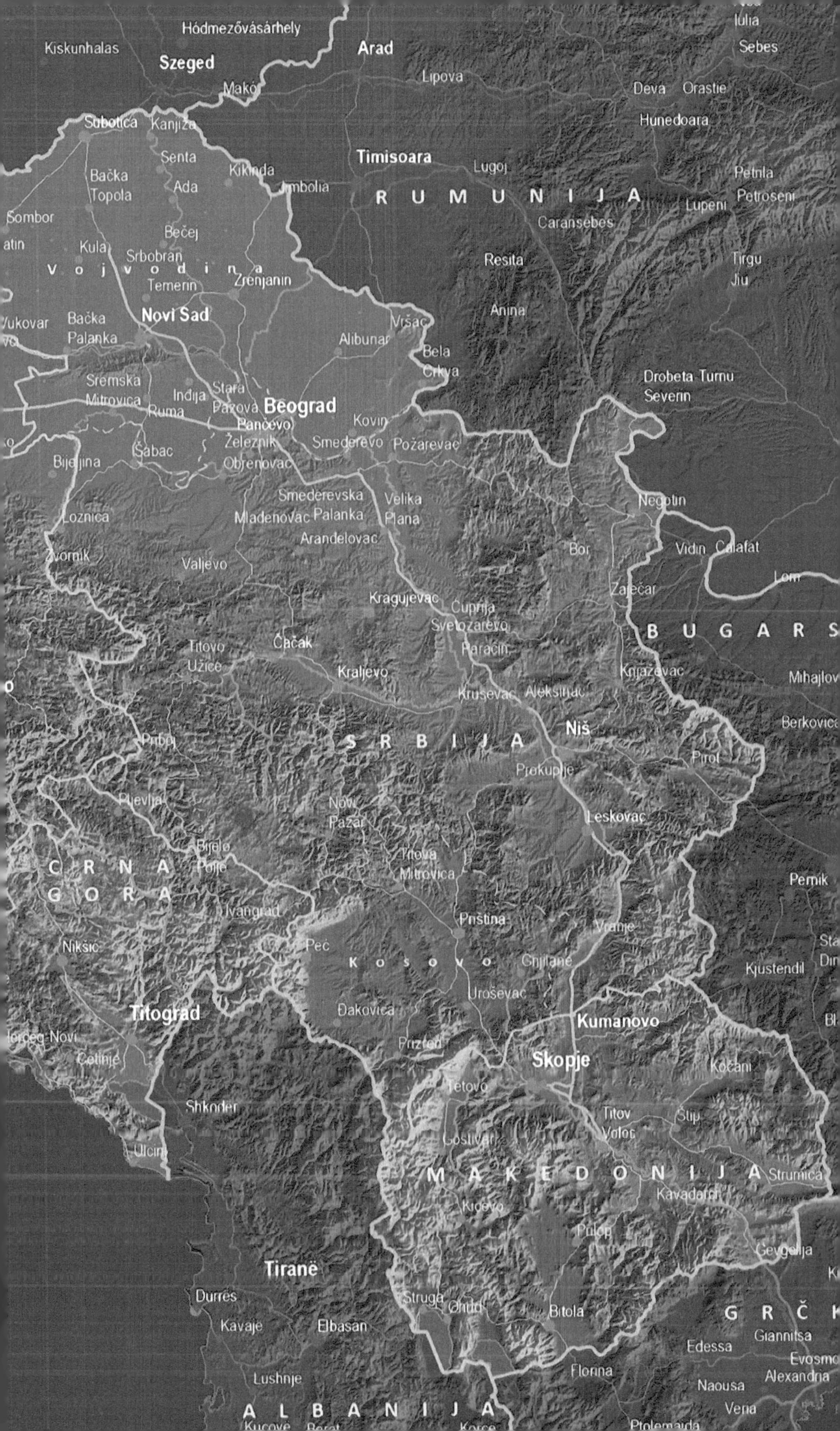

Kiskunhalas
Hódmezővásárhely
Szeged
Arad
Lipova
Iulia
Sebes
Makó
Deva
Orastie
Subotica
Kanjiža
Hunedoara
Senta
Ada
Kikinda
Timisoara
Lugoj
Petrila
Petroseni
Bačka
Topola
Jimbolia
R U M U N I J A
Caransebes
Sombor
atin
Bečej
Resita
Tirgu
Jiu
Kula
Srbobran
V o j v o d i n a
Zrenjanin
Temerin
Anina
Vukovar
vci
Bačka
Palanka
Novi Sad
Vršac
Alibunar
Bela
Crkva
Drobeta Turnu
Severin
Sremska
Mitrovica
Indija
Stara
Pazova
Beograd
Kovin
Ruma
Pančevo
Negotin
Železnik
Smederevo
Požarevac
Šabac
Obrenovac
Bijeljina
Smederevska
Palanka
Bor
Vidin
Calafat
Loznica
Mladenovac
Velika
Plana
Zaječar
Lom
Zvornik
Arandelovac
Valjevo
Kragujevac
Cuprija
B U G A R S
Titovo
Užice
Čačak
Svetozarevo
Paraćin
Knjaževac
Mihajlov
Kraljevo
Kruševac
Aleksinac
Berkovica
Priboj
S R B I J A
Niš
Pirot
Prokuplje
Pljevlja
Novi
Pazar
Leskovac
Bijelo
Polje
Titova
Mitrovica
Pernik
C R N A
G O R A
Ivangrad
Priština
Vranje
Niksic
Peć
K o s o v o
Gnjilane
Kjustendil
Sta
Din
Uroševac
Titograd
Đakovica
Kumanovo
Herceg Novi
Prizren
Bl
Cetinje
Skopje
Kočani
Tetovo
Titov
Veles
Stip
Shkoder
Gostivar
Ulcinj
M A K E D O N I J A
Strumica
Kavadarci
Kicevo
Prilep
Gevgelija
Tiranë
Durrës
Struga
Ohrid
Bitola
G R Č
Kavaje
Elbasan
Florina
Giannitsa
Edessa
Lushnje
Evosmo
Alexandria
Naousa
Veria
A L B A N I J A
Kucove
Berat
Korce
Ptolemaida

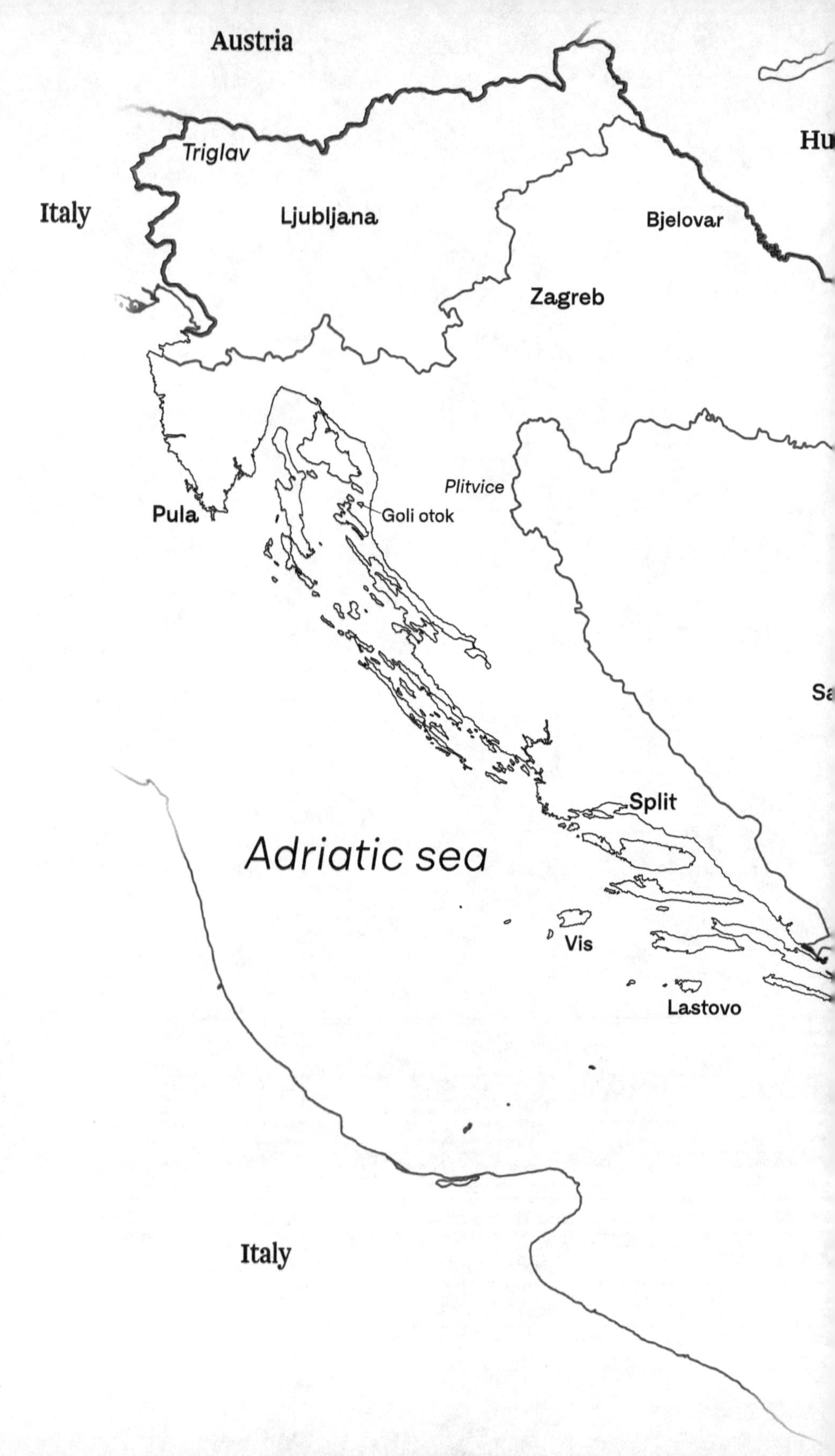

Austria
Hu
Triglav
Italy
Ljubljana
Bjelovar
Zagreb
Pula
Plitvice
Goli otok
Sa
Split
Adriatic sea
Vis
Lastovo
Italy

Media Landscape of SFRJ: Map of SFRJ

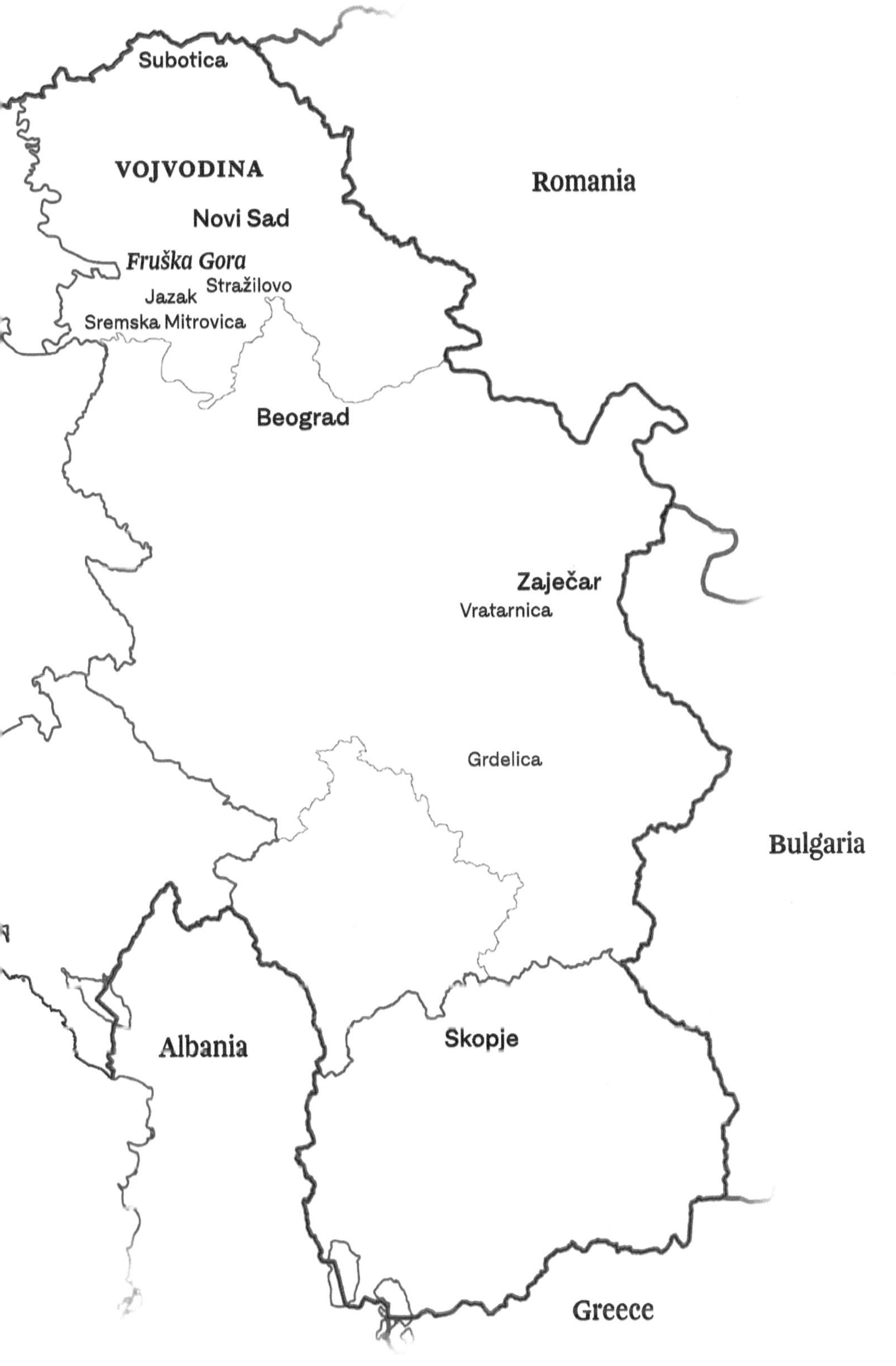

Media Landscape of SFRJ: Film Production Houses

Avala Film ★ Yugoslavia's oldest and largest film company, founded in 1946 in the capital Belgrade by the State Committee of Cinematography, part of the Government of the Socialist Federal Republic of Yugoslavia tasked with establishing new film production companies throughout the country.

Filmske novosti ★ Started on October 20, 1944, the day Belgrade was liberated, from the Office of the President of Yugoslavia, Josip Broz Tito, as a film production office attached to the cinema magazine *Vrhovačke produkcije*, with the goal of capturing all important events related to political, economic and cultural development of the country along with activities of President Tito.

Neoplanta Film ★ Film company based in Novi Sad, founded in September 1966 by decree of the Assembly of the Socialist Autonomous Province of Vojvodina, building on the practice of amateur cinema clubs. 1971 saw a turning point in company management when a political decision changed the production climate, radically deviating from previous practice. Neoplanta film lost its reputation, and following the catastrophic failure of the film *Great Transport* (*Veliki transport*) in 1985, it was shut down by political decision in 1986.

Jadran Film ★ Film production studio and distribution company founded in 1946 in Zagreb, Croatia. Between early 1960s and late 1980s one of the largest and most notable film studios in Central Europe, producing some 145 international and 120 Yugoslav productions. Amid the breakup of Yugoslavia in the 1990s the company experienced a sharp decline through privatization, most of its property either sold or falling into disrepair. Jadran Film continues to produce films, at a much lower rate: a handful of films a year, mainly Croatian and regional co-productions.

Viba Film ★ Film production company established in 1956 in Ljubljana, Slovenia. In 1994 the Government of the Republic of Slovenia designated Viba Film Studio the national technical film foundation.

Bosna Film ★ Bosnian film company founded in 1947 in Yugoslavia. Bosna Film d.d. Sarajevo was founded in 1983 as Permanent Film Union Bosna Film, which later grew into a mixed stock corporation. In 1990, the state-owned company Bosna Film became a joint-stock company with 50.46% private ownership. In late 1999 it was completely privatized, and state-owned stocks were purchased by a group of company workers.

Youth Forum (Tribina mladih) ★ Founded in 1954 in Novi Sad as the Youth Department of the People's University which began operating the same year. After several years the Youth Forum merged with Sonja Marinković Cultural and Youth Center, and the new institution became the Cultural Center of Novi Sad in 1984. ●

Media Landscape of SFRJ: Some Periodicals of SFRJ

Politika (Politics) ★ Founded in 1904 by Vladislav F. Ribnikar, still publishing in Belgrade, the oldest daily newspaper in circulation in the Balkans. After the demise of the Milošević government in 2000, the ownership share of *Politika* was taken over by the German media concern WAZ, which went on to buy a number of reputable and influential newspapers in Southeastern Europe. Ten years later, WAZ began to withdraw from the Balkans, and in 2012 sold its ownership stake to the East Media Group company registered in Russia.

Dnevnik (Daily) ★ Serbian daily newspaper, published in Novi Sad, started illegally by anti-fascists from the region of Vojvodina on November 15, 1942, during Hungarian occupation. Originally *Slobodna Vojvodina (Free Vojvodina)*, it was printed in an illegal underground print shop on the (then) outskirts of Novi Sad and covered politics under the auspices of the Provincial People's Liberation Committee of Vojvodina until 1952. From 1953, it was published under the name *Dnevnik*. It remained a public newspaper owned by the Assembly of the Autonomous Province of Vojvodina until 2003, when the majority owner became the German media company WAZ (Dnevnik Vojvodina Press).

Vjesnik (Herald) ★ Croatian state-owned daily newspaper published in Zagreb. Originally established in 1940 as a wartime illegal publication of the Communist Party of Croatia, it built and maintained a reputation as Croatia's newspaper of record for most of its post-war history. Following Croatia's independence and the breakup of Yugoslavia in the early 1990s its circulation began to dwindle, as the paper came under the control of the Croatian Democratic Union (HDZ), the conservative party that won the first elections in independent Croatia. It briefly changed its name in 1992 to *Novi Vjesnik* (New Herald) in an attempt to distance itself from its communist history. The paper was reduced to an online portal and stopped updating in 2012.

Borba (Struggle) ★ Daily newspaper first published in Zagreb 1922 as an outlet of the Communist Party of Yugoslavia, banned in

1929. Publishing continuously through the years of WW2, it became the official gazette of the League of Communists of Yugoslavia (LCY) until 1954, and then of the Socialist Alliance of Working People of Yugoslavia until its dissolution. During WW2 *Borba* was published in the Republic of Užice, a short-lived liberated Yugoslav territory and the first liberated territory in World War II Europe; after liberation publication moved to Belgrade. At the onset of the Yugoslav Wars, *Borba* journalists took an anti-war stance: in 1992 and 1993 the paper became one of the most important strongholds of opponents to the war policies of Slobodan Milošević. After the government takeover of the offices in 1994, the staff started *Naša Borba* (Our Struggle), from which emerged *Danas* (Today), still publishing today. After 2000 *Borba* went through a murky process of privatization and ceased printing in 2009 having lost all of its readership.

Politika Ekspres (Politics Express) ★ Daily newspaper published in Belgrade from 1963 till 2005, started as an evening newspaper or digested edition of the authoritative *Politika*. In the late 1980s, like *Politika*, its editorial policy hewed close to the positions of Slobodan Milošević and his regime, causing numerous controversies and public debates.

Danas (Today) ★ Daily newspaper published in Belgrade, Serbia, established in 1997 after a group of discontented journalists from *Naša borba* walked out in protest against the paper's new private majority owner. A left-leaning outlet, *Danas* promotes social democracy and European Union integration, and vocally supports the work of Serbian NGOs advocating for human and minority rights protection. The paper is published and managed by an entity called Dan Graf d.o.o., a limited liability company based in Belgrade. In 2021, the company was sold to the Luxembourg-based group United Media.

NIN • Nedeljne Informativne Novine (Weekly Information Magazine) ★ Weekly magazine of culture and politics established in Belgrade in 1935, and banned the same year having published 26 issues. Sixteen years later, a group of journalists from *Mladi Borac* (Young Fighter), a youth newspaper, advocated for the magazine's relaunch; *NIN* appeared again in Belgrade in 1951. During the late 1980s Slobodan Milošević and his associates recruited prominent publications such as *NIN* as media outlets for Serbian nationalism. *NIN* was privatized in 2007; Ringier AG became its majority owner in 2009.

Mladina (Youth) ★ Weekly left-wing political youth magazine founded in 1920 in Ljubljana as the official outlet of the Youth Section of the Communist Party of Yugoslavia in Slovenia. After the 1921 ban on the Communist Party, the journal kept circulating semi-illegally. In this period it was read by Communist and other radical leftist and anti-capitalist youth. In the 1930s *Mladina* ceased to exist due to government repression and was re-established in 1943. After 1945, it again became the official paper of the Youth Section of the Communist Party of Slovenia. After 1976, the publication profile changed such that it increasingly criticized the established political order. Still active and publishing.

Polja (Fields) ★ Academic journal for literature and theory, publishing since 1955 in Novi Sad as part of the Novi Sad Youth Forum, known for promoting new, avant-garde tendencies in art and especially literature at the time. In the early 1990s, the journal was discontinued, to be relaunched in the late 1990s as part of the publishing activity of the Cultural Center of Novi Sad.

Perspektive (Perspectives) ★ Created two years after the violent termination of *Magazine 57* in Ljubljana, Slovenia, as its successor with a new editor and new publisher, the State Publishing House of Slovenia. The state simultaneously published *Sodobnost* (Modernity), a newspaper for the older generation with a distinctly "liberal" orientation, and *Perspektive* as the outlet for the new "critical generation." The magazine called itself "a monthly magazine for culture and social issues," a broader ambit than *Magazine 57*, a "magazine for literature and culture."

Új Symposion (New Symposium) ★ Literary and artistic magazine in Hungarian with a courageous critical stance, founded in 1965 in Novi Sad by Hungarian writers from Yugoslavia as a supplement to the Hungarian-language newspaper *Ifjúság* (Youth) based in Novi Sad. The magazine died in 1992, the second year of Yugoslav wars. In 1993 its former editors founded the journal *Ex Symposion*, which preserves the legacy of *Új Symposion*, in Veszprém (Hungary).

Vojno delo (Military work) ★ State-supported military publisher and science journal publishing scholarship on security and defense. Founded in Belgrade in 1948 by the order of the Supreme Commander and the Minister of National Defense of the Federal People's Republic of Yugoslavia, its first issue was published on February 1, 1949. Today it is the "scientific and theoretical journal published by the Ministry of Defense of the Republic of Serbia serving as an open forum for the publication and cultivation of innovative thinking and critical exchange of experiences at all levels of security and defense, in the national and international contexts." ●

One Timeline

As a genre of graphic design, the time line combines pictorial and textual composition. Typically written in a terse, telegraphic style, the time line substitutes the rhythm of chronological order for the flow of traditional narrative. The time line visualizes history in a way that conventional prose does not, distributing words across a grid that regulates their placement...In the interest of brevity and clarity, the time line masks the interpretive character of historical narrative—hence its emphasis on "facts" and "information." The objective tone commonly used in time line and the exclusion of critical commentary obscure the presence of an active author. Time lines are rarely "written" but are more often compiled, researched, and designed...

   — **Ellen Lupton & Abbott Miller:** *Design Writing Research: Writing on Graphic Design* (London: Phaidon, 1999), 168

This timeline draws on *The Communist Manifesto: The Spectre Is Still Roaming Around* [*Komunistički manifest: Bauk još uvijek kruži*], trans. Moša Pijade (Zagreb: Arkzin, 1998); *A Lexicon of YU Mythology* [*Leksikon YU mitologije*], eds. Đorđe Matić and Vladimir Arsenijević (Zagreb: Postscriptum, and Belgrade: Rende, 2004); and the authors' partial selection of widely available information.

Abbreviations used in One Timeline

BCMS	The primary language of Serbia, Croatia, Bosnia and Herzegovina, and Montenegro
BH	Bosnia-Herzegovina
HR	Croatia
MK	North Macedonia
ME	Montenegro
NYC	New York City
RS	Serbia
RU	Russia
SL	Slovenia
SFRJ	Socialist Federal Republic of Yugoslavia
USA	United States of America
USSR	Union of Soviet Socialist Republics
UK	United Kingdom
XK	Kosovo
YU	Yugoslavia

AIDS	Acquired Immunodeficiency Syndrome
CERN	Conseil européen pour la Recherche Nucléaire
COVID	Coronavirus Disease
EEC	European Economic Community
EU	European Union
FDR	Franklin Delano Roosevelt
GNU	Gnu's Not Unix
HIV	Human Immunodeficiency Virus
ICTY	International Criminal Tribunal for the former Yugoslavia
IMF	International Monetary Fund
INF	Intermediate-Range Nuclear Forces Treaty
KPJ	Communist Party of Yugoslavia (Komunistička partija Jugoslavije)
LCY	League of Communists of Yugoslavia
NAM	Non-Aligned Movement
NATO	North American Treaty Organization
NSA	National Security Administration USA
NYSE	New York Stock Exchange
POTUS	President of the United States of America
WTO	World Trade Organization
WTC	World Trade Center

	Yugoslavia	**The World**
2023		▸ Gaza conflict ▸ Finland joins NATO
2022		▸ Ukraine War
2020		▸ COVID-19 lockdowns ▸ **George Floyd, Breonna Taylor** killed by police; worldwide protests
2019	▸ Dušan Makavejev dies [b. 1932]	▸ political crisis in Venezuela ▸ USA withdraws from INF Treaty
2018	▸ MK renamed North Macedonia	▸ Referendum in Ireland repeals abortion ban
2017	▸ ICTY: **Ratko Mladić**, life; 4 BH Croats, 10-25yrs, one immediately commits suicide by poisoning	▸ #metoo on social media
2016	▸ ICTY: **Radovan Karadžić**, 40 yrs	▸ Panama Papers: 11.5m documents, money laundering, tax evasion, and shell corporations ▸ Turkey: coup attempt ▸ migrant crisis: seven EU states withdraw from Schengen ▸ terrorist attacks in Europe, Turkey, Middle East ▸ TikTok ▸ **Donald Trump** elected POTUS
2015		▸ LIGO and VIRGO: direct observation of gravitational waves ▸ USA: same-sex marriage legal
2014	▸ HR legally recognizes same-sex partnerships	▸ Black Lives Matter; #blacklivesmatter; #BLM
2013	▸ HR joins EU	▸ **Edward Snowden**, NSA file leak ▸ **Pope Benedict XVI** resigns ▸ same-sex marriage legal in UK
2012	▸ Standard & Poor downgrades HR credit rating to BB+/B. ▸ ICTY acquits HR generals **Ante Gotovina** and **Mladen Markač**	▸ CERN, Higgs boson particle
2011	▸ First Gay Pride in Split HR canceled for homophobic attacks ▸ ICTY: HR generals **Ante Gotovina** and **Mladen Markač** guilty of participating in a joint criminal enterprise	▸ civil war in Syria ▸ Occupy Wall Street ▸ "Arab Spring"
2010		▸ Eurozone and IMF, severe austerity measures on Greece ▸ instagram

▶ **Chelsea Manning**, USA military information leak to WikiLeaks

2009
▶ HR student protests demanding free tuition
▶ HR joins NATO

▶ vinyl records back in stores
▶ noncommercial media licenses, Creative Commons

2008
▶ HR ceases mandatory military service
▶ XK declares independence

▶ Great Recession, global financial crisis
▶ **Barack Obama** elected POTUS
▶ expansion of social networks

2007

▶ iPhone
▶ Bulgaria and Romania join the EU

2006
▶ ME declares independence
▶ **Slobodan Milošević** dies in ICTY detention

▶ **Julian Assange**, WikiLeaks
▶ Google in China; debates about censorship
▶ twitter
▶ **Tarana Burke**, "me too" about sexual violence and harassment

2005
▶ last screening at the Zagreb Cinematheque

▶ YouTube

2004
▶ Slovenia joins NATO

▶ facebook
▶ EU expansion: 10 new member states
▶ **Joe Darby**, photos of prisoner torture by USA military at Abu Ghraib

2003
▶ Federal Republic of YU "Serbia and Montenegro"
▶ **Zoran Đinđić**, RS prime minister, assassinated

▶ USA invasion of Iraq; toppling of **Saddam Hussein**
▶ last flight of the Concorde

2002

▶ Euro replaces national currencies of 12 countries joining Eurozone

2001
▶ RS **Slobodan Milošević** extradited to ICTY
▶ RS Belgrade Pride Parade canceled, police and protesters clash

▶ 9/11 terrorist attacks on WTC and Pentagon
▶ **George W. Bush** POTUS,
▶ war on Afghanistan; War on Terror
▶ **Jimmy Wales**, Wikipedia
▶ Napster sued; file-swapping programs, Gnutella
▶ mp3 players
▶ dot.com stock market bubble and devaluation

2000
▶ RS **Slobodan Milošević** overthrown
▶ HR joins Partnership for Peace, WTO

▶ Prague: anti-globalization demonstrations
▶ Napster file-swapping system, music industry shutdown campaign

1999 ▸ NATO intervention in RS and XK

▸ 20m websites; dot.com crash

▸ Czechia, Hungary and Poland join NATO
▸ anti-globalization protests; battle in Seattle

▸ RU: **Vladimir Putin**, Prime Minister

1998 ▸ EU "Western Balkans:" Albania, BH, XK, ME, MK, RS

▸ **Larry Page** and **Sergey Brin**, Google
▸ 150th anniversary: *The Communist Manifesto: A Modern Edition*, intro **Eric Hobsbawm**, cover **Komar&Melamid** (London, NYC: Verso)

1997

▸ EU: Stability and Growth Pact
▸ wireless internet

1996

▸ Tamagotchi

1995 ▸ Paris: Dayton Agreement ends hostilities in BH; HR, BH, YU commit to implementing permanent peace and stability in the region
▸ Genocide in Srebrenica BH

▸ Schengen Agreement: gradual removal of inner EU border controls

▸ **Želimir Žilnik, Teddy Award, Berlin Film Festival for *Marble Ass***

▸ Netscape and Internet Explorer: war of browsers
▸ .com boom
▸ amazon.com

1994 ▸ YU hyperinflation: 22mo, peak 300m% monthly
▸ RS decriminalizes homosexuality

▸ Mexico: Zapatista rebellion
▸ USA: sale of personal computers outstrip sales of TVs
▸ Internet primary computing platform; junk email
▸ Yahoo!

1993 ▸ Croat vs. Muslim conflict begins in BH

▸ Treaty of Maastricht; EEC becomes EU
▸ CERN: world wide web wins over other internet technologies; free

1992 ▸ war begins in Bosnia
▸ Federal Republic of YU
▸ YU: hyperinflation begins
▸ EU recognizes independent SL and HR
▸ EU and USA recognize independent BH
▸ Siege of Sarajevo BH

▸ **Bill Clinton** elected POTUS

1991
- Dissolution of SFRJ
- MK declares independence
- SFRJ FIBA EuroBasket gold, men's basketball
- USSR dissolves
- Gulf War

1990
- LCY dissolves
- multi-party elections in SL, HR, RS
- FIBA World Cup gold, men's basketball
- world wide web
- **Mikhail Gorbachev**, President of USSR
- Germany reunified, NATO member

1989
- founding of political parties in all parts of SFRJ
- FIBA EuroBasket gold, men's basketball
- NAM conference in Belgrade
- Fall of Berlin Wall
- Romanian TV Revolution, fall of **Nikolae Ceausescu**

1988
- mass demonstrations, rise of nationalism
- Lepa Brena, "Jugoslovenka"
- TAT-8, transatlantic telephone cable uses optical fibers
- first World AIDS Day

1987
- SFRJ rejects offer to join EEC
- **Labin HR: miners' strike,** longest since WW2
- 9,351 domestic and 1,268 foreign book titles published; 68m volumes total
- first lesbian organization, Lilit
- **Ronald Reagan** and **Mikhail Gorbachev** sign INF Treaty, Washington, DC
- Single European Act: single European market
- Mathias Rust flies Cessna airplane into Red Square
- **Andy Warhol** dies

1986
- Chernobyl disaster

1985
- Live Aid, a multi-venue benefit concert
- GNU Manifesto, Dr. Dobb's Journal of Software Tools
- Schengen Agreement
- USSR: Perestroika; **Mikhail Gorbachev** leads Communist Party
- **Emir Kusturica**, Grand Prix Cannes, *While Father was Away on Business*

1984
- investment programs on hold in SFRJ
- Ljubljana SL: first gay culture festival in YU; first gay organization, Magnus
- high US$, interest rates; Euro-stagnation, debt in developing countries
- Apple Macintosh, $2,495
- UK miners' strike
- Sarajevo BH: Winter Olympics, first in a socialist nation

1983
- *Time* magazine, personal computer person of the year
- compact disc
- HIV identified as cause of AIDS

▸ **Richard Stallman**, GNU: fully functional Unix-compatible operating system completely free of copyrighted code

1982

▸ highest unemployment in developed world since Great Depression
▸ Falklands War

▸ French magazine *Actuel*, best Euro albums: **VIS Idoli**'s *Defense and the Final Days* [*Odbrana i poslednji dani*]

▸ **Ridley Scott**, *Bladerunner*

1981

▸ USA recognizes first AIDS cases
▸ *This Bridge Called My Back: Writings by Radical Women of Color*, eds. **Cherríe Moraga**, **Gloria E. Anzaldúa** (Watertown: Persephone)

1980
▸ **Josip Broz Tito** dies in Ljubljana
▸ Olympic gold, men's basketball
▸ First hardcore film in SFRJ cinemas: *Come to my Bedside* [*Der maa vaaere en sengekant*] (dir. **John Hilbard**, Denmark, 1975)

▸ oil crisis; oil-rich countries start development projects
▸ Iran-Iraq war
▸ **Ronald Reagan** elected POTUS

1979
▸ **Edvard Kardelj** dies, ideologue of workers' self-management

▸ **Ayatollah Khomeini** returns to Iran, Islamic Revolution
▸ USSR invades Afghanistan
▸ UK: **Margaret Thatcher**, first woman PM
▸ **Francois Lyotard**, *La condition postmoderne*
▸ Sony Walkman
▸ **John Paul II** visits Poland, first Pope in a communist country

1978
▸ First feminist conference in Belgrade
▸ FIBA World Cup gold, men's basketball

▸ Red Brigades kill **Aldo Moro**

1977
▸ **Danilo Kiš**, *A Tomb for Boris Davidovich*
▸ SFRJ FIBA EuroBasket gold, men's basketball
▸ Conference on European Security and Cooperation in Belgrade

▸ **Steve Jobs** et al., Apple Corp.
▸ The Combahee River Collective Statement
▸ **Stormtrooper** becomes **Crass Art Collective** and anarcho-punk band

1976
▸ **Rolling Stones** play two concerts in Zagreb

▸ **Rodolfo Marcenaro**, comics version of *The Communist Manifesto*

▶ Mao Zedong dies
▶ UK punk: Malcolm McLaren & The Sex Pistols
▶ The Gang of Four, band in Leeds UK, named for Maoist faction
▶ Rock Against Racism
▶ USA Copyright Act: all works in fixed form, life of author+fifty years

1975
▶ Treaty of Osimo: definitive division of Free Territory of Trieste between Italy and YU
▶ FIBA EuroBasket gold, men's basketball
▶ Vietnam War ends
▶ Francisco Franco, fascist caudillo of Spain, dies

1974
▶ New SFRJ Constitution, inscribes abortion rights
▶ *Praxis* journal, Korčula summer school banned
▶ Richard Nixon POTUS resigns
▶ Joseph Beuys, Free Int'l University for Creativity and Interdisciplinary Research

1973
▶ FIBA EuroBasket gold, men's basketball
▶ Chile: military coup, General Pinochet
▶ oil crisis

1972
▶ Watergate

1971
▶ FEST, Belgrade, largest Balkan film festival
▶ 9k domestic, 1k foreign book titles, 55m volumes
▶ Switzerland: women can vote
▶ Guy Debord, *Society of Spectacle*
▶ Josip Broz Tito, SFRJ's President-for-life
▶ Dušan Makavejev, *W. R. Mysteries of Organism*
▶ Tito meets Richard Nixon

1970
▶ FIBA World Cup gold, men's basketball
▶ industrial workers: majority employed population in developed world
▶ 231m TV sets
▶ Salvador Allende, first Marxist elected president in a liberal democracy in Latin America
▶ Baader-Meinhof Group

1969
▶ Peak of Black Wave YU film
▶ *Battle on the Neretva* [*Bitka na Neretvi*] (dir. Veljko Bulajić), starring Orson Welles, Yul Brinner, Franco Nero, Sergei Bondarchuk, Hardi Krüger
▶ Neil Armstrong and Buzz Aldrin walk on the Moon
▶ Želimir Žilnik, Grand Prix, Berlin Film Festival for *Early Works*

1968
▶ Student demonstrations, clashes with police in Belgrade; protests in other cities
▶ Prague Spring; Berkeley; Paris
▶ Pope asks Tito to intercede to stop Vietnam War

▶ Martin Luther King assassinated
▶ Warsaw Pact invades Czechoslovakia

▶ **Želimir Žilnik, Grand Prix, Oberhausen for** *The Unemployed*

▶ Pigasus the Immortal, **Pigasus J. Pig**, nominated POTUS by Yippies
▶ **Stanley Kubrick**, *2001 Space Odyssey*

1967 ▶ **Želimir Žilnik, first film,** *Newsreal on Village Youth*, **in Winter**
▶ BITEF (Belgrade International Theater Festival)

▶ race riots: Newark, Detroit
▶ Israel occupies West Bank and controls Gaza

▶ **Aleksandar Petrović**, *I Even Met Happy Gypsies* [*Skupljači perja*], Oscar nomination, Best International Feature; Golden Globe, Best Foreign Language Film; Grand Prize of the Jury, FIPRESCI at Cannes

1966 ▶ State Security: **Aleksandar Ranković** removed
▶ SFRJ participates in Miss World

▶ Cultural Revolution in China
▶ **Andy Warhol**, The Factory, **Velvet Underground**
▶ **Michelangelo Antonioni**, *Blow Up*
▶ **Huey P. Newton** and **Bobby Seale**, Black Panther Party

1965 ▶ International edition of *Praxis*
▶ Museum of Contemporary Art, Belgrade

▶ **Phil Ochs**, "I Ain't Marching Anymore"
▶ Chicago: Association for the Advancement of Creative Musicians
▶ Los Angeles: Watts Race Riots
▶ **Malcolm X** assassinated

1964 ▶ Zagreb: marxist philosophers, *Praxis* journal

▶ USA: Civil Rights Act, Lyndon Johnson POTUS
▶ Vietnam war escalation
▶ **Beatles** in America
▶ New York Race Riots

1963 ▶ New Constitution, new name: SFRJ
▶ Tito vs. western "decadence" in art and culture
▶ Skopje MK: catastrophic earthquake

▶ JFK assassinated

1962 ▶ personal banking current accounts
▶ **Orson Welles** films *The Trial* in Zagreb

▶ Cuban missile crisis

▶ **Adolf Eichmann** hanged in Israel
▶ Algeria independent from France

▶ **Dušan Vukotić**, Oscar, animated film *Surrogate* [*Surogat*]

▶ laser diode
▶ fluxus
▶ Telstar satellite

1961
- Catholic publications ahead of Vatican Council
- Economic reforms, stronger market economy
- Zagreb Music Biennale
- first New Tendencies exhibition
- Belgrade YU: First NAM summit
- Ivo Andrić, Nobel Prize for literature
- Yuri Gagarin, space flight
- Berlin Wall

1960
- 20k TV sets
- Olympic gold, national soccer team
- JFK elected POTUS
- New York Pop Art
- Krzysztof Penderecki, *Threnody to the Victims of Hiroshima*

1959
- 110+k translated books published in SFRJ
- homosexual anal intercourse still criminalized
- Cuban Revolution, Fidel Castro
- 1000 editions of *The Communist Manifesto* in 86 languages to date

1958
- Tito re-elected SFRJ President
- Abortion legalized, birth control discussed
- "temporary work abroad"
- Berlin crisis
- Motown

1957
- No visa required to enter SFRJ
- SFRJ citizens can leave for work abroad
- Sputnik, first artificial satellite
- Internationale Situationniste
- Louis Malle, *Ascenseur pour l'échafaud*, soundtrack by Miles Davis
- Treaty of Rome: European Economic Community (later EU)

1956
- Tito visits USSR, different paths to socialism
- regular national TV programming
- Belgrade: exhibition of USA modern art
- Brioni HR: Josip Broz Tito, G. A. Nasser, Jawaharlal Nehru meet; peaceful and active coexistence; NAM initiative
- USSR Nikita Krushchev, de-stalinization
- Hungarian uprising; USSR intervention
- *This is Tomorrow* exhibit, Whitechapel Gallery, London
- Bertolt Brecht dies
- Suez canal nationalized
- Elvis Presley, "Heartbreak Hotel"

1955
- Nikita Khrushchev visits Yugoslavia, normalizing relations
- First Film festival in Pula
- national radio network using ultrashort waves
- Warsaw Pact
- Federal Republic of Germany joins NATO
- Disneyland
- James Dean in *Rebel Without a Cause* (dir. Nicholas Ray)
- Bill Hailey & His Comets, "Rock Around The Clock"

1954
- Italy, UK, USA, YU: Free Territory of Trieste
- ▶ USSR liberalizes abortion
- ▶ Jonas Salk, inactivated polio vaccine
- ▶ War in Algeria

1953
- "social property" and workers' self-management
- NYC Ivan Meštrović, monument to Warsaw Ghetto Uprising
- ▶ J. V. Stalin dies

1952.
- KPJ renamed League of Communists of YU
- abortion legalized
- ▶ hydrogen bomb explosion

1951
- domestic typewriter: cyrillic+Latin keyboards
- Exat 51, geometric abstraction vs. soc-realism
- ▶ Marshall McLuhan, *The Mechanical Bride*

1950
- Law on workers' self-management
- USA economic aid renewed
- ▶ Billy Wilder, *Sunset Boulevard*, end of old Hollywood

1949
- 8-yr elementary education
- Belgrade: Yugoslav Cinematheque
- ▶ NATO
- ▶ USSR atomic bomb
- ▶ George Orwell, 1984

1948
- Tito+KPJ reject Stalin+Cominform
- Persecution of USSR supporters; Goli otok
- Brotherhood-Unity highway construction
- ▶ State of Israel; Al-Nakba
- ▶ standardized vinyl single (7" at 45) and LP (12" at 33 1/3 rpm)

1947
- Belgrade, *Kosmaj 47*, first domestic radio receiver
- First feature films in socialist YU: *These people will live* (dir. Nikola Popović), *Slavica* (dir. Vjekoslav Afrić)
- ▶ independence and partition of India, decline of British Raj
- ▶ Cold War begins
- ▶ Joseph McCarthy, Committee on Anti-American activities
- ▶ Marshall Plan
- ▶ Alexander Muirhead, fax machine
- ▶ Christian Dior, New Look

1946
- Nationalization Law
- First post-WW2 YU Constitution
- Avala and Jadran, film production companies
- ▶ 50 countries sign UN Charter
- ▶ Vespa 50

1945
- liberation and socialist governance; Federal People's Republic of Yugoslavia
- ▶ USA atomic bombs: New Mexico, Hiroshima, Nagasaki
- ▶ WW2 ends; liberation of Auschwitz; May 9 Victory Day

1944
- Moscow: secret meeting Tito, Stalin
- Naples, Italy: Tito, Winston Churchill informal recognition of new YU
- ▶ Soviet army pushes Nazi units out of USSR

▸ **Kandinski** dies in Paris,
Mondrian in New York
▸ France: women can vote
▸ FDR re-elected POTUS, fourth
term

1943 ▸ Democratic Federal Yugoslavia

▸ Third Communist International
[Comintern] dissolves
▸ **Michael Curtiz**, *Casablanca*

1941 ▸ First Proletarian Brigade, first
formalized partisan unit in
occupied YU

▸ *Kleine Bücherei des Marxismus-
Leninismus* (Moscow: Verlag fur
fremdsprachige Literatur);
includes *The Communist
Manifesto* with all of **Engels**'s
prefaces
▸ **Hedy Lamarr** and **George Antheil**,
radio frequency hopping

1940
▸ FDR re-elected POTUS, third term

1939
▸ Germany invades Poland;
World War 2
▸ Russo-Finnish war
▸ **Victor Fleming**, *The Wizard of Oz*
in Technicolor

1938
▸ Germany annexes Austria
and Czechoslovakia
▸ Volkswagen "beetle"
▸ "Kristallnacht"

1937
▸ "Entartete Kunst," Nazi exhibit of
"degenerate art," Munich

1936
▸ Berlin Olympics; **Leni Riefenstahl**,
Olympia (1938)
▸ Spanish Civil War
▸ **Stalin**'s Great Terror
▸ FDR re-elected POTUS

1935
▸ Italy invades Abyssinia
▸ **Wallace Hume Carothers**, nylon,
first fully synthetic fiber

1934 ▸ Marseille: **King Alexander** of YU assassinated
▸ **Mao Zedong**, Long March
▸ **Stalin**'s purges

1933
▸ USA New Deal
▸ Germany: **Adolf Hitler**; book
burnings; concentration camps
▸ USSR bans abortion

1932 ▸ *Surrealism here and now*, Belgrade
▸ *Impossiblo! [Nemoguće!]*, surrealist magazine

▸ *The Communist Manifesto,*
collected works of Marx+Engels
▸ UK and USA communist parties,
"hundreds of thousands" of copies
▸ FDR elected POTUS

1931

▸ Second Spanish Republic

1929 ▸ renamed Kingdom of Yugoslavia

▸ "Black Friday" at NYSE; global
economic crisis

1928 ▸ Tito on "Bombing Plot Trial" for
communist activities; five years
in prison

▸ **Luis Buñuel+Salvador Dalí,**
Un Chien Andalou
▸ **Walt Disney,** *Mickey Mouse*
▸ UK: women with property
qualifications can vote
▸ **Alexander Fleming,** penicillin

1927

▸ **Fritz Lang,** *Metropolis*
▸ **Philo Taylor Farnsworth,** television
▸ **Alan Crosland,** *The Jazz Singer,*
first sound film

1925

▸ **Sergei Eisenstein,** *Battleship
Potemkin*
▸ NYC world's largest city

1924

▸ **V. I. Lenin dies**

▸ **André Breton,** *Manifesto of
Surrealism*

1922

▸ Italy: Fascists in power,
Benito Mussolini
▸ USSR: **Arseny Avraamov,**
Symphony of Sirens, Baku

1921 ▸ Vidovdan Constitution
▸ *Zenit,* avant-garde monthly
for art and society

▸ USSR: Kronstadt rebellion
▸ **Frederick Banting** and
Charles Best, insulin
▸ **Ludwig Wittgenstein,** *Tractatus
Logico-Philosophicus*

1920 ▸ Communist Party banned
▸ regular radio programming

▸ USA 19th Amendment:
women can vote
▸ USSR legalizes abortion
▸ **Robert Vine,** *Das Kabinett des
Doktor Caligari*

1919 ▸ Socialist Workers' Party of
Yugoslavia (Communist);
renamed KPJ in 1920

▸ Treaty of Versailles
▸ Bauhaus
▸ Communist Party USA
▸ Third Communist International
▸ **Rosa Luxemburg** and
Karl Liebknecht murdered
▸ **Frank Watson Dyson+Arthur**

		Stanley Eddington, solar eclipse observation confirms **Einstein's** theory of relativity
1918	▶ Kingdom of Serbs, Croats, and Slovenes, later YU	▶ Great War ends: Austro-Hungarian, Ottoman, German empires collapse
1917		▶ Russian/Bolshevik/October Revolution
1916		▶ DaDa, Cabaret Voltaire
1915		▶ **Albert Einstein**, theory of general relativity: gravitational waves propagate as ripples in spacetime
1914	▶ Sarajevo BH: Archduke Franz Ferdinand assassinated	▶ World War 1 (Great War) begins; zeppelin air raids ▶ Panama Canal completed
1913		▶ **Henry Ford**, line production ▶ **Igor Stravinsky**, *The Rite of Spring* ▶ **Luigi Russolo**, *L'arte dei Rumori*, futurist manifesto
1912		▶ RMS Titanic sinks
1910		▶ 2/3 of German citizens live in cities ▶ London UK world's largest city
1909		▶ **Filippo Tommaso Marinetti**, *Manifesto of Futurism* ▶ NYC: Women's Day march organized by Socialist Party of America
1908		▶ Ford Model T
1907		▶ **Leo Baekeland**, bakelite, first synthetic resin ▶ **Baden Powel**, Scout movement
1906		▶ Grand Duchy of Finland independent from Russia, universal suffrage
1905		▶ First Russian Revolution ▶ **Albert Einstein**, *annus mirabilis*, four papers on modern physics
1903		▶ Panama Canal construction begins
1902		▶ **Georges Meliès**, *Voyage to the Moon*

1901		▸ Jacques Lacan born
1900		▸ Max Planck, quantum theory
		▸ Friedrich Nietzsche dies
1899		▸ Sigmund Freud, *Interpretation of Dreams*
1898		▸ Marie Curie and Pierre Curie, radium
1896		▸ Henri Becquerel, radioactivity
		▸ Guglielmo Marconi, wireless telegraphy
1895		▸ brothers Auguste and Louis Lumière, film camera
		▸ Friedrich Engels dies
		▸ Wilhelm Roentgen, x-ray
		▸ first International Art Exhibition, La Biennale di Venezia
		▸ Ferdinand von Zeppelin, rigid airship
1893		▸ Friedrich Engels, *To the Italian Reader*
		▸ New Zealand: women can vote
1892	▸ Josip Broz Tito born	▸ Friedrich Engels, *Foreword to Polish edition*
		▸ Rudolf Diesel, diesel engine
1891		▸ Otto Lilienthal, airglider flight
1890	▸ Moša Pijade born: Yugoslav revolutionary, painter, journalist; translates *Das Kapital* and *The Communist Manifesto* during 14 yr prison term	▸ Friedrich Engels, *Foreword to* (fourth) *German edition*
		▸ Julius (Groucho) Marx born
1889		▸ *The Communist Manifesto*, Italian edition
		▸ Second International
1888		▸ Brazil: slavery abolished
1887		▸ Emil Berliner, gramophone
1886		▸ Haymarket Riot
		▸ Cuba: slavery abolished
		▸ Nikola Tesla, electric motor
		▸ John Pemberton, Coca-Cola
1885		▸ internal combustion motor
		▸ hysteria treatments: surgical removal of ovaries (Paris); surgical clitoridectomy (London and Vienna); burning (Heidelberg)

1883		▸ Karl Marx dies in London
1882		▸ second Russian translation of *The Communist Manifesto*
1881		▸ Jenny von Westphalen Marx dies (b. 1814), collaborator+wife to Karl
1880		▸ Labor and socialist parties founded in developed countries
1879		▸ Thomas Edison, incandescent bulb
1878	▸ Treaty of Berlin: Kingdom of Serbia recognized; Austria-Hungary occupies BH in Ottoman Empire	
1877		▸ Thomas Edison, phonograph ▸ R.G. Bell, telephone
1874		▸ impressionism
1872		▸ Internationale moves to New York ▸ Prosecution of W. Liebknecht, R. Bebel, R. Hepner: publicity for *The Communist Manifesto*; mass publication, standardized text+title
1871	▸ BCMS translation of *The Communist Manifesto* in journal *Pančevac*	▸ Paris Commune ▸ Eugène Pottier, *L'Internationale*
1870		▸ V. I. Lenin born
1869		▸ USA transcontinental railroad ▸ Russian edition of *The Communist Manifesto*, trans. Mikhail Bakunin ▸ Suez Canal, "eighth world wonder"
1867	▸ Principality of Serbia, independent from Ottoman Empire	▸ Russia sells Alaska to USA ▸ Karl Marx, *Das Kapital* ▸ Alfred Nobel, dynamite ▸ Fyodor Dostoyevski, *Crime and Punishment*
1865		▸ Gregor Mendel, genetic experiments ▸ Juneteenth (June 19), enslaved people in Texas hear of Emancipation ▸ US Civil War ends ▸ Lewis Carroll, *Alice in Wonderland*

1864	▸ First International
	▸ **Louis Pasteur**, germ theory
	▸ German edition of *The Communist Manifesto*, London

1864
- ▸ First International
- ▸ **Louis Pasteur**, germ theory
- ▸ German edition of *The Communist Manifesto*, London

1863
- ▸ **Abraham Lincoln** POTUS, Emancipation Proclamation abolishes slavery

1861
- ▸ RU abolishes serfdom
- ▸ USA Civil War begins

1859
- ▸ **Charles Darwin**, *On the Origin of Species*; theory of evolution

1858
- ▸ **Jagadish Chandra Bose**, ultra-short radio waves

1857
- ▸ **Karl Marx**, *Grundrisse*

1854
- ▸ **Henry Bessemer**, steel converter

1853
- ▸ Crimean War; **Florence Nightingale** organizes modern nursing
- ▸ pedal bicycle

1851
- ▸ **Lord Kelvin**, second law of thermodynamics

1850
- ▸ **Herman Meville**, *Moby Dick*
- ▸ *The Communist Manifesto*, first English ed., in *The Red Republican*, London, trans. **Helen MacFarlane**, Scottish Chartist feminist

1848
- ▸ **Marx+Engels**, *Manifest der Kommunistischen Partei*, drafted 1847 for Communist League in London; trans. into French and Swedish
- ▸ Revolutions: Germany, Hungary, Austria, Italy; France: 2nd Republic
- ▸ **Karl Marx**, editor, *Neue Rheinische Zeitung*

1846
- ▸ planet Neptune discovered

1845
- ▸ Ireland: Great Famine propels mass emigration

1841
- ▸ Hong Kong declared British territory

1838
- ▸ UK Chartism

1837		▸ Samuel Morse, electric telegraph
1833		▸ UK+most colonies: Slavery Abolition Act
1832		▸ UK Great Reform Law
1830		▸ Eugène Delacroix, *Liberty Leading the People*
1822		▸ Joseph Nicéphore Niépce, photography
1821		▸ Napoleon Bonaparte (51) dies on St. Helena
1819		▸ UK: Peterloo Massacre, crowd of 60,000 demanding parliamentary reform charged by cavalry; 18 dead, 400–700 injured
1818	▸ Vuk Stefanović Karadžić, *Srpski Rječnik [Serbian Dictionary]* (Vienna: P. P. Armeniern), basis for modern BCMS	▸ Karl Marx born in Trier, Germany
1812		▸ (Napoleon Bonaparte) France invades Russia
1807		▸ abolition of slave trade in British Empire ▸ G. W. F. Hegel, *Phenomenology of Spirit*
1804		▸ Haiti declares independence Napoleon Bonaparte declared Emperor
1803		▸ Ludwig van Beethoven, *Eroica*
1802		▸ Napoleon Bonaparte re-introduces slavery in France and colonies
1799		▸ Napoleon in power in France
1793		▸ The Terror
1791		▸ Haitian Revolution, first successful insurrection by self-liberated slaves against French colonial rule in Saint-Domingue
1789		▸ France: Bourgeois Revolution; *Declaration of the Rights of Man and of the Citizen*; slavery abolished; women not citizens

Memory of the World

Suggestions for further reading embedded in the QR codes in the margin direct readers to resources available through Memory of the World.

When the dominant idea of freedom in an epoch is that of freedom regulated by markets, the collective capacity
to pursue autonomy, equality, and welfare becomes
reduced to the freedom of capital flows, the freedom
of competition, and the freedom of consumer choice.
Under the coercive invisible hand of the market, the freedom of
journalism tends to transmogrify into sensationalist
media acting at the behest of commercial and political interests; the freedom of expression into officially
condoned hate speech; the freedom of research and
education into sky-rocketing student fees, precarious academic labor, and intellectual self-censoring.
When the idea of freedom as regulated by markets meets the
idea of political freedom as self-assertion of ethnic
domination, as was the case over the last three decades in the countries of former Yugoslavia, then the
sensationalist media, normalized hate speech, and
intellectual self-censorship turn a blind eye when
books are purged from the libraries, documents are
disappeared from the archives, and monuments are
blasted into the air.
Purging, disappearing, and blasting are violent acts of erasure
from our collective memory of a past in which peasants and workers, communists and anti-fascists defeated—even if temporarily—Nazism, racism, and the
exploitation of the underclasses. In their toleration
of such material acts, the media, the public, and the
intellectuals are complicit in rewriting the history of
that emancipatory past. The monoethnic identity of
new capitalist nation-states thus descends into a
self-justifying spiral of historical revisionism.
Countering the revision of history requires the work of librarians,
archivists, and historians. To counter the revision
of history, their work requires access to documents
and books disappeared and purged by nationalism,
access to critical scholarship denied by the market.
To counter the revision of history, their work requires
overcoming the intellectual property regime. ●

https://library.memoryoftheworld.org

Past: An Introduction to the Problem
Želimir Žilnik on Film, Communism, and Former Yugoslavia
Boris Buden in collaboration with kuda.org, Olivera Jokić and others

THE BOOK WAS PRODUCED BY

Boris Buden, who wrote the essays and conducted conversations with Želimir Žilnik

Želimir Žilnik, who answered Boris Buden's questions, orally and in writing

Hito Steyerl, who recorded conversations between BB and ŽŽ

Olivera Jokić, who translated the book into English, re-edited and significantly improved the text

kuda.org, the book's initiators, who edited, redacted, and coordinated the work of book creation

PUBLISHERS   New Media Center_kuda.org
              Braće Mogin 2 • po box 22 • Novi Sad • Serbia
              office@kuda.org
              https://kuda.org
              https://zilnikzelimir.net

              Multimedia Institute — MaMa
              Preradovićeva 18 • Zagreb • Croatia
              mi2@mi2.hr
              https://mi2.hr/

              Iskra Books
              Madison • Wisconsin • USA
              inquiries@iskrabooks.org
              https://iskrabooks.org//

RESEARCH ADVISORY Emil Kerenji
                   Sarita Matijević Žilnik, Playground produkcija Novi Sad

COPYEDITING Taylor R. Genovese, Iskra Books

DESIGN & LAYOUT Dejan Kršić
TYPEFACES Bara Micro • Chairman • Link [ALL BY NIKOLA ĐUREK / TYPOTHEQUE]

PRINTING Tiskara Zelina • Croatia

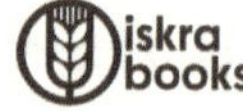

The book *Past: an Introduction to the Problem* is part of the "Peripheral
Visions project—towards trans(l)national publishing culture," a partnership
project implemented by the Kulturtreger, Maska, eipcp, kuda.org, Kontrapunkt,
Multimedia Institute, and financed by the European Union, the Ministry of
Culture of the Republic of Serbia, the City of Novi Sad Administration for
Culture and the Foundation for Arts Initiatives.

The book *Past: an Introduction to the Problem* is also a part of the research
program of Center_kuda.org and associates that examines the social, cultural,
and intellectual heritage of former Yugoslavia, Vojvodina, and Novi Sad.
This work is carried out through the projects "The Continuous Art Class,"
"Media Ontology," and "Political practices of (post-)Yugoslavian art."
These projects provide a new reading of the progressive practices of the
Neo-Avant Garde for today, and open a new way of communication between
these practices and contemporary art production.

Funded by the European Union. Views and opinions expressed are however
those of the author(s) only and do not necessarily reflect those of the
European Union or European Education and Culture Executive Agency (EACEA).
Neither the European Union nor the granting authority can be held responsible
for them.

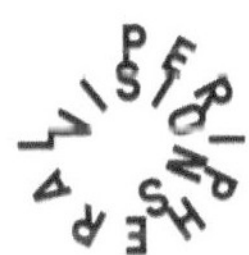

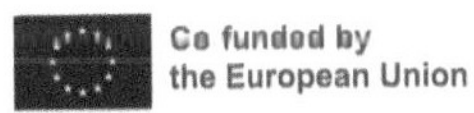

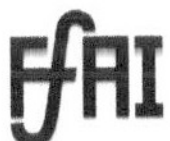

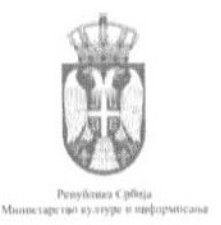

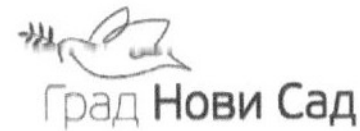

Želimir Žilnik on the set of *Freedom or Comics* (1971)
• PHOTO ANDREJ POPOVIĆ

CIP - Каталогизација у публикацији

Библиотеке Матице српске, Нови Сад

BUDEN, Boris, 1958-

Past: an introduction to the problem : Želimir Žilnik on film, communism, and former Yugoslavia / Boris Buden, kuda.org, Olivera Jokić ... [et al.] ; [translation Olivera Jokić]. – Novi Sad : New Media Center_kuda.org ; Zagreb : Multimedia Institute MaMa ; Madison : Iskra Books, 2024 (Hrvatska). – 245 str. : ilustr. ; 24 cm

ISBN 978-86-88567-41-1 (kuda.org)
ISBN 978-953-8469-13-8 (MaMa)
ISBN 979-8-8691-9071-0 (IB)

1. Žilnik, Želimir, 1942- [интервјуисана особа]
а) Жилник, Желимир (1942-) — Интервјуи б) Југославија — Културна историја

COBISS.SR-ID 140900361

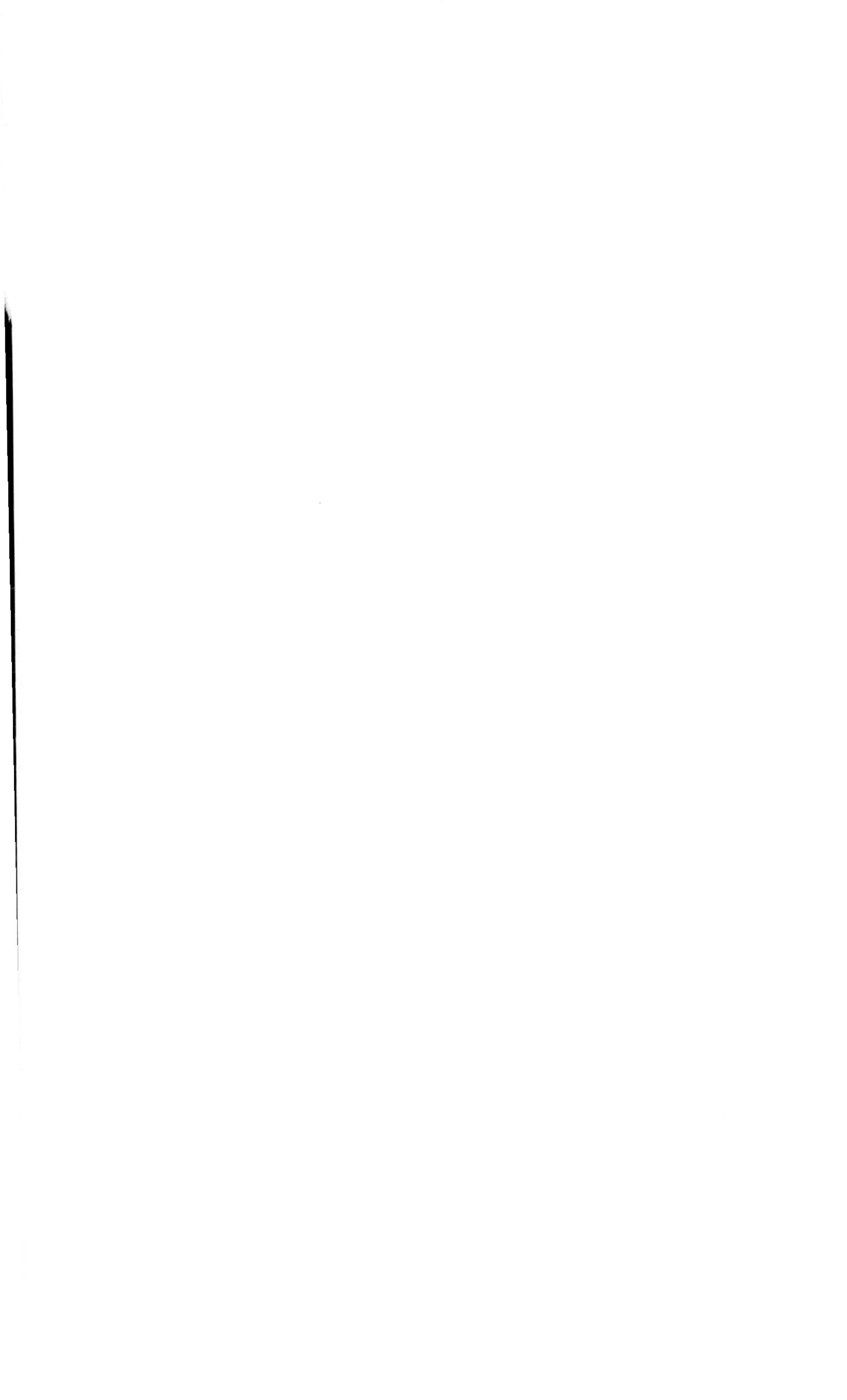